The Practice of Ethical Leadership

This book considers ethics as a practical discipline at the heart of decisions, reasoning, shaping, and ordering organizations. Both engaging and accessible, it offers effective suggestions for selecting and developing ethical leaders and invites readers to self-reflect and understand how to build ethical cultures within their organizations and beyond.

Examining the many characteristics of ethical leadership, including love and authenticity, the book uses factual evidence to explore both its positive and negative characteristics. It offers readers an in-depth insight into how ethical decision making can help determine the right thing to do, supported by directly applicable ethical lessons that help leaders become more conscious going forward. The authors provide concrete suggestions for action, as well as ways to develop and understand what is needed to become an ethical leader. Each chapter encourages readers to reflect on their own experiences, as well as engage in discussion with others, and challenge basic assumptions. The book concludes by offering a long-term oriented outlook at future challenges for ethical leaders.

Rooted in extensive psychological, philosophical, entrepreneurial, and business experience, *The Practice of Ethical Leadership* will appeal to leaders, human resource professionals, and Board members across a wide variety of organizations. This book will also benefit academics as well as anyone who is invested in the fields of leadership, management, business, and industrial–organizational psychology.

Claas Florian Engelke is a leadership advisor and senior consultant with Korn Ferry who operates both nationally and internationally. Florian is based in Berlin, Germany. He holds degrees in linguistics and religious studies, is a leadership developer and diagnostician, lover of music, literature, and critical geopolitical analysis.

Richard B. Swegan brings to this book over 30 years of experience as a consultant and salesperson focusing on leadership. He resides in Pittsburgh, Pennsylvania, USA, and operates his own consulting firm, ARCH Performance which specializes in identifying leadership talent.

The Practice of Ethical Leadership

Insights from Psychology and Business in Building an Ethical Bottom Line

Claas Florian Engelke and
Richard B. Swegan

Routledge
Taylor & Francis Group

NEW YORK AND LONDON

Cover Image: © Getty Images

First published 2024
by Routledge
605 Third Avenue, New York, NY 10158

and by Routledge
4 Park Square, Milton Park, Abingdon, Oxon, OX14 4RN

Routledge is an imprint of the Taylor & Francis Group, an informa business

Library of Congress Cataloging-in-Publication Data
Names: Engelke, Claas Florian, author. | Swegan, Richard B.,
1949– author.
Title: The practice of ethical leadership: insights from
psychology and business in building an ethical bottom line /
Claas Florian Engelke and Richard B. Swegan.
Description: New York, NY: Routledge, 2024. | Includes
bibliographical references and index. |
Identifiers: LCCN 2023040283 (print) | LCCN 2023040284 (ebook) |
ISBN 9781032397191 (paperback) | ISBN 9781032397245 (hardback) |
ISBN 9781003351078 (ebook)
Subjects: LCSH: Leadership—Moral and ethical aspects.
Classification: LCC HD57.7 .E538 2024 (print) |
LCC HD57.7 (ebook) | DDC 658.4/092—dc23/eng/20230830
LC record available at https://lccn.loc.gov/2023040283
LC ebook record available at https://lccn.loc.gov/2023040284

Graphics by Ava Bonam and Melissa Farr of Back Porch Creative

ISBN: 978-1-032-39724-5 (hbk)
ISBN: 978-1-032-39719-1 (pbk)
ISBN: 978-1-003-35107-8 (ebk)

DOI: 10.4324/b23260

Typeset in Optima
by codeMantra

Contents

About the Authors

Claas Florian Engelke

Claas Florian Engelke holds a strong fascination with geopolitics and political studies that go beyond the daily news coverage, progressive music, nineteenth-century (Gothic) literature, anthropology, history, and ethical leadership. He holds degrees in Religious Studies, German, as well as English Linguistics. Despite the fact that he studied religion, Florian likes to take a less anthropocentric view and tends to put things into a naturalist perspective. Florian loves and cherishes nature, solitude, and real dialogue. He is based in Berlin, Germany, where he lives with his wife, Ava Bonam, who is a trained cultural scientist, voracious reader, and runs her practice of naturopathy and vocal coaching.

Florian provides consulting services in the fields of leadership advisory, assessment, and leadership development. If possible and appropriate, he prefers to bathe in dialogue, cut to the chase, pause diplomacy, and put things on the right track to do good. An advocate of discomfort, Florian invites his friends and clients to question themselves and what they take for granted in order to foster incessant learning and aspire to be the best versions of themselves. Being a proponent of agency, self-reliance and self-development, he helps his clients establish and constructively question their leadership cultures.

Florian can be reached via email at florian_engelke@web.de

Richard B. Swegan

Rick Swegan is the founder and principal consultant of ARCH Performance. He developed an interest in the effects of culture on moral reasoning during his time in graduate school and has maintained that interest. In addition to *The Practice of Ethical Leadership*, Rick has authored *The Memories of Thomas M'Clintock: A Quiet Warrior for Women's Rights and the Abolition of Slavery* and co-authored with Debra Dinnocenzo *DotCalm: The Search for Sanity in a Wired World.* With a background in human resources and safety, Rick provides consulting to a variety of organizations on the developmental needs of potential leaders and makes recommendations on whether or not they should be hired.

A graduate of The College of Wooster (B.A. in Sociology) with a master's degree in counseling from Ohio University, Rick completed Ph.D. Coursework at The Ohio State University. During his career, he has worked as Vice President of Human Resources, Manager of Regional Consulting, Global Accounts Manager, and Senior Consultant for a variety of leadership development and training companies.

Rick and his wife, Debra, divide their time between Pittsburgh PA (USA) and the Chautauqua Institution where they have homes. A quiet observer of life's foibles, Rick has also written a satire and parody newsletter for more than a decade.

Rick can be reached via email at rick@rickswegan.com or by visiting our website www.ethicalbottomline.com/

Acknowledgments

Jointly, we would like to thank the staff at Routledge, particularly Zoe Thomson and Maddie Gray, who were and are unflagging in their support for our efforts. They answered our numerous questions patiently and promptly while being a constant source of support and understanding. They made the entire publishing process clear and easy to follow.

Our copy editors, Pamela Guerrieri of Proofed to Perfection, and Jenni Swegan, were extremely helpful prior to our submitting our manuscript by cleaning up our writing, offering frequent suggestions, and generally making our writing better. Likewise, our graphics people, Ava Bonam and Melissa Farr, provided clear creative solutions to the various concepts we wished to present visually. They made the book stronger and more appealing. Thank you kindly.

On a more personal note, we would like to thank Profil M, the company that Florian worked for when we met. Without our mutual relationship with the firm we would not have met and begun our collaboration.

Each of us has individuals we want to thank, and our personal acknowledgments follow.

Florian

I would like to extend my gratitude to Mother Earth, Gaia, and life as such. These are the basic conditions that provide, nurture and must be revered.

First of all, I would like to thank my mother, Ulrike-Brigitte Engelke, for planting the seed of constructive subversion, not to take anything for granted, and the urge to lovingly question everything past and present. I am grateful to my father, Kurt Kai Wilhelm Karl Engelke, for introducing me to literature, language, critical thinkers, and the motivation to strive and create. You both instilled an incessant desire to learn as well as a productive dichotomy of stillness and unrest inside of me. Thank you.

My thanks to Norbert Müller, Lille Gruber, Dr. Rolf Krökel, Rafal Fedro, Aylin Kaiser, Marta García-Marcos, and Jan Ferdinand for their trust, friendship, and the innumerable fruitful conversations (professional, personal, and artistic/creative) we enjoyed over the years.

I would like to thank my co-author, Rick Swegan, for his patience, flexibility, helpful feedback, and—eventually—for being a friend. Furthermore, I am grateful to both Debra Dinnocenzo and Jennimarie Swegan for their valuable feedback and stylistic advice. You are awesome!

When it comes to professional organizations, I would like to thank Profil M, Korn Ferry, FPK Unternehmensentwicklung, Kienbaum Consultants, and the Boston Consulting Group for challenging, welcoming, and pushing me.

Finally (and certainly claiming the concluding and most relevant position of my acknowledgments here), I would like to thank my beautiful wife and most precious comrade, Ava Bonam, for her intelligent, relentless, broad, profound, oftentimes surprising, and loving insights. Without you, this project wouldn't have been possible for me.

Rick

More than anything else, I would like to thank my friends who provided support, encouragement, and the occasional glass of wine over the course of this project. While there are many who were supportive several stand out and, at the risk of offending those I unintentionally omit, here they are. Phil and Melissa Carl, friends extraordinaire, Jay Summerville and Michael Forst, Mike Mangan, Rick and Susie Rieser, and Twig and Barbara Branch. There are others, but as an introvert I tend to stick to a small group.

Two in particular stand out for me. I have worked with Mike Mangan in three different firms and over time he has become a valued friend. I appreciate the thinking he has provided to this project. He has always been willing to donate his time and intellect. The other is Twig Branch (yes, that is his real name). For over a decade he has been my partner in mischief, a thoughtful friend who always provides perspective, and someone who always makes me laugh. It is a friendship I treasure.

Lastly, my thanks to my family, my wife Debra Dinnocenzo, and my daughter Jennimarie Swegan. They have put up with my being distracted and preoccupied, provided continual support, and appropriately gentle feedback on the contents of the book.

Introduction to the Forewords

As the present book is a journey of discovery and exploration of the domain of ethical leadership and it marries our different perspectives on the subject, we are pleased to have a group of diverse voices shedding some light on the topic from their unique perspectives. We appreciate these different vantage points, as they are a clear representation of the multifaceted approach we sought to employ when embarking on this exciting voyage. Enjoy.

Forewords

On the Various Dimensions of Ethical Leadership—and Their Real-World Implications

In today's complex and interconnected world, ethical leadership is more crucial than ever. Leaders are faced with numerous challenges and dilemmas (VUCA world) that require them to make difficult choices. They must navigate through ethical gray areas, balancing the needs of their organizations with the expectations of society.

Ethical leadership refers to a leadership style that emphasizes the importance of moral values and principles in guiding the actions and decisions of leaders. It involves leading with integrity, honesty, and fairness, while considering the well-being and interests of all stakeholders.

Ethical leaders set the tone for their organizations by establishing a strong positive ethical culture. They lead by example, demonstrating ethical behavior and holding themselves and others accountable for their actions. They prioritize transparency and open communication, fostering an environment where ethical concerns can be raised and addressed.

Ethical leadership also involves making decisions that are in the best interest of all stakeholders, not just the bottom line. Leaders must consider the impact of their decisions on employees, customers, communities, and the environment. They must strive to create a positive and sustainable impact and foster trust and collaboration.

Furthermore, ethical leaders recognize the importance of diversity and inclusion. They value different perspectives and actively seek input from a diverse range of individuals. They promote fairness and equality, ensuring that everyone has an equal opportunity to succeed and contribute.

Political leadership, on the other hand, refers to the leadership provided by politicians and government officials. Political leaders play a crucial role in shaping economic policies and regulations that can either promote or hinder economic success. Effective political leadership involves making informed decisions, collaborating with stakeholders, and implementing policies that support economic growth and development.

Pathological leadership, also known as toxic leadership, refers to a leadership style characterized by abusive, manipulative, and self-serving behavior. Pathological leaders create a toxic work environment that undermines employee morale, engagement, and productivity. They often engage in unethical practices, such as fraud or corruption, which can lead to legal and financial consequences for organizations. Pathological leadership can also result in high turnover rates and difficulty attracting and retaining talented employees.

Economic success is influenced by various factors, including market conditions, technological advancements, and global economic trends. However, leadership plays a crucial role in determining how organizations and economies navigate these factors. Ethical leadership and effective political leadership can contribute to economic success by fostering trust, stability, and sustainable growth.

From my many years of experience as a manager and entrepreneur I can reflect that ethical leadership and behavior have a significant impact on the return on investment (ROI) of a company Here are some ways in which ethical leadership and behavior will influence the ROI:

1. Reputation and brand value: Ethical leadership and behavior contribute to building a positive reputation and strong brand value for a company. This will attract more customers, investors, and business partners, leading to increased sales and higher ROI.
2. Employee morale and productivity: Ethical leaders create a positive work environment where employees feel valued, respected, and motivated. This will result in higher employee morale and productivity, leading to improved efficiency, reduced turnover, and ultimately, higher ROI.
3. Customer loyalty and trust: Ethical behavior builds trust and loyalty among customers. When customers perceive a company as ethical, they are more likely to continue doing business with them, recommend their products or services to others, and become repeat customers. This will lead to increased sales, customer retention, and higher ROI.
4. Risk management: Ethical leaders prioritize compliance with laws, regulations, and ethical standards. By doing so, they minimize the risk of legal issues, fines, and reputational damage that can negatively impact a company's financial performance. Effective risk management can protect the company's assets and investments, ultimately contributing to higher ROI.
5. Long-term sustainability: Ethical leadership focuses on long-term sustainability rather than short-term gains. This includes considering the impact of business decisions on the environment, society, and future generations. By adopting sustainable practices, companies can reduce costs, enhance their reputation, and attract socially conscious customers, leading to improved ROI in the long run.

Overall, ethical leadership and behavior create a positive business environment that fosters trust, loyalty, and productivity. These factors contribute to increased sales, reduced costs, improved risk management, and long-term sustainability, all of which can positively impact a company's return on investment.

This book aims to explore the various dimensions of ethical leadership and provide insights into how leaders can cultivate and practice ethical behavior. It delves into the ethical challenges faced by leaders, the importance of ethical decision making, and the role of values and ethics in shaping organizational culture.

Through real-life examples, case studies, and practical strategies, this book aims to inspire and empower leaders to become ethical role models. It encourages leaders to prioritize ethical considerations in their decision-making processes, foster a culture of trust and transparency, and promote ethical behavior throughout their organizations.

Ultimately, this book seeks to contribute to the development of a new generation of leaders who not only achieve success but also make a positive difference in the world. It is my hope that readers will find value in the ideas and principles presented here and be inspired to embrace ethical leadership in their own lives and organizations.

Dr. Rolf Krökel (Managing Director at DEKRA Certification GmbH) has twenty years of experience in corporate development, mainly within the TIC (testing, inspection and certification) and automotive sector (manufacturing and service) as well as in financial and consulting industries. This includes the development of growth strategies and their successful operational execution in domestic and international markets (organic and inorganic/M&A). Furthermore, Rolf is equipped with sound experience and proven success in establishing and expanding international locations. He has successfully realized restructuring projects with a focus on organizational, processual, and personnel adjustments but also on product and service-oriented changes.

***

... with love

Love is a word overused.

The word love has been used and misused in claims and advertisement, used and misused in romantic relationships and family dynamics. What is love? Maybe something too broad to be actually lived.

But what happens when you add a preposition: *with* love? Can you talk to someone *with love*? Can you drive your car *with love*? Can you make your coffee in the morning *with love*?

Not from a place of love, not because of love, not because you need to love, but *with love*.

With love is a companion of softness. *With love* can signal you instantly and physically where you hold harshness in your mind and in your body. It's a plea to your own perception of yourself in your environment: your eyes look within, at the same time as you see yourself from the outside, at the same time as you let your eyes wander outward. *With love* can offer a holistic perspective on yourself.

With love doesn't exclude fierceness and decisiveness—instead it adds a quality. Making tough decisions *with love*, taking on great responsibility and doing so *with love*, adds a layer to your being that is neither cognitive nor mental. You don't have to engage your head in thinking to do something in a loving or kind way, it's not an effort to be figured out mentally.

With love is an enactive entity that is making decisions with you. And these decisions will be different from the ones made with harshness and rigidity. Letting go of the need to control everything solely with your head and reaching a place where you engage your whole body in the process of decision making will always be an extra effort in our revenue-driven society. But one worth it and in great demand.

With love can act as a bridge to living a more embodied, ethical life, both personally and career-wise—and this book may be an important cornerstone in this regard.

Ava Bonam is a naturopath and cultural scientist. She focuses on body therapy and the relationship between the world of ideas and the phenomenal world. She is based in Germany.

***

Ethical Leadership as an Approach Going Beyond Traditional Leadership Styles

It is with great pleasure and a profound sense of honor that I contribute a Foreword to this enlightening book on ethical leadership. As a leader in the telecommunications industry, I have witnessed firsthand the pivotal role that ethical leadership plays in shaping the trajectory of our organizations and the lives of those we serve, as well as its profound importance in our ever-connected world. Throughout my journey as a leader, I have come to realize that ethical leadership is not just a buzzword but a moral imperative that shapes the very essence of our organizations.

Ethical leadership, to me, means leading with integrity, empathy, and a deep sense of purpose. It goes beyond traditional leadership styles, transcending the focus on results and profits, to prioritize the well-being of our employees, customers, and the communities we serve. In the fast-paced and dynamic telecommunications industry, ethical leadership becomes a compass that guides us through the complexities and challenges, ensuring that we remain true to our values and principles. I believe that what sets ethical leadership apart from other styles is its unwavering commitment to doing what is right, even when faced with difficult decisions. It is not about seeking shortcuts or sacrificing long-term benefits for short-term gains. Instead, ethical leadership is about fostering an environment of trust and collaboration, where open communication and mutual respect flourish, enabling our teams to thrive and innovate. As a leader in the telecommunications industry, ethical leadership is of utmost importance to me because I recognize the impact our decisions have on the lives of millions of people. We are entrusted with the responsibility of providing essential communication services to individuals, businesses, and governments, and this responsibility demands ethical leadership that prioritizes the greater good over personal gain.

To *do good* in the sense of ethical leadership is to act with a sense of purpose and to be mindful of the implications of our actions on various stakeholders. It involves actively seeking ways to contribute positively to society, whether it's by ensuring data privacy and security, bridging the digital divide, or empowering our employees to reach their full potential. This commitment to doing good permeates every aspect of leadership, including the development of our employees. Nurturing a culture of ethical leadership through coaching, mentorship, and training instills in our teams the values of empathy, integrity, and responsibility. By empowering our employees to make ethically informed decisions, we cultivate a workforce that is not only skilled but also compassionate and principled.

In the interconnected world we live in today, the impact of ethical leadership extends far beyond the boundaries of our organizations. The considerations and actions we take as ethical leaders influence the well-being of communities, economies, and the global society. By prioritizing ethical leadership, we create a ripple effect of positive change, leaving a legacy that benefits the world at large. Nevertheless, the path of ethical leadership is not without dilemmas. Balancing the interests of stakeholders, addressing privacy concerns, and navigating the ethical implications of emerging technologies can be challenging. In the case of the relocation of Russian colleagues following the Russian war of aggression on Ukraine, I was in a position to experience at first hand how people in leadership might find themselves facing complex moral decisions. Balancing the well-being and safety of employees with broader geopolitical concerns requires careful consideration and empathy. It is in these challenging situations that ethical leaders must demonstrate courage and resilience, making decisions that reflect the best interests of their employees and the broader community.

I am convinced that the purposeful commitment to ethical leadership considerations is rewarding and a benefit on several levels. When taking a principled stand, like closing branches in politically challenging environments or supporting colleagues who seek a better life outside of them, we contribute to a more just and compassionate world. These actions demonstrate to our customers, stakeholders, and the global community that ethical leadership is not just a slogan, but something that we live by.

Dominik Schüle, MBA (Chapter Lead System Engineering Mobile Devices at Deutsche Telekom AG) holds a Master's Degree of Business Administration for Business Innovation from the European School of Management and Technology in Berlin and a Bachelor of Engineering in Information and Communication Technology from the Hochschule für Telekommunikation—University Applied Sciences in Leipzig. He joined Deutsche Telekom in 2007 and has since served the Group in various leadership and expert positions. His passion is mobile communications, both anchoring his professional life and his academic interests.

***

Reason Behind the Reason: Ethical Leadership as a Possibility

Business ethics do not seem to exist as such, but only as a norm (Luhmann[1]). Assuming this as a starting point, we can question whether it is good that people engage in developing business ethics, and this would be a moral question. However, we can also ask what the motivations are when engaging in developing business ethics. Therefore, the answer to this question reveals the reasons behind the norm of business ethics, behind its imperative. It may be true that one of the problems of modern ethics has to do with the problem of regressus ad infinitum: every reason leaves us with the question for the reason of this very reason. But if we do not want to try to find some sort of *ultimate ground* in our thoughts (or assume a platonic heaven of ideas), we can also lean on those who give us those reasons—in an empirical way, that is. And we can compare: are their reasons ours?

The result may not only be instructive for one's personal cognitive purposes. It can also have consequences for the one doing business. If one shares these reasons, one can decide whether or not to act accordingly. The reasons can be purely economic: *A business is more efficient when employees are happy*. It can also be more ethical: *The employees are entitled to a good life*. By implication, the *ultimate ground* would be the nexus between these two recommendations, a reason which is both economic and ethically convincing. It would not only reach more addressees, it would also implement ethics in the *unconscious* of someone who merely thinks in economic terms. As a consequence, business ethics will potentially meet its goal: this goal does not entail avoiding regressus ad infinitum but to change common practice. The *shall* can become a *be*.

Whether and to what extent this book can provide such *ultimate ground* is left to the reader and depends on their own approach. One may ask whether and in what way one *oscillates* between an economic and an ethical perspective. The only thing certain is that this book goes beyond platitudinous advice, which may reveal how priorities are set; for instance, when it is said: *ethical business management pays off.* Setting such handy but simplified formulas aside, the following chapters offer a deeper thinking. It not only provides reflections based on C. G. Jung's *Archetypes* (Chapter 5) or Lawrence Kohlberg's *Theory of Moral Development* (Chapter 8), it also sheds some light on the difference between good and evil as well as the significance of love as the cornerstone of leadership (Chapter 3). And the reader will certainly derive some benefit from this.

However, a utilitarian mindset alone may not be sufficient to get to the core of the following chapters. Reflections such as those presented in this book inherently leave answers open, especially the question whether ethical leadership is a possibility at all. This openness, in turn, reflects that the decisive factor might just be that questions are asked (and not answered), and this may apply to theory as well as to practice. Personal experience with this practice certainly shapes the basis of the following chapters—and personal consequences drawn from this practice. This book is one of those consequences.

Jan Ferdinand (Political and Social Scientist) is a social scientist working in Berlin and Koblenz, Germany. He is primarily concerned with memory on a social level and related issues: ethics, conceptions of time, political narratives of the past, and the relationship between theory and practice.

Note

1 Niklas Luhmann and Detlef Horster, *Die Moral Der Gesellschaft* (Suhrkamp EBooks, 2008). http://ci.nii.ac.jp/ncid/BA85779729.

Preface

The Practice of Ethical Leadership essentially started as a question. At its most basic, we were both intrigued by the question of why otherwise ethical people misbehave in certain circumstances. In other words, why do good people do bad things? In asking this question, we fully recognized that some people may have psychological disorders that remove guilt or that they are criminals. By and large we are not talking about them. Our focus is on those that are otherwise ethical and the individuals that lead them. More to the point, our focus is on leaders—those that aspire to be ethical, those that want their organizations to be ethical, and the organizations who want to hire and develop ethical leaders.

This book has been an extended journey. During our time writing *The Practice of Ethical Leadership* we have gone through a pandemic, experienced the death of parents, marriage (not to each other), job changes, and an album release, all while carrying on a long-distance relationship with each other via Zoom. Physically we have not seen one another since the onset of this project but our relationship and friendship has continued to develop and expand.

We share similarities and differences. Both of us have spent the bulk of our careers with consulting companies that specialize in assessing individual leadership skills for promotion or development. In fact, we first met when Florian came to the United States to conduct a development center and Rick was one of the consultants on the project. That meeting was followed by a visit by Florian to Rick and his wife, Debra, in Pittsburgh, USA, where we discovered more that we had in common and began to develop our friendship which has grown and developed over the intervening years. This book project sprang from that beginning when Florian, via email, raised a question about ethical leadership, Rick responded, and we were off.

We have differences as well. Some we knew at the outset—we differ by age, nationality, tastes in music, number of tattoos or earrings—which were apparent at the beginning, while others we discovered as we wrote, argued

DOI: 10.4324/b23260-1

points of view, or debated topics in the book. By and large, our differences balance each other out—for example, Florian is more philosophical, and Rick tends to be more practical—which has turned out to be a blessing as we explore various issues. Otherwise, we differ on the essential nature of mankind which simply serves as fodder for debate.

We started our project with more questions than answers. Among the questions we asked were:

- How do I define the common good for my business and certainly beyond mere business objectives? In what way does it matter for my clients, my employees, the community where my business is located, my investors, and my supporters?
- How do I make sound ethical decisions? How do I scrutinize a situation and make a decision that positively contributes to the greater good?
- What incentives can I install and communicate that promote veritable ethical behaviors?
- How do we deal with dilemmas? In what way do we raise awareness for such paradoxes and how do we reconcile them? What happens if identification of dilemmas turns out to be unfavorable for our business?
- What is my impact on society? In what way is it political? Is marrying politics and doing business admissible? If so, what is my leeway? If not, why?
- What kinds of structural conditions or company policies do I need to put in place to foster an ethical culture? How will I track, quantify, and monitor the ethical practices of my business?
- In what way may climbing the corporate ladder have an impact on my authenticity? In what way does this impact my ethical reasoning and acting?
- In light of relevant future developments, what will my ethical responsibility be?

In our book we will ask many questions to ponder. To get started, let us take a look at these fundamental considerations right off the bat. Do you want to be a leader or work with one who

1. Focuses on the organization, works to maximize the mission of the organization, and is concerned about the well-being of the people in the organization.
2. Focuses on your organization, works to maximize the mission of the organization, is concerned about the well-being of the people in the organization while making sure that the organization complies with the laws of the land.

3. Focuses on your organization, works to maximize the mission of the organization, is concerned about the well-being of the people in the organization, makes sure the organization complies with the laws of the land, and demonstrates concern for all people, the environment, and the community.

We suspect that most people would opt for the third. People search for and want a higher calling. They strive for a higher loyalty. They want to feel they are contributing to the greater good and well-being of others. That group, regardless of the type of organization they work in, is who we are writing to—those that aspire to more.

What This Book Is Not

If you are looking for a book on compliance and ethics, this is not the book for you. While we have a great deal of respect for organizations that have a compliance group or ethics officers, we intentionally stayed away from that arena. Fundamentally, we believe that compliance and ethics are a necessary starting point. Particularly if one is in or working with a large organization, moving toward compliance is crucial. At a bare minimum, organizations should strive to obey the laws of their land and expect that their employees will do the same. And we know that is not always an easy task. Moving toward legal equilibrium can be a challenging task. For many leaders of fast moving, entrepreneurial organizations, moving to compliance can be a daunting task as the organization culture may encourage pushing legal and ethical boundaries in the name of growth.

On Process Ethics

Be not simply good—be good for something.

(Henry Thoreau)

We think true ethical leadership transcends compliance and ethics policies. True ethical leadership takes moral decision making and action beyond rule obedience. Put another way, probably you will have heard of the phrase, *I would follow him or her into battle.* We suspect that that phrase is seldom used because a leader was great at getting people to follow the rules. More often, it is applied to those leaders who elevated the standard and expectations.

Likewise, we have our own personal views on right and wrong that will probably be transparent to the reader. Certainly, we believe in some transcendent truths, not harming others, revering life, questioning and developing self, but we have attempted to refrain from being overly "preachy" or pedantic. Rather, we have focused more on what we would call *process ethics*. We don't actually use that term much in the book, but it serves as an undercurrent of our perspective. We think each ethical leader needs to be reflective about matters of right and wrong, engage in discussion with others, and challenge basic assumptions.

Overview of the Book

We have divided this book into four major sections, although you may see overlap among some sections. These sections are:

I.   Definitions of Ethical Leadership and Its Importance
II. Conceptual Framework of Ethical Leadership
III. Practical Applications of Ethical Leadership
IV. Thoughts for the Future

Section I, which is comprised of Chapters 1 and 2, focuses on building the case for ethical leadership and begins a definition of terms, i.e., what is ethical leadership. This portion of the book also explores normative ethics—laying out a foundational argument of the book that some values, some decisions, and different ethical choices are better than others. The idea that there is a hierarchy of values and choices permeates the book and subsequent chapters.

Section II continues in Chapters 3 through 6 and introduces what we think are the foundations for ethical leaders—love and authenticity. We believe that coming from a place of love and being authentic are crucial aspects of ethical leaders. Without being true to oneself and having a large vision of humanity it is difficult, if not impossible, to make the right decision and lead others to the right place. This section also looks at the darker side of leadership and in the last two chapters of this section we explore the pathology of leadership and leadership as a political concept. In effect, placing road signs along the journey, noting pitfalls to avoid.

Section III, Chapters 7 through 11, directs attention toward the practical aspects of ethical leadership. While proposing both a stage model of ethical leadership and a hierarchy of values that can be applied to ethical behavior and decision making. Interspersed among those chapters, we also look at the question of hiring and developing ethical leaders, in both cases, offering practical solutions to hiring and development.

Section IV, contained in the last chapter of the book, looks at the future of ethical leadership through the lens of the various trends leaders will face in the near future. From climate change, individualization, artificial intelligence to aging populations, and other stops along the way, we explore some of the challenges ethical leaders will face, along with their organizations.

You will also notice as you move through the book that each chapter ends with a series of questions to ponder. While not a workbook in the traditional sense, we strongly believe that exploring personal reactions and insights as you read, particularly as it relates to ethics, is important.

Final Thoughts

There are many ways to look at or read a book. It can be information, a story, or multiple other options. We see this book as a dialogue. We lay out a framework for ethical leadership that is a reflection of our research, personal experience, and our opinions. We welcome and invite discussion, disagreement, and hearing your opinion. You can find our contact information and links to our website later in the book.

Enjoy

March, 2024
Florian and Rick

Section I

Definitions of Ethical Leadership and Its Importance

Chapter 1

Why Ethical Leadership?

Why not whip the teacher when the pupil misbehaves?

(Diogenes)

Leadership is a beautiful act. It involves responsibility, movement, making decisions, driving change that matters, and shaping the future. Mature leaders do not simply display ethical egoism as Adam Smith would have it. Rather the opposite: today's leaders should ponder the ethical consequences their decisions will have on individuals, teams, organizations, markets, the environment, and society. Sustainability, the social as well as ecological footprint, and most certainly the effects products and services will have on life (in the human as well as the animal realm) are subject areas leaders ought to think about. These are no mere buzzwords, but actual realities. If you think back one or two decades and sincerely consider what change inventions and new habits have initiated, you will realize we are seated in a bullet-train. With power comes responsibility. That is why ethics matter—and that is the main thrust of this chapter. Ethical leadership matters!

Starting Point and Motivation of This Book

Divorced from ethics, leadership is reduced to management, and politics to mere technique.
(James MacGregor Burns—historian, political scientist, presidential biographer)

This is a striking thought by James MacGregor Burns, and it highlights one of the key ideas we would like to underline in the following pages: ethics are at the very core of accomplished leadership. So let us delve right in: one could argue that we are in a cycle of divisiveness, chaos, and anger

DOI: 10.4324/b23260-3

around the world. People seem polarized by their differences and increasingly isolated from one another. Add to those dramatic life-and-death changes such as climate change, war, geopolitical tensions, power shifts as well as demographic challenges, and individuals, organizations, and leaders are left to ponder what direction to go in and what to do about the world. Certainly, it is a bit of a trite trope to say that times have never been more challenging. However, the challenges we face in the social, economic, and ecological domain are abundantly clear. Against this background, it is our contention that ethical leaders are needed and critical to the earth's future.

Ethical Consciousness and Moral Dilemmas

These times are marked by moral lapses. Deliberate misinformation and corporate scandals are rampant. We find ourselves asking:

- Who are these leaders?
- What do they stand for?
- What might be a positive outlook?
- What might a coherent skillset look like, ascertaining more ethical conduct and leadership?
- What might a comprehensive concept look like that goes beyond traditional business metrics and leadership behaviors?

This concern of ethical consciousness comes at a time when public trust in corporate governance or administrative institutions is extremely low, and leadership legitimacy is questioned.[1] Taking a look at society and the political domain, data gathered by the Organisation for Economic Co-operation and Development (OECD) suggests that, between 2018 and 2022, trust in the governance's work has been at 31% in the US, 35.4% in Italy, 39.5% in the United Kingdom, 45.7% in the Russian Federation, 50.7% in Canada, 60.8% in Germany,[2] 77.5% in Finland, 63.6% in Norway, and 83.8% in Switzerland.[3] In our view, this data raises some serious questions.

   Doing the right thing is not only a notion that gets raised on a regular basis in plays, movies, and books—it is at the very heart of the paths we choose on a daily basis. The question about what is fair and right is as old as humankind. Religious scripture has scrutinized the question of what is *good*, and philosophers such as Immanuel Kant, Søren Aabye Kierkegaard, Henry Thoreau, Lao-Tse, and Arab philosopher and polymath, Al-Kindi, have pondered on what is *right*.

Some people might consider ethics an intimate and an ultimately confidential matter. If our actions are legal and legitimate, the question of how we achieve our goals might not seem important at all. Some may even hold that ethics has no connection to leadership.

In our view, the opposite is true. Let us look at where leaders come from. A number of driving forces propel people into leadership positions. Based on the international experience we both share—and extending over a period of several decades of selecting and qualifying leaders—we believe that leaders typically feel motivated by a few factors:

- Achievement and a sense of accomplishment
- Giving guidance to others
- Perceived freedom and autonomy
- A sense of power and creative leeway
- Community and teamwork
- Driving positive change
- Influence
- Strategic work and vision
- Human development
- Visibility.

Virtually everyone is also driven by personal values and an innate sense of goodness. However, like many forces that guide behavior, these values are often intuitive and realized in an unconscious way.

Leaders enjoy an elevated status. People naturally look up to those in leadership positions and observe their behaviors closely—and the observers sometimes give that behavior symbolic meaning. Why is the CEO's door closed suddenly? Why does the company take a certain direction? What does a certain communication indicate? What does lack of communication indicate? People tend to give special scrutiny to decisions and statements by people who exert influence. No matter how flat the proclaimed hierarchies within organizations, leadership always matters—and it is our contention that leadership should always be ethically sensitive. This is one of the key motivations of this book.

When we hear position-related inconsistencies from a head of state, we might find it difficult to embrace what she or he stands for. We might even find it difficult to accept a high-ranking officer as representing our home country or the company we work for—especially so, if their values seem inconsistent.

Goodness, justice, rectitude, and honour—humans have always wondered about and scrutinized these things, but we've failed to clearly define them. Oftentimes, the best we can come up with are empty platitudes. It's too easy to compromise values based on platitudes, as founder of the research and consulting firm, Rainmaker Thinking, Bruce Tulgan, describes in his article "Values-Driven Leadership Is About More Than Just Platitudes." Winning and speed do not suffice.[4]

Ethical behavior (and leadership) is a tough job. It is usually time-consuming and uncomfortable. Over and above of this, it is equally satisfying and perilous to challenge oneself to conduct oneself ethically. Nobody is exempt from ethical scrutiny—from individuals steering global organizations or countries to grocery store clerks and kindergarten teachers.

In our point of view, people in leading positions will probably always be looked at a little more closely. That is why it is worthwhile to be ethically conscious. A firm ethical basis will help you not only maximize profit and progress, but also live an honorable, dignified, and humble life.

Life and leadership are full of moral dilemmas—those situations where the rules for action are not clear. Whether you are in a business, contribute to a spiritual institution, adhere to a specific philosophical discipline, or work in government, we all face choices where the answers and the way forward are anything but clear. The situations we are confronted with might be debatable, and at times downright ambiguous.

If you are a member of a business, there are daily situations where you must ask yourself whether (or not) you are behaving as the organization would expect. Now imagine you are the leader of that organization. You must constantly question yourself as to whether you are sending the right message to your people, and whether they are acting in a manner consistent with that message. And, if you are in a position to hire and lead leaders, are you selecting the people who will lead according to the values and expectations you deem relevant? It no secret that bad hires cost companies a fortune: global talent management consultants Talent Intelligence are getting to the heart of the matter by stating,

> from managing poor performance, damage to team morale, drain on productivity and—in the worst cases—poor customer service and reputational costs, the impact of one bad decision can be hard to reverse. In some cases, "bad hires" are actually strong candidates who have simply been placed in the wrong roles. This is also bad news—a single good hire leaving the company because a position isn't a good fit will cost the company, on average, 6–9 months of their salary.[5]

Let us look at an example of that kind of situation to see what we mean.

The company you work for has spent years developing a new, innovative product. The company has spent large sums on a product which management believes will be cutting edge. Forecasts look promising and indicate the device will be highly profitable. It goes without saying the company will gain a dominant position in its industry.

The CEO has already shared a prototype of the product with the business press, along with a production date. Expectations are extremely high for the product. The company has a growing sense that the product could be wildly successful, and that failure would be disastrous.

You work in an engineering group that is responsible for several components of the new product. You have final sign-off on the components in terms of quality and reliability. Recently, you discovered a small flaw in one of the component parts. While not a fatal flaw, your analysis suggests that the part might fail in less than 2% of the products. That failure would result in the product not functioning and would require warranty repairs.

You go to your supervisor with your concerns, and you're told not to pursue the issue, because reworking the part would significantly delay getting the new products to the marketplace.

What would you do?

Note: *Throughout this book, we will use various scenarios, case studies, and moral dilemmas. Where these refer to specific, real-life situations, we have cited the company or organizations.*

To be clear, no absolutely right answer exists for the above situation. Multiple variables and much more information about the situation would guide us in making a decision.

What we can agree on is that this dilemma raises a host of questions on ethics, right and wrong, and organizational expectations. In a nutshell, it raises the issue of ethical leadership and organizational culture. These might be some interesting (yet challenging) questions to ask when analyzing the above scenario:

- Do we want leaders who encourage ethical behavior?
- How does leadership affect the organizational culture?
- How will that engineer respond to the issue when there is no one looking over their shoulder?
- How will the engineer respond when problems occur eventually?

- What effect will potential issues have on the relationship of both leadership and employee?
- What might be a possible reaction on the part of the CEO?
- What general ethical principles come into play here?
- What is at stake, what are possible trade-offs, and which values have to be weighed here?

This is a simple yet significant dilemma of which there are many in ethical leadership. In our opinion, three different trends seem relevant to the generations preparing to take over the world:

1. There appears to be a growing dissatisfaction with the *old* way of doing things by institutions, governments, spiritual institutions, and leaders. The younger generations (millennials and younger) often show an angry sense of dissatisfaction and/or alienation, particularly as they face an uncertain future. Even though employee engagement is on the rise in the US,[6] other sets of data suggest otherwise: "More than half—51%—of all respondents said they're actively looking for a new job; 53% of respondents told Gallup that it's a good time to search for a new job. That's 8% higher than last year, indicating that "deeply unhappy workers are able to leave bad workplaces and find a career they like, according to the company."[7]
2. The younger generations—such as Gen Z—care a great deal about a range of ethical issues including social justice, climate change, and the distribution of wealth. One in four Gen Z employees are dissatisfied with their current job.[8] It appears that they will make decisions in politics, religion, and employment based on how those institution address their concerns.[9]
3. The traditional approaches to leadership—focused on goals achievement, using metrics to measure success—are incomplete and may have missed the mark relative to what people want and expect from their institutions. All the evidence seems to suggest that the younger generations (see above) will hold both higher standards *and* different standards for their leaders than the generations that preceded them.[10]
4. Put another way, the leadership models of the past—whether they focused on behaviors or traits or attributes—might be inadequate for leading in the future. More than the bottom-line results will be critical to success. Citizens, employees, consumers, and community members of the future will expect a focus on ethics or morality.

In most cases, that's not an area of emphasis for leaders today. Here's the crux of our discussion: we have no issue with the long-standing approaches to leadership that focus on achievement of bottom-line results. "Being ethical pays …,"[11] as Professor of Economics, Andrew Leigh, rightly states in his seminal book "Ethical Leadership."[12] But alongside Leigh and other researchers on the subject, we think that model is insufficient for the future—and it might have failed us in the past.

In our view, ethics does not simply raise the question of what is good and fair. It is not merely a discipline applied in courts, legal committees, and education. Ethics also serves as an ideal, something to strive for. As human beings, we want to grow, and most of us have a (transcendent, long-term, and overarching) north star to strive for.

Ethical leaders are *advocates of becoming* in a complex world. They should care for their people, but also have a sound footing when it comes to accountability toward society. That is one reason why ethical leadership matters.

As *Warrior for Life* and author, Dr. Israel W. Charny, accurately observed in *Psychology Today*,

> the obviously correct answer to the question 'is man good or bad?' is that both are very true. Man[kind] indeed is wonderfully good, caring, and creative: our species is an incredible leap forward on the evolutionary scale. Yet simultaneously man is one rotten manipulator, exploiter, abuser, and killer.[13]

Too often, we have seen spectacular ethical lapses on the part of businesses (think Banco Intercontinental, Boeing, Facebook, Uber, Equifax, or Volkswagen), religion (Inquisition, Irish Civil War, Luther on Judaism, or *nikāḥ al-mut'ah* (pleasure marriages which are condoned in some Islamic countries), institutions (Boy Scouts of America), and governments (turning over states, unjustified wars, genocide, and so forth). Just look at populist leaders around the world who ostensibly lead by demonizing others, building on fears, or supporting xenophobia (for instance, think of the rise of German right-wing party Alternative für Deutschland[14]).

The pandemic crisis caused by the coronavirus (COVID-19) between the end of 2019 and early 2023 represents a genuine ethical dilemma. On the one hand, business leaders need to be concerned with the health and well-being of employees, stakeholders, and customers, while still being concerned about the long-term economic viability of the business organization. This is uncharted territory. Leaders have clearly experienced uncountable dilemmas, trying to assume responsibility for both their employees, society, and their organizations. That is why ethical leadership matters and should be refined further.

Moving One Level Deeper: Why Ethics Matter

Until he extends the circle of his compassion to all living things, man will not himself find peace

(Albert Schweitzer—physician, theologian, musician)

Article 1 of the *Charter of Human Rights* of the United Nations says "all human beings are born free and equal in dignity and rights. They are endowed with reason and conscience and should act towards one another in a spirit of brotherhood."[15] On reflection, it becomes clear that leadership—just like other disciplines—must deal with dichotomic opposites. The above quote in its essence sounds accomplished. The realities surrounding us do not match up to this ideal—for a plethora of reasons which are anything but simple. It is true indeed that all human beings are (or should be) born in freedom and equal in dignity and rights. Leadership can grant freedom and help others self-actualize and reach for the stars. But one would be naïve to conjecture that leadership does not compromise certain freedoms. Dealing with such complexity, ambiguity, and dilemmas is the objective of ethical leadership. That is why we decided to work on this book.

Whether it is done explicitly or implicitly—and even though it is questioned and criticized by prominent personalities and top executives such as internet activist and computer engineer, Wael Ghonim[16], or the authors of the *Starfish and the Spider*, Ori Brafman and Rod Beckstrom—leadership always entails rules, standards, reporting lines, and legal accountability[17]. Someone or a group of stakeholders own the business, and they might employ a strategist who at least initiates the discussion of where to direct the organization in the future. This person might pull the proverbial strings together in order to then decide. However, the idea of contemporary and acceptable leadership is subject to dynamic developments. In our view, ethical leaders can navigate these purpose-driven discussion best—and that is why we decided to work on this book.

In discussions—no matter how constructive, equitable, and utterly lacking in hierarchy—certain individuals will always be particularly vocal about their viewpoints, even if they haven't been thought through sufficiently. When someone aggressively pushes an agenda, someone else's freedom will be constrained, even when the first article from the United Nations Charter holds true: all human beings are born free and equal in dignity and rights. Does this not translate into the corporate world as well? Of course, it does. So, again: such paradoxes must be dealt with and carefully navigated. This is where ethical leadership plays a role.

Indeed, the world is far away from this ideal. This is clearly observable in the unequal distribution of resources within organizations, the very fact of the poverty in most of countries worldwide, the over-exploitation of nature (clearly observable in repercussions such as pandemics, global warming, or social unrest), and troubling employee satisfaction rates in the often-quoted Gallup Studies (see above).

According to the *Worldwatch Institute*, in 1992, governments made a historic commitment to sustainable development—development that promotes the maintenance of well-being of both people and ecosystems.[18] Yet more than twenty years and several summits later, humanity has never been closer to ecological collapse. One-third of humanity lives in poverty and another two billion people are projected the join the human race over the next forty years. How will we move toward sustainable prosperity, equitably shared among all, even as our population grows, our cities strain to accommodate more and more people, and our ecological systems decline? We believe such situations call for ethical leadership.

Further Complexities

If you're not confused, you're not paying attention.
(Tom Peters—author, advisor, leadership expert)

To be clear: confusion over complexity must not function as an apology for refraining from profound analysis. This might be the intention of Tom Peter's thought-provoking quote above. Pick any organization or institution—a business, a religious institution, or a community organization. In almost every case, large or small, that organization has a mission statement about their overall direction and the values they and their members hold. In many of those statements, there is some reference to *integrity* as a value, usually referring to doing the right thing relative to customers, stakeholders, and employees.

In other words, almost every entity *says* they value some form of ethical behavior. But against that backdrop, we see a continual litany of misbehavior on the part of otherwise respected organizations. Why is that? Why do organizations that we often respect engage in immoral—or in many cases criminal—behavior? Even though this might not be a comfortable question, it is of the utmost importance—and answers do not come easily.

The answers to those questions are obviously complex, and we'll talk about many of them in the coming pages. However, we believe the fundamental issue is the failure of leaders to be ethical and to maintain ethical standards in their organizations. In some cases, that failure is intentional and even criminal (witness various Ponzi schemes or fraudulent organizations). Mind you, though, such failure can also be due to lack of attention, lack of follow-through, situational biases, or misplaced emphasis on the wrong rewards having unintended consequences.

We can and will look at those ethical standards which are unique to membership in a particular group—whether it is a business organization or some other institution. This is analogous to participating in a sport and following the rules of the game. Within the context of the game, we behave in a manner that is consistent with the rules. Should we misbehave (commit a foul), an objective third party (the referee) will mete out punishment. This third party has to reduce complexity and get to a verdict or judgment somehow: and that is why ethical leadership clearly matters.

To put it in another context, I can behave in a manner consistent with the norms of my peer group and be considered ethical within those confines. That is one standard of measuring ethical behavior—am I behaving in a manner that is consistent with the ethical standards of my community, country, or business?

However, the standard of my community or peer group might not represent ethical behavior as society generally defines it. In fact, our standard might directly oppose generally accepted standards of ethical behavior. I could be a member of a criminal gang and behave in accordance with the ethical standards of the gang while being in direct opposition to the generally accepted norms of society (think of the Mafia's creed "la cosa nostra"). Or, in an example closer to most of us, I could work for a company that is a major polluter and still be considered ethical within the organization, even if I am a social pariah outside the company because of who I work for and what they represent to the broader community.

Organizations have many ways to measure ethical behavior and ethical leadership, which we will address throughout the book. However, that still leaves us with the question of *why* people who are generally good sometimes misbehave.

Think about the following quotes or statements for a moment:

- "Management does not want to hear bad news or be challenged."
- "I was under pressure to meet my goals."
- "I was incentivized to cut corners or tell customers things that weren't true in order to make more money or meet expectations."
- "I had the chance to make a lot of money quickly."

While the list could go on, the key point is that, in almost every case of organizational misbehavior (other than those cases of criminal activity by an individual), something the leaders did or did not do contributed to the ethical lapses or provided the rationale for a lapse.

Too often, it seems, we celebrate leadership based on return to stakeholders, growth in revenue, and other traditional business metrics without tying that success to *doing the right thing*. Here's a hypothetical case to make the point.

Company X has a storied history. Founded more than 100 years ago, the company has grown steadily both through acquisition as well as organically. Over the last twenty years, the company has been run by the same individual, who has been celebrated in the business press for his visionary leadership as a result of the exponential growth the company has seen in international revenue, expanding business lines, and value returned to shareholders. The company's leader has achieved celebrity status with vast numbers of the population as a result of this effort, as well as his significant personal wealth.

But now another side of the company's success is receiving growing attention by the alternative press. The press has published several articles that focus on the company's record in its treatment of employees, based on low wages and massive layoffs. Its constant focus on profit has resulted in business being shifted to off-shore locations and putting pressure on suppliers. The company's environmental record is also under scrutiny for its significant impact on climate change.

While the above example may be overwrought for emphasis' sake, it makes the case that an organization has successfully met its *financial bottom-line* but has failed, either covertly or overtly, to meet its *ethical bottom-line*. Dealing with such complexities requires ethical sensibility—and we try to give guidance with this book.

Past, Present, and Future

Marry your future, court your present, and divorce your past.
Matshona T. Dhliwayo—philosopher, entrepreneur, author)

Organizations have always changed. In his ground-breaking work *On the Origin of Species by Means of Natural Selection, or the Preservation of Favoured Races in the Struggle for Life*, Charles Darwin's (1809–82) argued that every organism needs to adapt and modify in order to survive.[19] Newer factors might become more important, including competencies such as having an agile mindset and the capacity to be a credible activist, a cultural steward, or a strategy architect. Corporations might adopt these over the more traditional corporate values such as *entrepreneurial thinking, conflict management,* or *self-development*.

Competencies are constructs of ideal behaviour. Thus, whenever behaviour is measured, this happens against the background of an ideal. Good leaders are curious individuals who want to become the best versions of themselves. But as sure as Adam Smith's (1723–90) economic theories were geared toward healthy, ethical egoism[20], leaders ought to have a clear ethical foundation on which to consciously make decisions. They also must analyse their own behaviour and actively accept accountability for society as a whole.

Two famous authors took this position: the pursuit of self-interest is the best way to promote the general welfare. Bernard Mandeville (1670–1733) in his work *The Fable of the Bees*[21] and the aforementioned Adam Smith in his pioneering work on economics, *The Wealth of Nations*,[22] posited that what's good for the individual was good for the nation.

This very notion needs to be put in historic context, of course, and might be complemented by notions such as the acceptance of responsibility for future generations, the capacity of relinquishment, and the humble capacity of a leader to be open to the idea that he or she might sometimes err. During these times, discussions about *what's good for me* might include alternative compensation models. Millennials raise the question of life purpose as a high personal value. This also needs to be taken into account. In our view, modern leaders must assume responsibility toward society, mother nature, and generations that will follow. This raises challenging questions—and might even call our own behaviors into question. That is why ethical leadership matters.

Compliance and Oversight

Ensure compliance and be responsive to the feedback.
(Anne McLellan—entrepreneur, leadership expert)

As we progress on our journey, let us be clear about one other item. Simply having a code of ethics, an ethics officer, or a compliance staff is not enough and is not the answer to the above challenges. So, in a way, we would like to complement McLellan's statement above. Certainly, codes of ethics and compliance officers help reinforce the ethical culture and provide clarity on what individuals should and should not do. But fundamentally, compliance happens under the overarching umbrella of ethical leadership. Compliance and codes are just one step in the right direction.

The same is true of oversight by a professional association, trade association, or regulatory agency. To expect that an outside agency will monitor ethical behavior or reinforce that behavior is naïve. As a case in point, let's look at safety. We think safety is an ethical issue, because providing a safe environment for employees should be crucial to the success of any leader. In the US, employee safety is monitored by OHSA (Occupational Health and Safety Agency), a government-funded watchdog. OHSA is vigilant and active, but they can't be everywhere all the time. Regardless of their intense oversight, people are still killed and injured on the job. Ultimately, safety should be a local issue driven by leaders and a culture that cares. As some of the cases outlined above, ambiguity and economic pressures oftentimes cause dilemma. Leaders should be attuned to an ethical compass in order to resolve such dilemmas and proceed in a reasonable way when it comes to escalation, communication, and deriving lessons learned.

What Is Different About Ethical Leadership?

Leading with positive ethical values builds trust and brings out the best in people, which brings out the best in the organization, which leads to great results.
(Linda Fisher Thornton—entrepreneur, author)

Leadership has many definitions and traditions. Researchers, leaders, HR experts, consultants, and politicians alike talk about servant leadership, humble leadership, neuro leadership, directive leadership, democratic leadership, and transformational leadership.

For the sake of simplicity, let us assume that leadership is the ability to influence others to achieve a desired goal (whilst establishing team morale, purpose, motivation, and vision). Ronald Reagan once said, "The greatest leader is not necessarily the one who does the greatest things. He or she is the one that gets the people to do the greatest things."[23] In other words, leaders are measured by their effectiveness in getting things done through and with other people.

Many view leadership as a series of traits (like author Steve Covey[24]) while others see it as a combination of competencies a leader can easily re-sort to and apply at a high maturity level. Competency models tend to look at what effective leaders *do* and describe the behaviors of effective leaders.

There is nothing inherently wrong with the trait or competency model approach to leadership. Both approaches provide a means for individual development, training, and/or selection practices. But these models often speak of ethics in aspirational terms, i.e., a leader should be honest, pos-sess integrity, and/or be of good character.

Ethical leadership might be even trickier to define, although this topic has been researched (see Ahmad and Gao, 2017 for an overview[25]). Some ethical leadership definitions speak to the characteristics of ethical leaders (integrity, trustworthiness, honesty, transparency, future-orientation, etc.) while others connect the ethical leader to a system of ethics or beliefs.

For our purposes, we will define ethical leadership this way:

Ethical behavior is defined as the conscious moral reasoning that guides the behavior of human beings regarding what is right and wrong. This in-cludes personal conduct as well as decision making. Ethical demeanor considers the individual's best interest but also takes into consideration the best interest of those impacted. Ultimately, ethics does not only deal with philosophical understanding, but also inspires us to "improve how we live" (Alex Voorhoeve, 2009[26]) and respectfully fit into the natural world. In our view, by being ethical, we enhance our lives and the lives of others. Or, as Aristotle famously stated in *The Nicomachean Ethics*, "the good for man is an activity of the soul in accordance with virtue, or if there are more kinds of virtue than one, in accordance with the best and most perfect kind."[27]

Tangible Consequences and Return on Ethics (ROE)

We must shift our thinking away from short-term gain toward long-term investment and sustainability, and always have the next generations in mind with every decision we make.

(Deb Haaland—politician)

Leadership of self and others must be credibly and effectively sustainable – and that is why Deb Haaland rings in this section on the Return on Ethics (ROE). Twenty years ago, the idea of ethical investing or ethical investment strategy was either unknown or scoffed at. The general argument was that avoiding oil companies or tobacco companies was short-sighted and would always return less than the general approach to investing. Indeed, companies paid little or no attention to the ethical investing niche.

This may be changing. Organizations such as Morgan Stanley are now producing material strongly suggesting that ethical investing is, in fact, both profitable and sustainable. A 2009 research by Ethisphere[28] demonstrated that the world's most ethical companies see their stock grow twice as fast as conventional companies. Ethisphere annually analyzes how the share value of publicly traded honorees compares to the large cap index. They concluded in 2020 that the world's most ethical companies had outperformed the large cap sector, over five years, by 13.5%.[29]

It appears that strategies considering ethics are becoming more attractive to individuals who want to do good while doing well—and we suspect that more and more companies and their leaders are paying attention.

In short, the evidence is increasing that the *ethical bottom-line* might be just as important as the traditional *financial* bottom-line.

There is likewise a body of evidence that unethical or bad behavior on the part of organizations and institutions does have a direct impact regarding company value, public perception, investigative scrutiny, and consumer confidence. To mention a few:

- **Negative public perception:** public perception and the support of buying consumers may drop dramatically. Recent scandals regarding the Boeing 737Max or Boy Scouts of American bankruptcy[30] might be the tip of the iceberg.
- **Employee engagement:** employee engagement and retention may drop following unethical behavior, resulting in decreased productivity and/or increased turnover.

- **Investigative scrutiny:** public or legislative investigations may follow perceived malfeasance or criminal activity.
- **Consumer confidence:** consumers of services and goods do pay attention to a company's ethics—and when consumers lose confidence, it directly impacts the bottom line.

(Ethical) Culture Is Crucial

Culture is the arts elevated to a set of beliefs.

(Thomas Wolfe—author, novelist)

While we discuss leadership, we would be remiss if we did not also talk about organizational culture. In fact, we have dedicated one entire chapter to culture. For the moment, let us use the premise that *culture* is determined by the principle of "we are what we repeatedly do," which is a well-known notion (and misattribution to Aristotle). In other words, culture is the sum of the consistent, observable patterns of behavior in an organization.

To that end, we believe that:

1. An organization's culture is a crucial aspect of whether the organization will behave in an ethical manner. Put another way, the culture defines what is and is not ethical behavior and practice. Consider the Catholic Church and its problems with sexual abuse of children. The Church espouses a claim to morality and the teachings of Jesus, yet its day-to-day operations have created a culture where child abuse was brushed under the carpet and pedophiles have been supported and/or protected from prosecution by civil legal authorities. Put bluntly, the church's *culture* has been stronger than the moral teachings of the church.
2. That leads to our second belief. The stated culture as described in the organization's documents, mission, and values might be quite different from the actual culture. In other words, an organization might say that it values integrity and honesty in all its public pronouncements, and yet, in actuality, it might tolerate breaking the law.
3. Points 1 and 2 lead to our fundamental belief and one of our core premises: *Leaders shape culture.* Leaders define the ethical nature of the organizational culture by their actions and words.

We will further discuss organizational culture as it relates to ethics, but we think it is significant to introduce the idea early on. Leaders define and shape the culture around them. A leader does not lead in a vacuum. A leader's actions and behaviors have a direct impact on the behaviors and actions of others.

The Greats on (Ethical) Leadership: What They Teach Us Still

The mediocre teacher tells. The good teacher explains. The superior teacher demonstrates. The great teacher inspires.

(William Arthur Ward—author)

George Orwell (1903–50) and Aldous Huxley (1894–1963) painted dystopian views of the future in books like *Animal Farm, 1984, Brave New World*, and *Island*. At the same time, they both advocated for a dignified and humane life. Today's leaders must demonstrate a similar grasp of current realities (and occasionally read some Orwell and Huxley). They must be up to speed politically and in terms of self-critique, market trends, societal developments, and the question about what is good and fair. That is why, we are convinced, ethical leadership matters.

We can find many clues in what has been said about leadership over the past 3,000 years: the great Chinese philosopher Lao Tse, in his well-known work *Tao Te Ching*, told us: "Water is fluid, soft, and yielding. But water will wear away rock, which is rigid and cannot yield. This is another paradox: What is soft is strong."[31] Alexander the Great (356 BC–323 BC) exclaimed his gratitude toward his teacher and educator, the legendary philosopher Aristotle: "I am indebted to my father for living, but to my teacher for living well."[32] Saladin (1138–93), the great Muslim leader who fought against Richard the Lionheart (1157–99), King of England, and engaged in vivid correspondence with his foe, stated: "I have become so great as I am because I have won men's hearts by gentleness and kindliness."[33] Eleanor Roosevelt (1884–1962), the great American first lady and leader, famously remarked: "Do what you feel in your heart to be right—or you'll be criticized anyway."[34] Jacinda Ardern (1980–present), who became fortieth Prime Minister of New Zealand and led the country through one its greatest tragedies when the Christchurch shootings happened on March 15, 2019, said of her country:

> We are a proud nation of more than 200 ethnicities and 160 languages, and amongst that diversity, we share common values. And the one that we place currency on right now is our compassion and the support for the community of those directly affected by this tragedy and secondly, the strongest possible condemnation of the ideology of the people that did this. You may have chosen us, but we utterly reject and condemn you.[35]

All these observations refer to the notions of goodness, righteousness, responsibility toward others, dignity, and respect. By researching the deeds and lives of these and other individuals, we can get clarity on our own cultural background, values, and upbringing. This might lead to judgment or identification. In any case, all the above statements are rooted in ethical foundations. These are the words of great leaders. As William Arthur Ward observed, the great teachers (or leaders) inspire and kindle a spark within. These leaders have accepted a path toward giving guidance to others. Leaders are given power and leeway, and this should be used to create goodness. The intention of this book is to provide a sound foundation, framework, and guideline for ethical leadership, while raising essential questions with which every human being—and especially those in powerful positions—must grapple.

Questions to Ponder

He who has a why to live for can bear almost any how.
(Friedrich Nietzsche—philosopher)

If you are *not* a leader:

1. Do I work for a leader who is ethical? Will they do the right thing? Do they care about me as a person? Do they care about the environment, society, and the great good?
2. Is the organization I belong to ethical and moral? Am I proud to tell others that I am a member of the organization?
3. If I made the choice in my organization to report the problems, would the organization support me?
4. Is there anything I can contribute personally in order to make the organization I work for greater? Whom could I approach? What specifically could I do?
5. We all consider ourselves to be righteous and good, but objectively speaking, in most cases there is room for improvement. Is there anything I could work on to become a better version of myself?

If you *are* a leader in an organization:

1. Do I do the right thing when I am faced with ethical issues? Do I reinforce doing the right thing with the people who work with me?
2. How could I get a more objective view of myself? If I ask someone, will they tell me the truth or just confirm what I want to know? Who would be bold enough to critique my demeanor so that I might learn a relevant lesson about myself?
3. Do the people who work with me do the right thing when I am not present?
4. What systems, processes, or tools do I use to reinforce ethical behavior? Do I recognize and reward the ethical choices others make?

If you are a board member, CEO, or otherwise lead an organization:

1. Do we expect our leaders to be ethical and moral? Do we create reward systems that support ethical behavior?
2. Would it be feasible to introduce a key performance indicator that takes ethical conduct into consideration? What criteria would we base it on?

3. What positive impact does my organization have on society now and on future generations to come? Is this wishful thinking? If so, what can I do about it?

4. Bearing in mind that the *Dark Triad* (powerful people's tendency toward narcissism, psychopathy, Machiavellianism) described by Paulhus and Williams[36] is often present and might affect me as well: how can I get candid feedback to help me work on myself as a leader in a position of power whose actions matter to others?

5. Do we consider ethical leadership when we hire or promote employees?

Notes

1 Robert M. Fulner, "The Challenge of Ethical Leadership," *Organizational Dynamics* 33, no. 3 (August 1, 2004): 307–17. https://doi.org/10.1016/j.orgdyn.2004.06.007.

2 Data gathered by Statista and others in the summer of 2023 suggests that 42% of Germans are not particularly satisfied and 33% are not satisfied at all. Compare: https://de.statista.com/statistik/daten/studie/2953/umfrage/zufriedenheit-mit-der-arbeit-der-bundesregierung/

3 OECD, "Trust in Government." https://data.oecd.org/gga/trust-in-government.htm

4 Bruce Tulgan, "Values-Driven Leadership Is about More than Platitudes," *Forbes*, March 31, 2022. www.forbes.com/sites/brucetulgan/2022/03/31/values-driven-leadership-is-about-more-than-platitudes/?sh=5880915fb8b3.

5 Talentintellig, "Why Do Companies Keep Hiring the Wrong People?—Talent Intelligence," Talent Intelligence. September 8, 2022. www.talentintelligence.com/why-do-companies-keep-hiring-the-wrong-people/.

6 Jim Harter, "Employee Engagement on the Rise in the U.S.," *Gallup.Com*, April 5, 2023. https://news.gallup.com/poll/241649/employee-engagement-rise.aspx.

7 Cf: https://edition.cnn.com/2023/06/13/business/stressed-disengaged-workers-gallup-poll/index.html

8 Camille Bello, "1 in 4 Gen Z Employees Are Unhappy at Work and 20% Are Considering Quitting Their Jobs, Study Finds," *Euronews*, April 19, 2023. www.euronews.com/next/2023/04/14/1-in-4-gen-z-employees-are-unhappy-at-work-and-20-are-considering-quitting-their-jobs-stud.

9 Harter, "Employee Engagement on the Rise in the U.S." .

10 Lloyd Chrein, "The Moral Leadership Report 2022 | The HOW Institute for Society." The HOW Institute for Society, January 26, 2023. https://thehowinstitute.org/the-moral-leadership-report-2022/.

11 Andrew Leigh, "Why It Pays to Be an Ethical Company," *Real Business*, September, 2018. https://realbusiness.co.uk/why-it-pays-to-be-an-ethical-company.

12 Andrew Leigh, *"Ethical Leadership:* Creating and Sustaining an Ethical Business Culture" (London: Kogan Page, 2013).

13 Cf: www.psychologytoday.com/us/blog/warrior-life/201803/the-nature-man-is-man-nature-good-or-basically-bad.

14 Zeitung, *Süddeutsche*, "AfD Watershed, 5 Reasons For The Far Right Rising In Germany," *Süddeutsche.De*, May 2018. www.sueddeutsche.de/projekte/artikel/politik/afd-5-reasons-for-the-far-right-rising-in-germany-e403522/.

15 United Nations, "Universal Declaration of Human Rights," United Nations, n.d. www.un.org/en/about-us/universal-declaration-of-human-rights.

16 HarvardCPL, "Leadership & the Internet: Wael Ghonim," 2012. www.youtube.com/watch?v=CSJTb8uD1Gw.

17 Ori Brafman and Rod A. Beckstrom, *The Starfish and the Spider: The Unstoppable Power of Leaderless Organizations* (New York: Penguin US, 2006).

18 The WorldWatch Institute, Rockefeller Brothers Fund. 1974. www.rbf.org/about/our-history/timeline/worldwatch-institute.

19 "Charles Darwin," History and Society, *Encyclopedia Britannica*, July 8, 2023. www.britannica.com/biography/Charles-Darwin/On-the-Origin-of-Species.

20 Emrys Westacott, "What Is Ethical Egoism?" *ThoughtCo*, October 2019. www.thoughtco.com/what-is-ethical-egoism-3573630.

21 Bernard Mandeville, "The Fable of the Bees or: Private Vices, public Benefits" (1732). https://oll.libertyfund.org/title/kaye-the-fable-of-the-bees-or-private-vices-publick-benefits

22 "The Wealth of Nations," Adam Smith Institute, n.d. www.adamsmith.org/the-wealth-of-nations.

23 Alize Malik, "Leadership!" *Medium*, December 9, 2021. https://medium.com/@LizSwag/leadership-32e96675aa6c.

24 Marcel Schwantes, "How Stephen Covey's 'The 7 Habits' Guides Leaders in Times of Challenge and Uncertainty." *Inc.Com*, January 5, 2021. www.inc.com/marcel-schwantes/stephen-covey-the-7-habits-of-highly-effective-people-leaders.html.

25 Israr Ahmad and Yongqiang Gao, "Ethical Leadership and Work Engagement," *Management Decision* 56, no. 9 (2018): 1991–2005. https://doi.org/10.1108/md-02–2017–0107.

26 Alex Voorhoeve, "Hugh LaFollette: The Practice of Ethics," *Social Choice and Welfare* 34, no. 3 (2009): 497–501. https://doi.org/10.1007/s00355-009-0414-4.

27 *Nicomachean Ethics of Aristotle: Book I: The Good for Man*: Chapter 13. "Division of the Faculties, and Resultant Division of Virtue into Intellectual and Moral," n.d. www.sacred-texts.com/cla/ari/nico/nico013.htm.

28 Carlos Baez, "Ethisphere: Data and Community for Leading Integrity Programs," Ethisphere, March 13, 2023. https://ethisphere.com/.

29 Ethisphere, "Ethisphere Announces the 2020 World's Most Ethical Companies," New York, February 25, 2020. https://ethisphere.com/ethisphere-announces-the-2020-worlds-most-ethical-companies/.

30 Dietrich Knauth, "US Boy Scouts Exits Chapter 11 Bankruptcy after Abuse Settlement," Reuters, April 19, 2023. www.reuters.com/legal/boy-scouts-emerges-chapter-11-bankruptcy-2023–04–19/.

31 Elizabeth Yuko, "3 Leadership Lessons from Lao Tzu That Are Completely Relevant Today," *Thrive Global*, June 2023. https://community.thriveglobal.com/lao-tzu-ancient-wisdom-effective-leadership-lessons/.

32 Tal Gur, "I Am Indebted to My Father for Living, but to My Teacher for Living Well," Elevate Society, June 21, 2023. https://elevatesociety.com/i-am-indebted-to-my/.

33 "Saudi Aramco World : Saladin: Story of a Hero," n.d. https://archive.aramcoworld.com/issue/197003/saladin-story.of.a.hero.htm.

34 T. Emerson, "'Do What You Feel in Your Heart to Be Right—for You'll Be Criticized Anyway. You'll Be Damned If You Do, and Damned If You Don't.'—Eleanor Roosevelt." *Medium*, October 3, 2022. https://medium.com/be-bold/do-what-you-feel-in-your-heart-to-be-right-for-youll-be-criticized-anyway-b2457d5e7fba.

35 New Zealand Ministry of Foreign Affairs and Trade, "Statement from Prime Minister Jacinda Ardern on the Christchurch Terror Attacks—March 15." March 15, 2019. www.mfat.govt.nz/en/media-and-resources/statement-from-prime-minister-jacinda-ardern-on-the-christchurch-terror-attacks-march-15/.

36 Delroy L. Paulhus and Kevin L. Williams, "The Dark Triad of Personality: Narcissism, Machiavellianism, and Psychopathy," *Journal of Research in Personality* 36 no. 6 (2022): 556–63. https://doi.org/10.1016/s0092–6566(02)00505-6.

Chapter 2

What Is Ethical Leadership?

Ethics is knowing the difference between what you have a right to do and what is right to do.

(Potter Stewart)

In Chapter 1 we dug into the argument for why ethical leadership is important. Taking it one step further, discussing why a concept is important naturally leads to a desire for a more specific definition of the concept. In this case, let's define what ethical leadership is as we head toward an operational definition of ethical leadership which can be used for multiple purposes. However, a discussion of ethical leadership requires more than just a definition—it also requires some background and perspective. As Stewart, the former US Supreme Court Judge, notes in the quote above, knowing what is right and doing right are two different things. We will look at both sides of the equation in this and subsequent chapters.

When we first started to lay out this book, one of the publishers we approached turned us down with the simple statement that "books on ethics do not sell because everyone considers themselves to be ethical." Perhaps the publisher's statement is true. Most, if not all, people consider themselves to be ethical. However, when one becomes a leader responsible for setting direction, caring for people, and ensuring their well-being, production, and transcendent values, the leader's personal ethics may be insufficient. What may be right or wrong for me personally may be different when I lead others. Consequently, we believe ethical leaders consciously explore concepts of right and wrong as they apply to leading others and decision making.

German theologian Dietrich Bonhoeffer wrote a book titled *Ethics*, which states that the two ethical problems we all face are "How can I be good?" and "How can I do something good?"[1] An ethical leader asks themselves the same questions, which may or may not be grounded in religious beliefs. While *how to be good* may have religious overtones for some, the

DOI: 10.4324/b23260-4

discipline of ethical thought is not necessarily rooted in the *esoteric* (i.e., the spirit behind the form, such as Sufism, Yoga, or Brahmanism) or the *exoteric* (i.e., the unique stories and myths behind each of the great faiths, Christianity, Buddhism, Islam, Shintoism, Taoism, and so forth) traditions at all. Consider the French existentialist philosopher Simone de Beauvoir (1908–86), who wrote extensively on feminism, politics, and social issues.[2] Another example of how spiritual influence is not always a factor in ethics is evident with Bertrand Russell (1872–1970), the British philosopher, historian, and atheist social critic.[3] Or consider Ibn al-Rawandi (827–911 AD), a Persian philosopher who argued dogma to be antithetical to reason and who stated that miracles were fake, prophets just magicians, and paradise described by the Qur'an was not actually desirable.[4]

Other figures that come to mind include Friedrich Nietzsche (1844–1900), who evoked the *superman* in "Thus spake Zarathustra,"[5] Patricia Churchland (born in 1943), a Canadian American analytical philosopher known for her materialistic approach in the philosophy of mind,[6] or Ayn Rand (1905–82), the Russian-American founder of objectivism and a novelist who coined her take on love, stating,

> *to love is to value. Only a rationally selfish man, a man of self-esteem, is capable of love—because he is the only man capable of holding firm, consistent, uncompromising, unbetrayed values. The man who does not value himself, cannot value anything or anyone.*[7]

The critical questions are the ones Bonhoeffer raises, regardless of religious orientation. As we work towards a useable, operational definition of ethical leadership, some background is in order as we are essentially merging two concepts: ethics and leadership. You do not have to be an expert in the study of ethics, but some understanding of the history of ethics and various approaches to ethical issues is in order.

A Short History of Ethics: Background and Relevance

Prior to the twentieth century, reading and studying ethics was considered part of the education and preparation of future leaders. Often this consisted of reading classical writers or philosophers who addressed moral and ethical issues (such as Solon, Aristotle, and Sun Tzu, to name just a few). With the industrial revolution and rampant capitalism, that study seems to have fallen by the wayside. The trend appears to be changing as more and more schools, particularly political, business, legal, as well as medical programs, now contain an ethical component.

At its most basic form, ethics is the study of the moral principles that guide our behavior and decisions about what is right and wrong for individuals and society. As such, most philosophers use the terms *ethics* and *morals* almost interchangeably. You will find that we bounce back and forth in our use of the terms as well.

If ethics is about the determination of right and wrong, then the discussion of ethics has probably existed as long as the spoken word has existed. It's timeless. Most cultures have an oral or written tradition of myths. The Mesopotamian Gilgamesh epic, the Chinese Pangu myth, Siberian Tungusic creation myths, or the Norse mythology were documented in both the Prose Edda as well as the Poetic Edda, and contain stories that explore right and wrong through the tales of gods or ancestors. Our heritage as humans seems to be rooted in the exploration of correct behavior and how to pass those expectations down through generations. While that exploration of right behavior seems to be a constant, it is striking to note the inherent contradictions—war, slavery, brutality—that have existed along with more peaceable pursuits.

You can also read the history of ethics in the explorations of different religious faiths. Every faith and culture explores right and wrong in the context of faith and belief. The Jewish and Christian exploration of the Ten Commandments is a case in point where correct behavior is proscribed and defined. The Qur'an and the Hadith (a record of the words, actions, and the silent approval of the Islamic prophet Muhammad) outline moral commandments and guidance of a similar nature for Muslims. Likewise, the five precepts of Buddha provide guidance on correct behavior.[8] Whether you are an adherent of Eastern beliefs, Abrahamic faiths, or no organized religious structure, the faiths contain a moral system that provides guidance to believers on the dilemmas they face in daily lives. While some faiths are quite prescriptive and carefully delineate what is right and what is wrong, others are more fluid. Yet all faiths define some attributes of behavior that believers should act on and adopt. Bear in mind, we are not suggesting that one needs to be religious or spiritual in any way to be ethical. It's really just the opposite. There is a rich body of non-religious thoughts and discourse that has been geared toward giving ethical guidance throughout the ages and exploring the nature of goodness.

In the so-called Western world, much of the focus on ethics seems to have been on early Greek philosophers and the tenets of the various Abrahamic faiths with less attention paid to Eastern philosophies and religions in Western cultures. This book does not intend to explore that dilemma at great length or resolve the potential chauvinism involved. Rather, we simply acknowledge that there may be potential omissions in our review of ethics and its history.

Most Western philosophers, while potentially influenced by Judeo-Christian traditions, look at two main branches of ethics: normative ethics and applied ethics.[9]

Normative ethics explores the various codified approaches (i.e., established norms for behavior or action) to determining right and wrong behavior. Normative ethics can further be subdivided into various additional branches that look at a range of approaches to right and wrong. Each of these approaches uses a variety of methods for determining right and wrong. The often-referenced Utilitarianism and Social Contract Theory also fall under the umbrella of normative ethics.[10] Each in its own way attempts to provide a principled approach to making ethical decisions.

Most human beings operate under some form of normative ethics based on religion, culture, or other variables that define right or wrong for them. Ethical leadership requires a degree of introspection that makes it different from "just plain" leadership. Without taking a position on a particular branch of normative ethics, although we lean toward principled approaches, the study of ethics *is* important to those who aspire to be ethical leaders.

> In the United States, largely because of its constitutional separation of church and state, the religious faith of its elected leaders has always been a source of consternation, particularly when that faith is different from your own. Witness the debate in 2020 over the Supreme Court nominee (Amy Coney Barrett) who was considered a conservative Catholic.
>
> There is no question that when we consider someone for a significant position, we should understand their philosophies and beliefs. But perhaps the real question is why we do not place more value on people who have well-thought-out systems of belief.

Whether consciously or unconsciously, the underlying assumptions and beliefs one has about the nature of right and wrong (normative ethics) serve as the platform for ethical leadership. Applied ethics, which looks at specific issues such as business ethics or environmental ethics, tends to apply principles of normative ethics to specific situations. Hence applied ethics often considers principles of lawfulness, justice, or harm as they apply to specific moral dilemmas (such as the ethics behind euthanasia). Organizations often use applied ethics to define accepted behavior or actions. Most codes of ethics that one may see in various organizations are variations on applied ethics. They prescribe or proscribe specific actions in certain situations based on the underlying principles the organization follows.

We will return to the discussion of ethics in Chapter 10 when we discuss developing and selecting ethical leaders. Prior to that, several thoughts are in order:

1. Ethical leaders consciously think about, study, and debate the nature of right and wrong in their environment. While ethical leaders consider traditional metrics in their decision making, what keeps them awake at

night is the fundamental question of whether their decision is morally right. Think for a moment about your own knowledge of ethical lapses in organizations. Most, if not all, lapses come from excessive reliance on profit or greed. At a minimum, those organizations that do not get into trouble place a reliance on obeying the letter of the law as a standard of practice. While we do not believe that ethical leaders need to be philosophers, some study of different ethical concepts is in order. At a minimum, ethical leaders need to engage with others in debating the pros and cons of different decisions relative to ethical norms.

2. Many organizations have developed codes of ethics and compliance standards, and hire organizational officers whose responsibility is to ensure their organization complies with legal and ethical standards. While a positive step, these actions are not a substitute for ethical leadership. Compliance is inherently based on laws, rules, or codes of behavior. Their goal might be to avoid breaking the law, not nurturing ethical practices. No set of rules can cover the moral quandaries that ethical leadership encounters. Compliance may be, but is not always, ethical leadership.

3. In later chapters we speak about values and their role in ethical leadership. And, we definitely have our own views on values, hierarchies of right and wrong, and appropriate behavior. Fundamentally, however, we believe in what we call "process ethics," meaning that we think it is more important for leaders to engage with their organizations in defining right and wrong, debating specific decisions, and being transparent about reasoning and concerns. In that sense we are less concerned about absolute definitions of right and wrong, while being more concerned about the journey leaders and organizations take to determining right and wrong.

Relativism: Cultural and Otherwise

At one level, discussions about ethics or morality sound like debates between various approaches, beliefs, and values. Think of a political discussion between people who disagree with one another. Often, it sounds like the opposing sides are speaking different languages, not listening or agreeing on basic facts. This is a common-sense approach to what philosophers would refer to as *relativism*. *Oxford Reference* defines relativism as "the doctrine that knowledge, truth, and morality exist in relation to culture, society, or historical context, and are not absolute."[11]

What exactly does this mean? On the one hand, there are differences in cultures and how they may define right and wrong. Different cultures have varied mores, norms, and views on how right or wrong is judged, which are unique to each culture and heritage. Read any history book or look at the current news and it does not take long to find instances of discrimination or injustice that have been institutionalized as part of a particular culture. Look at instances of racial discrimination, discrimination based on religious beliefs, or all-too-frequent instances of genocide that occur all too often. One only has to witness the Persian Gulf crisis, the Syrian war, China–India skirmishes, the Yemen humanitarian crisis, or the expansion of detention camps that the Chinese government is pushing in an effort to suppress the Uighur Muslim minority in Xinjiang. In almost every case the local culture or country justifies that action based on tradition, history, or laws that support it.

> Look at the tension created by the rise of Islam (either through conversion or immigration) in North America and Western Europe. While most Muslims and Christians may be decent law-abiding citizens, the degree of fear, hostility, and mistrust created by different cultures and beliefs potentially erects bridges that cannot be crossed, even with the best of intentions.

However, cultural relativism is not justification for an ethical leader. Ethical leadership is built on a small range of moral principles that are universal—principles that cut across all cultures. While we can debate individual principles, we can all probably agree on a handful, such as: do no harm to others, social justice, non-aggressiveness, prohibition of initiation of force or violence against another person or people, freedom, and so forth. Almost all cultures at some level agree on such things in principle, if not in practice.

In short, ethical leaders act on moral principles that undergird their actions, not necessarily the norms and traditions of a specific culture.

The Question of the Nature of Goodness

"The arc of the moral universe is long, but it bends toward justice." A quote most often attributed to Martin Luther King, Jr., but in truth originated from Theodore Parker, a nineteenth-century American Unitarian and Transcendentalist, sums up ethical leadership.[12] While good and evil may exist in the world, ethical leaders work to bend their organizations and actions toward justice and the common good. Ethical leaders strive toward what is good. One can have long discussions about the nature of man, the existence of evil, and the natural order of things, but essentially, we believe all ethical leaders at least strive toward the good for all, regardless of their individual perspective on the nature of humankind.

When many of us conjure images of ethical leaders, we tend to think of big-picture moral leaders such as Gandhi, King, or Mandela. There is truth in that, as each of those leaders pushed toward justice, freedom, and the common good. And there is truth in looking at their lives as exemplars of ethical and moral leaders. However, one does not need to operate on the world stage to be an ethical leader. Ethical leaders come in all sizes, shapes, and nationalities. We tend to look at large-scale leaders who run large organizations who are featured in various news stories. However, we suspect that most of us can find more ethical leaders in our local communities running small businesses, leading non-profits, or local politicians than we can in our country or the larger world. Perhaps size and intimacy does matter when it comes to ethical leadership as leaders may be more oriented to the common good when they interact with the people affected by their decisions on a daily basis.

The overarching belief that ethical leaders strive toward that which is good is the central notion to our concept of ethical leadership. And that sense of good is not a narcissistic view of what is good for me, but a view of good that reflects concern for humanity, country, and community.

Ethical Leadership: Defining the Construct

A definition of ethical leadership must do three things: provide a framework for individual development, suggest a means for evaluating the ethical or non-ethical behavior of leaders, and provide a potential means for identifying leaders.

Simplistically, the ethical leader acts consciously and courageously to do the right thing while influencing and motivating others to act in an ethical manner. Or more formally, ethical leadership is acting consciously and courageously to do the right thing while influencing and motivating others to act in an ethical manner. A simple idea, but one full of complexities. Let us look at some of the components of our definition:

- Doing the right thing implies a level consciousness about the nature of right and wrong that goes beyond traditional business metrics of profit and loss. The ethical leader thinks consciously and deeply about his or her actions and their "rightness." As noted earlier in this chapter, the study of ethics and one's meditations on right and wrong are an important component of ethical leadership. One needs to be able to integrate notions of right and wrong while pondering successes and failures in the interest of being able to justify ethical action.
- The ethical leader acts on his or her beliefs and shares those beliefs with others. Acting unilaterally, without explanation, fails to build trust and does not build a basis for ethical behavior in others.

- Belief without action is not leadership. While one can utter inspiring or thought-provoking words that may lead others to think about their actions, how one acts as an ethical leader is crucial.
- The ethical leader is transparent about his or her thinking and thought process so that others can understand what is behind the decision or action. Ethical leaders are models for others as they bend their organization toward the arc of justice. A big part of that modeling is sharing insights and rationale.
- While not explicit in our definition, the ethical leader must be willing to challenge and confront others in order to influence them, engage them in a discussion of right and wrong, and as a model.
- The ethical leader models doing the right thing even when it is not the popular or easy choice. He or she demonstrates the behavior and motivations behind the actions that they expect of others in their organization.

One of the authors' ancestors who was a leader in the US abolition and women's rights movements used to say, "As for me, I must speak the truth and abide the consequences" (Thomas M'Clintock, 1792–1876).

Those words speak to ethical leadership and the components of action, courage, and belief.

- The ethical leader is empathic. One cannot act on justice and encourage others to do so as well without an understanding of the fears, values, and beliefs that drive others. One cannot impel ethical behavior and action without first having empathy.
- Doing the right thing reflects universal values and moral stances: doing no harm to others, minimizing harm to the environment, and maximizing the social justice implications of a decision. Might an ethical leader cause harm to others (such as in times of war)? Yes, but that is also why we speak of ethical principles rather than ethical rules.
- Doing the right thing as a leader is complex and intimidating, but it provides the opportunity for moral heroism. Being a moral leader implies a degree of courage as acting may go against commonly held beliefs and carries a touch of risk.
- The other side of the definition *motivating others to do the right thing* is much closer to traditional views of leadership that look at the leader's ability to influence others to achieve goals or a change in behavior—the major difference being an emphasis on influencing others to act in a way that is ethically correct and appropriate.

Defining whether a leader is doing the "right thing" is a complex and sometimes contradictory issue. We all can think of people who we would consider great moral leaders (M.L. King, Gandhi, etc.) who also had character flaws. That is not our core concern as we understand great moral leaders are also flawed human beings.

The greater complexity is in those cases where an individual is a moral leader in one area but immoral in another. Take the case of Elizabeth Cady Stanton, a great advocate for women's rights in the 1800s in the United States. On one hand her championing of women's rights and specifically the right to vote was a great moral cause and she provided significant leadership to that cause. At the same time, however, she appears to have been racist and xenophobic, opposing the vote for black men and foreign men, based on ignorance or race. Deciding whether she is an ethical leader is an ongoing question that highlights the complexity of the discussion.

Or you may think of Ghandi, whose racism is not necessarily well known to those who primarily praise his peaceful protest and stoicism. In 1903, when Gandhi was in South Africa, he wrote that white people there should be "the predominating race." He also said black people "are troublesome, very dirty, and live like animals."

There's no way around it: Gandhi was a racist early in his life, says his biographer, Ramachandra Guha. "Gandhi as a young man went with the ideas of his culture and his time. He thought in his 20s that Europeans are the most civilized. Indians were almost as civilized, and Africans were uncivilized," Guha once stated in an NPR interview.[13]

From this start, we are going to move on to discuss ethical leadership from a variety of perspectives, including actions you can take to reflect and grow as a moral leader. This can further lead you to hire moral leaders and understand how an ethical leader can create an ethical culture. Fundamentally, we stand on our conception of the ethical leader as one who reflects on ethical issues, acts with courage, inspires and influences others to beget good things, acts honorably and productively, and demonstrates dignity.

In subsequent chapters we will explore different aspects of ethical leadership including basic characteristics, how to select ethical leaders and related topics.

Questions and Actions for Your Consideration

1. If you have not already, spend some time reading about your faith tradition or various philosophers regarding the nature of right and wrong. The

critical question is not what they say but what your belief is about what they say, and what you are willing to put into practice.

2. Identify those moral dilemmas (where right and wrong are not clear) that exist in your workplace. How have they been handled, would you do anything differently, and what did you learn?

3. Talk to mentors or leaders you respect about moral and ethical issues they have faced in their careers. What have they learned and what would they do differently?

4. Analyze your own organization. Are you led by ethical leaders? Why or why not? What can you or are you willing to do about this?

5. Are you striving to be a (more) ethical leader? Why or why not?

Notes

1 Dietrich Bonhoeffer, *Ethics* (New York: Simon & Schuster, 1995).

2 "Simone de Beauvoir," *Stanford Encyclopedia of Philosophy*, January 11, 2023. https://plato.stanford.edu/entries/beauvoir/.

3 Ray Monk, "Bertrand Russell: British Logician and Philosopher," *Encyclopedia Britannica*, May 14, 2023. www.britannica.com/biography/Bertrand-Russell.

4 "Ibn Ar-Rawandi (c.910?)." n.d. www.muslimphilosophy.com/ip/rep/H035.htm

5 Robert B. Pippin and Adrian Del Caro, eds, *Friedrich Nietzsche: Thus Spoke Zarathustra* (Cambridge, UK: Cambridge University Press, 2006). www.cambridge.org/highereducation/books/nietzsche-thus-spoke-zarathustra/5E1FF7A96401587F59F12BDAEB9CEF93#overvie12095.

6 Sigal Samuel, "Patricia Churchland: Your Brain Invents Morality and Conscience," *Vox*, July 8, 2019. www.vox.com/future-perfect/2019/7/8/20681558/conscience-patricia-churchland-neuroscience-morality-empathy-philosophy.

7 Tom Bowden, "Voices for Reason—Ayn Rand on Love.," The Ayn Rand Institute, September 3, 2019. https://ari.aynrand.org/ayn-rand-on-love-2/.

8 "The Five Precepts—Buddhist Beliefs—Edexcel—GCSE Religious Studies Revision—Edexcel—BBC Bitesize," BBC Bitesize, n.d. www.bbc.co.uk/bitesize/guides/zf8g4qt/revision/9.

9 Libretexts, "6.1.1: Applied Ethics, Normative Ethics, and Meta-Ethics," *Humanities LibreTexts*, July 2021. https://human.libretexts.org/Courses/Cosumnes_River_College/PHIL_300%3A_Introduction_to_Philosophy_(Binder)/06%3A_Ethics/6.01%3A_Meta-Ethics/6.1.01%3A_Applied_Ethics_Normative_Ethics_and_Meta-Ethics.

10 "Utilitarianism and Social Contract Theories Essay," Free Essays, March 19, 2020. https://ivypanda.com/essays/utilitarianism-and-social-contract-theories/#:~:text=Utilitarianism%20is%20an%20expanse%20approach,the%20means%20of%20attaining%20it.

11 "Relativism: Scourge of a Nation and Religion," Burleson Church of Christ, September 14, 2017. https://burlesonchurchofchrist.com/relativism-scourge-of-a-nation-and-religion/.

12 NPR, "Theodore Parker and the 'Moral Universe,'" *NPR*, September 2, 2010. www.npr.org/templates/story/story.php?storyId=129609461.

13 https://www.npr.org/2019/10/02/766083651/gandhi-is-deeply-revered-but-his-attitudes-on-race-and-sex-are-under-scrutiny

Section II

Conceptual Framework of Ethical Leadership

Chapter 3

Leadership and Love

Preliminary Thoughts on the Notion of Love, and the Lessons It Holds on the Matter of Ethical Leadership

The function of leadership is to produce more leaders, not more followers.
(Ralph Nader—lawyer, political activist, writer)

Great leadership engenders ownership, inspiration, possibly contentment, and, as Nader puts it so beautifully in his quote above, more leaders. This chapter is a bold attempt at contributing the idea of leadership by love in a clear and emphatic manner. In this chapter we boldly attempt to zoom in on love with a historic as well as conceptual perspective. This chapter is supposed to give a direction as to how love can be taken up as a conscious choice by demonstrating or living the principles suggested herein. The idea is to provide a predictable paradigm to lead businesses in an unpredictable world, which is the (overly emphasized) characteristic of the current environment and is likely to continue in the long term. A paradigm, which gives basic and universal principles to help leaders deal with a novel situation in a novel way. It suggests positioning *love as a competency* which can be consciously acquired and practiced. So, this chapter will propose a simple model for leadership by love. Of course, we are well-aware that this kind of juxtaposition of two seemingly detached realms may be perceived as somewhat counterintuitive. So, the objective here is by no means to offer an exhaustive concept claiming to capture this most profound emotion. However, in our opinion, the discussion of love and leadership is an unfathomable source of inspiration.

Furthermore, the ambition here is certainly not to mechanize love which, of course, can be better captured by poetry, plays, and paintings. Our ambition, however, is to scrutinize love and to carve out the underlying competency, mindset, and behaviors that will enrich your leadership approach. When we talk about competencies, we base our considerations

DOI: 10.4324/b23260-6

on *Competence at Work*[1] by Spencer and Spencer, who distinguish between knowledge, skills, self-concepts, traits, and motives as constituting factors of the respective competency.

You may wonder why we include a chapter on love in this book on ethical leadership. As mentioned above, this seems counterintuitive at first glance and probably begs a brief explanation. Love is a fundamental emotion and has been explored by sociology, psychology, spiritualism, religion, and literature alike. Pitrim Sorokin, an eminent Harvard sociologist, who developed an intricate framework to understand what he called other-regarding or altruistic love,[2] stated,

> *hate begets hate, violence engenders violence, hypocrisy is answered by hypocrisy, war generates war, and love creates love. Unselfish love has enormous creative and therapeutic potentialities, far greater than most people think. Love is a life-giving force, necessary for physical, mental and moral health. Only the power of unbounded love practiced in regard to all human beings can defeat the forces of interhuman strife and can prevent the pending extermination of man by man on this planet.*[3]

Obviously, this observation has more far-reaching consequences than mere interpersonal connections. It can be applied to communities, federal tensions within a country, national politics, unnecessary political friction, malfeasance and misuse of political power, and geopolitical contexts. It is our contention that a human being who acts kindly and out of love will surely be a better, level-headed, more mature, and most certainly a more successful leader. Most probably, others will feel inspired to follow, go the proverbial extra mile, feel identified, and be more open in their hearts to consider criticism uttered by their leader if this is necessary. With that being said, let us take a plunge.

Raising the Young, Neuroscience, and the Kind Leader

> *I think probably kindness is my number one attribute in a human being. I'll put it before any of the things like courage or bravery or generosity or anything else.*
> (Roald Dahl—author, poet, fighter ace)

This quote by author Roald Dahl who wrote most touching books such as *Charlie and the Chocolate Factory* and *Matilda* is in perfect line with Ava Bonam's thoughts on love as an additional quality in everything you do: fix yourself a cup of coffee in the morning, make decisions, and lead. To begin, let us take a look at an example from the business world. Sir Richard Branson, British business magnate, investor, author, and philanthropist who founded the Virgin Group in the 1970s once stated in an interview conducted by *Big Think*—a think tank that helps individuals and organizations by catalyzing conversation around the topics most critical to the twenty-first century—that he was fortunate to be brought up by two very loving parents.[4] They were great believers in bestowing a lot of praise and encouragement upon their children, which equipped him with sound confidence. They put a lot of emphasis on the fact that their children would stand on their own two feet at a young age (which in Branson's case meant that his mother once put him out of the car and asked him to make his way back home for a three-mile foot walk somewhere in Surrey, England). If we take these intimate revelations Branson shares in the above interview by Big Think, and ponder them for a moment, the implications are powerful: instilling trust in others, establishing psychological safety, equipping others to succeed, stretching others in a loving way. In the buzz of the business world, however, such behaviors and, at a deeper level, such an ever-present personal philosophy of love may not be that self-evident. That is why the capacities of self-awareness, self-discipline, and self-reflection are significant as they allow us to be fully present and not to forego praise, recognition, integration, and acknowledgement. All of the above behaviors (and therefore competencies) engender love, motivation, and mutual trust, and make people surpass themselves.

To consider yet another insightful study on the subject of love, let us have a brief look at early child development and neuroscience. The linkages between leadership and parenting have been made frequently by leadership experts such as Simon Sinek, Scott Turansky, Marcie White, or Jamilah Smian and Ahmad Fakhri Hamzah in their beautiful book Leadership in Parenting[5] in which they zoom in on the significance of a proactive as well as purposeful parenting approach.

Psychotherapist Sue Gerhardt's clear-sighted assessment of child development coalesced in her powerful book *Why Love Matters*[6], when she goes where most in recent years have feared to tread: she takes the hard language of neuroscience and uses it to prove the soft stuff of attachment theory. Drawing on a substantive body of research and evidence from the field of neuroscience and neurochemistry, Gerhardt makes an engaging case that emotional experiences in infancy and early childhood have a quantifiable effect on how we evolve and develop as human beings. A child's earliest impressions and interactions with their parents are not simply laid down as fuzzy influences or reminiscences. In fact, they are transmitted into specific physiological patterns of response in the brain. These patterns then set the neurological rules by which we deal with our emotions and those of others for the rest of our lives. As usually is the case, the subject is more complex than we may expect and it is neither nature nor nurture, but both.

The way we are treated as babies and toddlers ordains the way in which we develop into who we are as a person. According to Gerhardt, "there is nothing automatic about it. The kind of brain that each baby develops is the brain that comes out of his or her experiences with people."[7] Gerhardt discusses fascinating instances where researchers examined the cerebral architecture of Romanian orphans through x-ray and detected spots where the orbitofrontal cortex should have been but were underdeveloped instead. These children had been left to cry in their cradles and cots from birth and experienced grave challenges of forming close bonds with adults. The orbitofrontal cortex is the part of the brain that enables humans to manage emerging emotions, to relate sensitively to other people, to enjoy pleasure and to be appreciative of beauty.

In neuroscience, a set of highly interesting findings has caused some stir in the business community over the past 20 years or so, ranging from *Willpower*[8] by Roy Baumeister and John Tierney to *The Mind and The Brain*[9] by Jeffrey Schwartz and Sharon Begley who focus on neuroplasticity, perseverance, decision fatigue, and courage. Another intriguing finding is that for our brains, feeling the shock and pain we sense when falling is essentially the same as experiencing social rejection by a group. We process such an experience in the same part of our brains. As a consequence, leaders should foster a work environment where people feel that they belong and are safe, can express themselves without any potential sanction or reprimand, and where company values are no lukewarm ideals but a tangible reality. A sense of purpose and being part of a common goal are aspects that are equally important. So, in other words, we are less likely to just respond automatically, but be aware, feel attuned to our emotions and present in the moment when a sense of belonging and purpose are established by leaders who focus on love.

To conclude, all the above should draw our attention to these simple, yet challenging insights:

1. Acting out of love engenders an environment in which people will want to take responsibility and work for the greater good, which is the ultimate goal of ethical leadership.
2. Love is one relevant cornerstone for mature behavior and it bears the potential to resolve (and prevent) conflict, conduct ourselves sensitively and consciously, and to foster mutual respect and purpose.
3. Loving leadership of parents has a positive impact on the brain development of children as it helps putting transmitters such as cortisol, adrenaline, and testosterone into the right equilibrium and enables children to develop trust, which, of course, is key in leadership also. It is essential to trust others. If you do not trust yourself as a leader, work on yourself.
4. Being aware of your own emotions as a leader helps you conduct yourself in a professional and warm-hearted way, which will have positive biochemical effects on the one hand and help foster an ethical culture within your organization on the other.

Emotional Intelligence, Love, and Leadership

What matters is hard work, and emotional intelligence.
(Mickey Drexler—businessman, investor)

Marry the two: ambition, thrift, and dexterity on the one hand and compassion, empathy, and love on the other. Mickey Drexler is right in this recommendation of his. Before delving more profoundly into the concept of love by taking a look at ancient scripture and philosophy and its connection to leadership and love, let us zoom in on one more force that we think is pivotal when it comes to developing love for self and others and, eventually, using this force to make others follow willingly—just as former US American president Dwight Eisenhower stated so fittingly: "Leadership is the art of getting someone to do something you want done because he wants to do it."[10]

This force is emotional intelligence, which is an integral capacity to foster love, become more aware and establish a loving environment. Emotional intelligence, also referred to as EQ, is a powerful facility that helps us grasp and explore our own emotions, as well as the feelings of others, more profoundly. If emotional intelligence is well developed, it also helps leaders act in a more understanding, warm-hearted, and loving way. Leaders who are well-versed at discerning the emotions behind other people's statements, signals, or verbal omissions are better at establishing real dialogue. Interestingly, they are also more skilled in managing their own emotions which are sent back to their discussion partners, peers, or co-workers. In order to establish a constructive environment—characterized by psychological safety and an overarching sense of belonging—it is key to train one's capacity of emotional intelligence.

Daniel Goleman—psychologist and award-winning author of *Emotional Intelligence: Why It Can Matter More Than IQ*—has developed an impressive case laying out the argument that the behavioral proficiency emotional intelligence brings about may outshine IQ as a determinant for life, self-love, and leadership success.[11]

Emotional intelligence is a set of competencies that enable us to appraise our own emotions as well as those of others. On the other hand, EQ can also help us regulate and control own emotions and feelings.[12] If well developed, EQ enables us to be distinctly aware of our own sentiments. As a consequence, emotions become lucid and can be controlled more in social interactions. Hence, it allows a person to handle their interpersonal relationships fairly and sensibly and makes leaders more successful when it comes to establishing an environment of belonging and mutual trust, and a space where people experience meaningful relationships.

Side note: we are perfectly aware that oftentimes people seek (and possibly find) fake identities in organizations, and that corporations promise some sort of family surrogate when advertising the metaphysical quantum leaps people will experience when joining their ranks. This, we believe, is a recent phenomenon and should be scrutinized critically. Work environments will most certainly never replace a loving family and the intimate feeling of safety and acceptance brought about by one's home (in the broadest sense including personal interests, one's homestead and closest friends). But still, it is a decidedly positive development that it becomes more and more relevant to promote meaningfulness and purpose in the workplace. Experiencing purpose triggers feelings of contributing and connection, which is essential for psychological health and ethical environments.

We all probably have experienced situations where we did not feel safe, appreciated, seen as a person, or taken seriously in our desires. For many of us numerous recollections will kick in straight away, and others may have developed mechanisms and self-images that make it hard to recall. It is one of a leader's key responsibilities to engender surroundings where people do not feel excluded but rather inspired and almost *compelled* to do their best. Emotional intelligence helps leaders to achieve just that. There is general agreement that EQ exists and that it is a determining factor when it comes to professional and personal success as well as the ability to foster an environment that can be considered psychologically safe.

Goleman's model distinguishes four dimensions that play an important role in order to develop mature ways of recognizing your own emotions and responding effectively to those of your counterparts:

Self-Awareness is the capacity that enables us to sense and recognize own emotions. Self-awareness also sheds light on the appropriateness, power, and downsides of own emotions. It takes their impact on others into consideration. People with highly developed levels of self-awareness profess an accurate self-assessment and are not wishful thinkers. They have developed a keen sense of own strengths and weaknesses. Furthermore, high levels of self-awareness determine a person's sense of self-esteem.

Self-Management helps us control our emotions. This involves suppressing, controlling, venting, or redirecting our disruptive emotions. Self-management also comes into play when adapting to changing circumstances is key in order to support and nourish relationships. It is indispensable to manage one's internal states and impulses. People with a stable level of self-management act congruently with their values. They strive for excellence and persist in pursuing their goals despite setbacks and pitfalls.

Social Awareness is the capacity that enables us to relate to another human being both cognitively as well as emotionally. If social awareness is highly developed, it clearly increases the probability of supporting others and showing compassion. The Greater Good Science Center[13] which researches the psychological, sociological, and neuroscientific aspects of well-being states that "empathy is a building block of morality."[14] Empathy is an integral ingredient of successful and loving relationships as it helps us to understand the vantage points, ideas, desires, fears, and perspectives of others.

Relationship Management is a person's facility or adeptness to induce desirable responses in others. People who excel in this skillset are alert to the development needs of others and can *rally the troops* as inspirational leaders. Proficient relationship managers establish an environment that is open to change and they are proficient when it comes to wielding influence. Furthermore, relationship management includes the skill to manage conflicts successfully and to establish performance cultures where people unite their energies in a concerted effort to strive for common goals.

In our point of view, this quote by businessman Mickey Drexler says it all: "What matters is hard work, and emotional intelligence."[15] Emotional intelligence and its different aspects such as self-awareness or relationship-management help experts evolve into great leaders who succeed in fostering a culture of cohesion, purpose, and belonging. This, we believe, is an essential building block and leadership prerequisite to sustain ethical (corporate) cultures.

Intermediate Result

As a preliminary result, we can say that acting out of love, being kind and seeing others for who they are or can potentially become, being aware of one's own emotions and acting emotionally intelligent are universal truths for a dignified life and should be taken to heart by leaders. It does not matter which guild you pride yourself to be part of. Leaders of pre-schools, family businesses, election districts, landscape gardening companies, construction companies, grocery stores, brokerages, or business consultancies will all enjoy greater success in life and their professional endeavors if they go about their jobs and conduct themselves with a *sense of love*. All these observations are backed by hard data as our brief neuroscientific digression has shown. Furthermore, the connection between love and leadership can be detected in personalities such as social activist, Mahatma Gandhi, New Zealand's former prime minister, Jacinda Ardern, Nobel Prize winner and political fighter, Aung San Suu Kyi, actress and humanitarian activist, Angelina Jolie, or CEO of Apple, Tim Cook. Developing and actively applying EQ is not just a soft skill (as we see it, this term seems outdated anyhow) but a real skill. Recognizing and regulating own emotions and, in addition, acknowledging the emotions of others are indispensable leadership skills that essentially stem from a place of love.

Ancient Insights That Matter and (Still) Move the World

Time is the wisest counsellor of all.

(Pericles—Athenian statesman and strategist)

Let us now take a closer look at three awe-inspiring quotations from history pondering love and scrutinize them later with respect to their significance to leadership, and ethical leadership in particular.

First, the Buddha once said: "If you knew what I know about the power of giving, you would not let a single meal pass without sharing it in some way."[16]

Second, in 1956, in his fifth talk, Krishnamurti stated in Bombay:

So, if you really want to stop wars, if you really want to put an end to this conflict within society, you must face the fact that you do not love. You may go to a temple and offer flowers to a stone image, but that will not give the heart this extraordinary quality of compassion and love, which comes only when the mind is quiet, and not greedy or envious. When you are aware of the fact that you have no love, and do not run away from it by trying to explain it, or find its cause, then that very awareness begins to do something; it brings gentleness, a sense of compassion. Then there is a possibility of creating a world totally different from this chaotic and brutal existence which we now call life.[17]

Third, in his first letter to the Corinthians, Paul stated,

Love is patient, love is kind. It does not envy, it does not boast, it is not proud. It does not dishonor others, it is not self-seeking, it is not easily angered, it keeps no record of wrongs. Love does not delight in evil but rejoices with the truth. It always protects, always trusts, always hopes, always perseveres.[18]

Clearly, a lot has been said about love as a most fundamental human emotion and driver. The above quotations have this essential human sentiment at their very core. In the following pages we will endeavor to connect the concept of love with leadership and provide further reasons why love is a prerequisite for effective and truthful leadership.

The Buddha says that the power of giving is vital. What can we learn from this concept? In Buddhism, there is the concept of relative *bodhicitta*. Bodhicitta describes the mindset of unconditional love. The person embracing this notion does not share wisdom in order to get something in return. Unconditional love—as the term suggests—is not linked to conditions, expectations, or some sort of trade. A leader who applies unconditional love shows a generative mindset and enjoys sharing information, offering support, developing others for the sake of development, and being able to let go (as in forgive, step back, or delegate). This does not mean that anything is possible. However, the mindset of bodhicitta can be felt straight away by the person receiving. The culture generated by unconditional love and giving is magical and able to create purpose, motivation, and high-performing teams.

What does the quote by Krishnamurti denote and teach us about leadership and love? Basically, this statement is the exact opposite of toxic positivity and self-indulgence. The concept Krishnamurti alludes to is about accepting the fact that there are fundamentally base energies residing in each one of us. We tend to put ourselves on a pedestal. This is especially true when conflicts occur, and we are part of it. In such situations, we rather pass on the buck to somebody else. Essentially, we externalize. In our opinion, a spiritually and morally full personality acknowledges his or her own shortcomings. This should not merely be an intellectual act, but an insight we embrace fully. Taking part in (corporate) rituals, playing by the rules, and fitting in does not suffice. Offering proverbial flowers to stone images does not make a leader complete, so to speak. What matters is to work on ourselves deeply and appreciate the fact that we are essentially nothing. This opens us up to insight, self-realization, and humbleness. Ethical leaders are attuned to such insights as they constitute humbleness, readiness to self-reflect, and become the best version of oneself.

When Paul shares in his letter to the Corinthians that "love does not delight in evil but rejoices with the truth. It always protects, always trusts, always hopes, always perseveres", he references a variety of a good person's qualities: love enables us to let go, move on, and to forgive. A loving leader welcomes the future and does not look back, bearing grudges. In his letter to the Corinthians, Paul also draws attention to the fact that community matters ("always protects"). He also emphasizes that the generative power of trust—possibly in oneself, others, and an external power, idea, or objective—works its magic when embraced. Finally, hope opens us up to the future and its potential. Such future objectives can only be achieved by willpower, persistence, and resilience ("always perseveres"). So, ethical leaders who draw their leadership actions from a place of love, may show such qualities as the ones described above: perseverance, forgiveness, future-orientation, constructiveness, and team-orientation.

Great leaders have proven time and again that the power of love can move the world. Love is native to all humans and is also clearly observable in the animal kingdom (think of humpback mothers protecting their calves or chimpanzees grooming one another). The greatest of leaders have shown us the connection of love and leadership. These leaders have demonstrated their love both for their followers and critics. They have demonstrated it through their altruism, one of the most famous examples being that of Mahatma Gandhi who is an accepted and revered leader.

Love is an emotion. People are bundles of emotions. Carnegie cautioned us to remember that people are not creatures of logic but creatures of emotions.[19] In our opinion, leaders have to lead through these emotions. Love then is an obvious choice of someone to lead others. Kouzes and Posner mentioned the philosophy of leadership, which is the first principle of leadership as expressed by General John H. Stanford: "Love them and lead them."[20] Now this is coming straight from a person who has led masses in the toughest of practical situations. So, it carries that weight.[21] Caldwell and Dixon[22] talked about suggestions given by several scholars (such as Covey) that when leaders consistently exhibit love, forgiveness, and trust in relationships, their employees will respond with increased commitment and loyalty. That is, in turn, employees love and value them: a mutually beneficial system emerges.

The Ancient Greeks coined and used several words for love, enabling them to distinguish more clearly between the different types: *eros, philia, storge, agape, ludus, pragma,* and *philautia.*[23] We will take a closer look at two of them as they play a central role when it comes to leadership: *agape* and *philautia.*

Agape is universal and unconditional love – a concept we scratched upon above. This may be the love for strangers, nature, or a greater purpose. *Agape* can be said to encompass the modern concept of altruism, as defined as unselfish concern for the welfare of others.[24] Recent studies link altruism with a number of benefits. In the short term, an altruistic act leaves us with a euphoric feeling, the so-called *helper's high.* In the long term, altruism has been associated with better mental and physical health, and even greater longevity. At a social level, altruism serves as a signal of cooperative intentions and of resource availability.[25] It also opens up a debt account, encouraging beneficiaries to reciprocate with gifts and favors that may be of much greater value to us than those with which we felt able to part. More generally, altruism, or *agape,* helps to build and maintain the psychological, social, and, indeed, environmental fabric that shields, sustains, and enriches us. If embraced fully, these insights can further equip ethical leaders to establish sustainable and lasting corporate cultures.

Philautia is self-love, which can be healthy or unhealthy. Unhealthy self-love is akin to hubris. In Ancient Greece, people could be accused of hubris if they placed themselves above the gods, or, like certain modern politicians, above the greater good. Many believed that hubris led to destruction, or nemesis. Today, hubris has come to mean an inflated sense of one's status, abilities, or accomplishments, especially when accompanied by haughtiness or arrogance. Anthropocentrism is typical human hubris: even though we know better, many of us place our fate at the center of (our) universe. In literature, *Frankenstein,* the well-known (Gothic) novel, published in January 1818 by Mary Shelley, is about human hubris unfettered: a scientist tries to be God and usurp the divine throne. It goes without saying, things go terribly wrong in the course of the story. Because it does not accord with the truth, hubris promotes injustice, conflict, and enmity. Healthy self-love, on the other hand, is akin to self-esteem, which is our cognitive and, above all, emotional appraisal of our own worth. Furthermore, it is the lens through which we deliberate, feel, and go forward. In everyday language, self-esteem and self-confidence tend to be used interchangeably. However, self-esteem and self-confidence do not always go hand in hand. In his article on "Self-Confidence versus Self-Esteem", psychiatrist and philosopher, Neel Burton, observed:

> In particular, it is possible to be highly self-confident and yet to have profoundly low self-esteem, as is the case, for example, with many performers and celebrities. People with sound self-esteem do not need to prop themselves up with externals such as income, status, or notoriety, or lean on crutches such as excessive, consumerism, neoliberal bigotry, alcohol, national chauvinism, drugs or sex.[26]

Furthermore, he rightly states,

> they are able to invest themselves completely in projects and people because they do not fear failure or rejection. Of course, they suffer hurt and disappointment, but their setbacks neither damage nor diminish them. Owing to their resilience, they are open to growth experiences and relationships, tolerant of risk, quick to joy and delight, and accepting and forgiving of themselves and others.[27]

Both *agape* and *philautia* play a central role when it comes to sustainable and authentic leadership as *agape* enables leaders to engender cooperation and an environment of belonging. *Philautia* can serve as the fabric for personal and psychological health and, indeed, the readiness to share love. Both universal love and healthy love of self, of course, are the prerequisites to be a mature and caring leader yourself.

Love as a Construct and, If Taken to Heart, a Competency

> There's a lot more to competence than a law degree and a modicum of courtroom skill.
>
> (Fred Thompson—politician, actor, attorney)

In our view, we oftentimes overestimate technical knowledge, expertise, and competencies that drive results. We agree with Fred Thompson when he says that there is a lot more to competence. From our research we extracted a set of broad principles as leadership constructs which are foundational in nature. Almost all these principles have been discussed by various authors and researchers in connection with leadership or related topics; although, they may have called it either a theorem, principle or an assumption, and in a few cases would have discussed them indirectly. While some or many of these principles may appear to be moral objectives or moral directions, we choose to call them *principles*, as they are universal, do not depend on time or context, and are foundational for love to be realized in situations of leadership. To conclude this chapter, we will attempt to suggest a simple model which incorporates these principles. A probable cause and effect relationship is thus proposed between these principles, love, and leadership.

Simply stated, the proposed principles are the independent variables which cause love to take place. Hence, love is a dependent variable here. While there may be some arguments that love leads to these principles and not the other way around, we take the position of love being a conscious choice which can lead to (or facilitate) the realization of love as a competency. So, love is the effect here. In turn, it is our contention that love leads to ethical leadership. We would like to emphasize once more that the principles proposed are broad, open, and flexible in nature. These principles do not represent a particular culture or country of origin.

As mentioned above, the term *competency* as per Spencer and Spencer includes five categories of behavior and attitudes: motives, traits, self-concept, skills, and knowledge.[28] The principles provided below are more illustrative than definitive and exhaustive. However, these illustrative behaviors and attitudes are important and helpful to understand how each principle is manifested in a leader's behaviors and what leadership lessons can be drawn from it. Some of these behaviors may overlap as—in our point of view—it is not mandatory to segregate attitudes on the one hand and human behaviors on the other.

In our experience, eight distinct principles determine loving leadership as an enabler for ethical culture: being accepting, being appreciative, being altruistic, being humble, being human, being open, being authentic, and being self-reflective (Figure 3.1.

Let us now take a look at each one of these principles and zoom in on some of the research that has been done on each principle, connecting it with attributes, skill sets that are relevant in this regard, motives, and attributes.

Being Accepting

"Leaders accept people as they are regardless of their actions and behaviour."[29] In our view, this is a concise and meaningful observation that Professor of Management and Professor of Psychology, Gerald R. Ferris of Florida State University, has made. Love accepts everyone and everything.

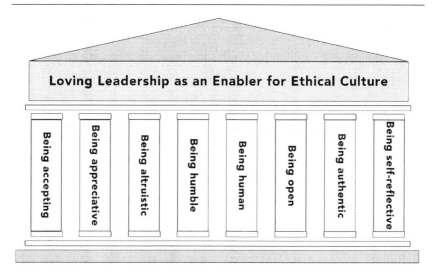

Figure 3.1 Loving Leadership as an Enabler for Ethical Culture

Correcting efforts are made, when required, out of love and not out of judgments or non-acceptance. When a leader accepts a person the way he or
she is, there is no judging and no calling of names. When discussing servant leadership, Robert K. Greenleaf establishes that "the servant always accepts and empathizes, never rejects."[30] When we accept others, there is no
threat to them. Rather the opposite: even in conflict, acknowledgement of
the opponent's view is present and mutual respect stays intact. This is great
leadership of self. Mahatma Gandhi loved everyone including British rulers
whom he resisted to free India from British rule. He gifted them hand-made
presents while he was resisting them. Consequently, the world remembers
him as one of the greatest (peaceful) leaders. In his article "Accessing the
Power of Love in the Workplace",[31] pediatric psychologist Roger Harrison
mentions that by not doing enough research on love in organizations, we
are depriving ourselves of its positive influences. Furthermore, Harrison
states "instead of trying to fix what's broken, appreciative process improves
systems by amplifying what is working. Appreciative change processes engage the people who need to be part of improving the organization in
identifying the best of what they do, celebrating and learning from it, working with people's intrinsic motivation to be competent, do their best and
be successful."[32] Leaders who embrace the notion and mindset of *accepting* are usually more resilient and level-headed; they establish a culture
of psychological safety, trust, and real positivity (as opposed to toxic positivity, which triggers the exact opposite by radically suppressing negative
emotions). Attributes (and what they constitute psychologically) that may

describe the mindset of *accepting* are welcoming, listening, accompanying, respect, support, cherishing, being present and calm, non-judgmental, forgiving, empathetic, and so forth. In our experience, these concepts shape ethically sound and dignified leaders when internalized fully.

Being Appreciative

When we love, we appreciate and do so genuinely. Famed author and lecturer, Dale Carnegie, once stated "be hearty in your approbation and lavish in your praise."[33] Can we love and not appreciate? Leaders praise others through their words and actions. And they do so consistently, and out of an incessant internal dynamic that almost compels them to do so. This genuine, consistent, and abundant appreciation has the power to move people as they feel seen and recognized. In *Transactional Analysis*, Canadian-born psychiatrist, Eric Berne, developed the so-called stroke theory.[34] He established that infants require units of recognition. They are touched, parents look after their child, cuddle, hum lullabies, and soothe. As adults we still require such units of recognition. This fundamental need does not wane. Berne's stroke theory and the mindset of appreciation are directly linked. Leaders who understand this give praise, acknowledge consciously, appreciate, and show real gratitude. A mindset of real appreciation harbors the potential to pull someone out of his or her negative rut. Such appreciation stems from a true feeling of profound gratitude. Dierendonck and Patterson introduced the idea that grateful leaders have a sense of abundance, humility, forgiveness, and they appreciate the contribution of others.[35] The attributes and actions that describe this principle may include: praise, highlighting positives, admire, compliment, commend, forgive, acclaim, applaud, cherish, perceive, respect, honor, acknowledge, and so forth. In our experience, leaders who embrace such a mindset of appreciation bring into being cultures and environments that are truly inspiring, motivating, and profoundly positive.

Being Altruistic

Who can be bigger examples of this than Mahatma Gandhi, Joan of Arc, Indira Ghandi, Jacinda Ardern, Eleanor Roosevelt, the Dalai Lama, and the likes? In leadership research, great minds like Matthieu Ricard and Charlotte Mandell wrote about altruism, compassion, and love that have the power the change oneself, and the world.[36] In their book, they make a strong case for compassion and altruism as the best means for strengthening ourselves and the people around us. Being altruistic is about having selfless concern for the well-being of others. Leaders who love always think of others first. Professors of Management, Cam Caldwell and Rolf D. Dixon, observed, "love, forgiveness, and trust convey a willingness of one party to give of one's self to invest in the other party."[37] They further established that love along with trust and forgiveness calls for one agreeing to be vulnerable in order to ensure the help for others. Being altruistic is also about bearing pain and difficulty for others. American businessman and author, Max De Pree, poignantly observed "leaders don't inflict pain, they bear pain."[38] In our view, this is a strong statement that bears truth. Altruistic leaders are more likely to establish ethical environments where people care for one another and collaborate more peacefully. Clearly, the concept of altruism may be debated and cannot be imposed as a universal. However, in our work as consultants, we have observed over the years that unconditional giving, and a mindset of altruism generate healthier cultures and work environments where people speak up, go the extra mile, feel safe, and share purpose. Attributes and actions which may describe this principle of altruism may include: sacrificing, thinking of others, defending others, putting others before you, taking pains for others, supporting others, sharing, and participation.

Being Humble

Humble leaders value others. They question themselves and recognize that haughty and arrogant behaviors sow the seeds of fear, mistrust, and selfishness. That is only possible by being humble and generative. A humble leader does not criticize critics. He or she welcomes different opinions. So even the critics experience love by such leaders. A leader does not treat anyone as less or inferior just because he or she is more experienced or knowledgeable. In their book on servant leadership, Sousa Milton and Dirk Van Dierendonck observed that humility is seeing oneself as no better or worse than others do.[39] Such leaders respect diversity, and they can find a way through cross-cultural challenges. Humble leaders consistently give due credit to others, consider themselves as part of a team, and enjoy the company of everyone alike. Humble leaders are not smug about their position. Rather the opposite is true: despite their position or power, they do not shy away from admitting their mistakes and apologizing when they need to. Being humble on the one hand and giving guidance on the other represents a powerful dichotomy, and it will most probably make a mature leader. In our experience as leadership advisors, we find humble leaders to be more convincing when establishing an ethical workplace where it is not just structures and rules that ascertain ethical behavior. Leadership personalities with a humble mindset emanate dignity and motivate others to follow their lead. The attributes, traits, motives, and actions which may describe this principle may be: modesty, simplicity, humility, acknowledgment of others' contribution, peaceful, including accepting one's limitations or mistakes, showing dignity, harnessing input from everyone, and respecting differences of opinions.

Being Human

Being human is about consistently being human with everyone and every-thing. Love is an innate energy for human beings (and animals alike). The greatness of a leader perhaps may be weighed by his or her ability to be that human. A person who strives to be the best version of himself or herself approaches life with love. In fact, they cannot not love. Love is innately leading. Great leaders know and have effectively demonstrated that it is love that binds teams, company cultures, and organizations. Of course, we are perfectly aware of the fact that economic necessities are key drivers as well. However, leadership that acknowledges fundamental human needs such as closeness, dialogue, personal development, appreciation, and co-hesion tends to be more successful. What we mean by successful here are qualities such as dignity, sustainability, absence of fear, and freedom. Toxic cultures may prove successful when it comes to market position or com-mercial achievements. However, such cultures are inherently unethical, and usually do not last. It is our hope that anti-human organizations will disappear one day. To us, a central human quality is the reverence for (all) life which, of course, is an allusion to Dr. Albert Schweizer's renowned philosophy of peace, compassion, and altruism. Some traits, motives, and actions that may describe this principle of being human may include: showing compassion, being natural, embracing life, being noble, being considerate, showing interest in others, being thoughtful.

Being Open

Great leaders love and they love abundantly. Social psychologist, Geral-dine Downey,[40] considers love as a process which involves understand-ing of others by showing interest in their views and by being open. Being open is a mindset that is characterized by a genuine interest in exploring and possibly discovering something new. Leaders displaying this mindset expand their ways, their networks, and possess a child-like openness to welcome people and ideas. They connect, give attention, and are open to change. Megan McDonough, CEO of the Wellbeing Institute observed[41] "loving leadership is that you lead with love. It describes the feeling of connecting, serving, and indeed, loving others. It is giving full attention to another—really looking at them, hearing their words, and connecting to them."[42] This is a fitting observation of what a mindset of openness can create in a leader. Leaders embracing this mindset of openness sincerely observe and feel the concern of others. Attributes, actions, skillsets, and motives that may describe being open may include: showing curiosity, ex-ploring, asking questions, showing tolerance, welcoming dialog, being in-quisitive, showing interest in learning, showing flexibility.

Being Authentic

What happens when leaders love? They don't need to negotiate, force, or coerce. They simply need to be authentic. Leaders who love remain true to themselves and authentic. Professor of Human Resources Management, Dirk van Dierendonck, expressed the idea that authenticity is about being honest and consistent about oneself.[43] Authenticity is consistency in thoughts, feelings, and actions. In our experience, authentic leaders do not need to persuade or insist. In his inspirational article, "Leadership by Love: A Divine Paradigm," Nishant Khandelwal, assistant professor at the Symbiosis Center of Management Studies (Deemed University), stated "business success flows from adherence to such old-fashioned virtues as trust, respect, honesty, loyalty, and love."[44] In our view, he is right. The above virtues enable an authentic work environment where people are transparent, real, and open about their viewpoints. Dialog is a necessity, and highly political organizations that suppress free expression of thought are likely to fail or suffer from brain drain. The authentic principle can be described by motives, actions, and attributes such as: showing vulnerability, expressing own feelings, establishing psychological safety, being welcoming, being truthful, avoiding political games, being transparent.

Being Self-Reflective and Knowing Oneself

Self-reflection presupposes not only thinking about what has happened or what should have happened. Self-reflection also compels the person reflecting himself or herself to act upon personal insights. Self-reflection or self-reflexivity are directly linked to self-development and self-knowledge. The capacity to reflect on what we have done influences the development of functional competencies. Self-reflexivity fuels conscious decisions, brought about and followed in an evaluative process. Self-reflexivity is considered one of the most popular means for introspection and for establishing social relationships. To attain self-reflexivity it takes endurance, perseverance, and attention. The challenge gets even bigger because self-reflexivity refers to a person's attitude towards an active meditation over her or his deeds and feelings, personal accomplishments and changes produced in her or his psycho-behavioral, affective, and volitional structure. Furthermore, two elements and capacities are key here: first, the capacity to meditate over one's abilities and the methodological approach which favors the critical analysis of activities and fosters personal growth. Whenever we develop or select leaders for critical positions in organizations, we focus on self-reflectivity as it is an indicator of future development. When certain competencies have not reached a sufficient level yet, self-reflexivity will be a reliable skill to consider as it propels personal growth. Leaders who embrace self-reflectivity are usually more agile, flexible, and broader in their interpersonal approach. Attributes, actions, and motives which may describe self-reflexivity may be: intrinsic aptitude, being a nimble learner, cognitive flexibility, behavioral bandwidth, showing curiosity, being bold and open, being open to criticism and corrective feedback, showing openness to try things out, generating multiple options to act upon.

To Conclude

So, to condense the above in a brief summary, we would like to close by drawing your attention to the following essential premise: leadership which is grounded in love truly makes a difference. It establishes an environment which makes people feel they belong. Love begets love, which can be translated into trust, reciprocity, responsibility for one another, accountability and ownership (some of the major challenges in organizations), support, and a positive vision. Loving leadership has a positive neuroscientific impact on others and love helps raising awareness of self and establishing a growth-oriented environment. The very premise and objective of ethical leadership is to *do good* – and love truly is a means to achieve just that.

Questions to Ponder

1. When was the last time you did something selflessly without expecting anything in return?
2. When was the last time you did something good without self-optimization at your deed's core?
3. What do you truly love about yourself?
4. How do you want to be remembered?
5. How are you going to serve the world more from today?
6. If this was your last day on earth, where would you go and what would you do?
7. What's true about you today, that would make your 8-year-old self cry? What could you possibly do about this?

Notes

1 Lyle M. Spencer and Signe M. Spencer, *Competence at Work: Models for Superior Performance* (New York, Wiley, 1993). http://ci.nii.ac.jp/ncid/BA20262819.
2 Anita Yourglich and Pitirim A. Sorokin, "The Ways and Power of Love: Types, Factors, and Techniques of Moral Transformation." *The American Catholic Sociological Review* 15, no. 4 (1954): 347. https://doi.org/10.2307/3709089.
3 Yourglich and Sorokin, "The Ways and Power of Love."
4 "Richard Branson," Big Think. September 14, 2021. https://bigthink.com/people/richardbranson/.

5 Jamilah Smian and Ahmad Fakhri Hamzah, 2018. *Leadership in Parenting: Real Stories, Examples and Practical Strategies to Enable You to Lead Your Child Better* (Bangi, Malaysia: Dezeek Media, 2018). ISBN: 978-967-10430-5-9.
6 Sue Gerhardt, *Why Love Matters: How Affection Shapes a Baby's Brain* (London: Routledge eBooks, 2004). https://doi.org/10.4324/9780203499658.
7 Sue Gerhardt, "Why Love Matters: How Affection Shapes a Baby's Brain," *Infant Observation* 9, no. 3 (2006): 305–9. https://doi.org/10.1080/13698030601074476.
8 Noel Ryan, "'Willpower: Rediscovering the Greatest Human Strength' by Roy F. Baumeister and John Tierney," *The Journal of Positive Psychology* 7, no. 5 (2012): 446–8. https://doi.org/10.1080/17439760.2012.711350
9 Jeffrey Schwartz and Sharon Begley, *The Mind and the Brain: Neuroplasticity and the Power of Mental Force* (New York: Harper Perennial, 2002). http://ci.nii.ac.jp/ncid/BB04623323.
10 Jeff Bussgang, "*Taking People With You*—Book Review," *Business Insider*, February 12, 2012. www.businessinsider.com/taking-people-with-you-book-review-2012-6.
11 Daniel Goleman, *Emotional Intelligence: Why It Can Matter More than IQ* (London, Bloomsbury, 1996). http://ci.nii.ac.jp/ncid/BA28658620.
12 John E. Mayer and Peter Salovey, "The Intelligence of Emotional Intelligence," *Intelligence* 17, no. 4 (1993): 433–42. https://doi.org/10.1016/0160-2896(93)90010-3.
13 "Greater Good: The Science of a Meaningful Life," n.d. *Greater Good*. https://greatergood.berkeley.edu/.
14 "The Psychology of Emotional and Cognitive Empathy" (Lesley University, n.d.). https://lesley.edu/article/the-psychology-of-emotional-and-cognitive-empathy.
15 https://www.fastcompany.com/90759802/the-ultimate-science-backed-guide-to-emotional-intelligence-at-work
16 Erika Andersen, "The Buddha: 10 Quotes for Leading (and Living) Well." *Forbes*, December 8, 2012. www.forbes.com/sites/erikaandersen/2012/12/07/the-buddha-10-quotes-for-leading-and-living-well/?sh=7406033c27e0.
17 Krishnamurti Foundation Trust, "The Observer and the Observed." Krishnamurti Foundation Trust, September 21, 2022. https://kfoundation.org/the-observer-and-the-observed/.
18 "1 Corinthians 13:4–8 (Niv)." n.d. Bible Gateway. www.biblegateway.com/passage/?search=1%20Corinthians%2013%3A4–8&version=NIV.
19 Dale A. Carnegie, *How to Win Friends & Influence People* (New York: Pocket Books, 1936). http://ci.nii.ac.jp/ncid/BB02478846?l=en.
20 James M. Kouzes and Barry Z. Posner, "Ethical Leaders: An Essay about Being in Love," *Journal of Business Ethics* 11, no. 5–6 (1992): 479–84. https://doi.org/10.1007/bf00870559.
21 Retired Colonel Jill Morgenthaler, "Love 'em and Lead 'em!" *SC Media*, March 15, 2016. www.scmagazine.com/news/careers/love-em-and-lead-em.
22 Cam Caldwell and Rolf D. Dixon, "Love, Forgiveness, and Trust: Critical Values of the Modern Leader," *Journal of Business Ethics* 93, no. 1 (2009): 91–101. https://doi.org/10.1007/s10551-009-0184-z.
23 Scott LaPierre, "What Is Agape, Phileo, Storge, and Eros Love? (John 21:15–17)." Scott LaPierre, April, 2023. www.scottlapierre.org/agape-phileo-storge-eros-love/.
24 "Altruism Definition and Meaning," *Collins Dictionaries*, 2023. www.collinsdictionary.com/dictionary/english/altruism.
25 Partha Dasgupta, "Altruism and the Allocation of Resources," on JSTor, *Social Service Review* 67, no. 3 (September, 1993): 374–87. www.jstor.org/stable/30012505

26 Neil Burton, "Self-Confidence versus Self-Esteem," *Psychology Today* (2020). www.psychologytoday.com/au/blog/hide-and-seek/201510/self-confidence-versus-self-esteem.

27 Neil Burton, "How to Increase Self-Esteem," *Psychology Today* (2020). www.psychologytoday.com/intl/blog/hide-and-seek/202010/how-increase-self-esteem.

28 Spencer and Spencer, "Competence at Work.".

29 Kathleen Ann Ahearn, Gerald R. Ferris, Wayne A. Hochwarter, Ceasar Douglas, and Anthony P. Ammeter, "Leader Political Skill and Team Performance," *Journal of Management* 30, no. 3 (2004): 309–27. https://doi.org/10.1016/j.jm.2003.01.004.

30 Robert K. Greenleaf, "Servant Leadership: A Journey into the Nature of Legitimate Power and Greatness," *Business Horizons* 22, no. 3 (1979): 91–2. https://doi.org/10.1016/0007–6813(79)90092-2.

31 Roger Harrison, "Accessing the Power of Love in the Workplace," (2009). https://bschool.pepperdine.edu/masters-degree/organization-development/content/poweroflove.pdf

32 Harrison, "Accessing the Power of Love in the Workplace.".

33 Dale Carnegie, "How to Enjoy Your Life and Your Job: Selections from How to Win Friends and Influence People, and How to Stop Worrying and Start Living," (1914). http://ci.nii.ac.jp/ncid/BA32752316.

34 Eric Berne, *Transactional Analysis in Psychotherapy* (London: Souvenir Press, 1996).

35 Dirk Van Dierendonck and Kathleen Patterson, "Compassionate Love as a Cornerstone of Servant Leadership: An Integration of Previous Theorizing and Research," *Journal of Business Ethics* 128, no. 1 (2014): 119–31. https://doi.org/10.1007/s10551-014-2085-z.

36 Matthieu Ricard, Charlotte Mandell, and Sam Gordon, *Altruism: The Power of Compassion to Change Yourself and the World* (New York: Little, Brown & Co., 2015).

37 Cam Caldwell and Rolf D. Dixon, "Love, Forgiveness, and Trust: Critical Values of the Modern Leader," *Journal of Business Ethics* 93, no. 1 (2010) 91–101. www.jstor.org/stable/40605330

38 Max De Pree, *Leadership Is an Art* (New York: Crown Publishers, 2004).

39 Milton Sousa and Dirk Van Dierendonck, "Servant Leadership and the Effect of the Interaction between Humility, Action, and Hierarchical Power on Follower Engagement," *Journal of Business Ethics* 141, no.1 (2015): 13–25. https://doi.org/10.1007/s10551-015-2725-y.

40 Geraldine Downey and S. I. Feldman, "Implications of rejection sensitivity for intimate relationships," *Journal of Personality and Social Psychology*, 70, no. 6 (1996): 1327–43.

41 Compare: https://wholebeinginstitute.com/megan-mcdonough/.

42 Megan McDonough, "Loving Leadership." Wholebeing Institute, September. https://wholebeinginstitute.com/loving-leadership/.

43 Dirk van Dierendonck and Inge Nuijten, "The Servant Leadership Survey: Development and Validation of a Multidimensional Measure." *Journal of Business and Psychology* 26, no. 3 (2011): 249–67. https://doi.org/10.1007/s10869-010-9194-1.

44 Nishant Khandelwal and Anil Mehta, "Leadership by 'Love': A Divine Paradigm," SSRN, March 20, 2018. https://papers.ssrn.com/sol3/papers.cfm?abstract_id=3144151.

Chapter 4

The Dilemma of Authenticity

A Plea for Authenticity and Authentic Leadership

It is never too late to try authenticity.

(Miranda Devine—columnist and writer)

Miranda Devine is right when calling on us to unfold authenticity. This thought represents the very essence of the following pages: authenticity is one of the most used terms in discussions around leadership. In our work as consultants who conduct leadership assessments, we frequently stumble across observations about whether a candidate shows sufficient authenticity. A person worthy of this label should be highly cognizant of her or his values, defend these if necessary, and should not shy away from being real and, ideally, unpretentious about personal qualities that matter. Authentic people speak the truth, they solicit feedback, they practice undisguised honesty with themselves and—if applicable—with others. Authentic leadership is in high demand and an absolute necessity, as purpose-seeking employees of the twenty-first century insist on being inspired by natural people—as opposed to *high chair tyrants* or arrogant bullies. *The high-chair tyrant*[1] is a notion that was coined by Moore and Gillette in their seminal book on Jungian archetypes, shadow aspects, and personal development. When in comes to individual personality structure and self-development, the term represents an aspect of the so-called *divine child*. The *divine child* may show shadow sides such as the attention-seeking, manipulative, and selfish *high chair tyrant* on the one hand. On the other hand, the so-called *weakling prince* may keep this archetype from perfect and mature fruition. Eventually (and if nurtured appropriately), the *divine child* may evolve into the *king* in his fullness, authenticity, and generosity. Typically, there is a distinction between male and female archetypes that can be developed in individuals. There is the mother, *the queen, the mystic* and so forth which are considered female. On the other hand, there are male archetypes such

DOI: 10.4324/b23260-7

as the king, the lover, or *the magician.* We do not refer to these concepts to trigger a discussion on gender or raise the question whether or not these concepts are scientific (which is not necessarily a sigil or label for everything good anyway). We refer to the Jungian archetypes as they are a profound source to self-reflect and work on one's personal development. Aspiring to become the best and most authentic version of oneself is a life's journey and must be taken into account when pondering the subject of authenticity. From our point of view, authentic leaders have developed an astute sense of emotional intelligence, and they are open to a diversity of viewpoints—in fact, they demand and invite cognitive dissonance in order to get to the best solution, drive creativity, solve problems, and challenge the status quo. A beautiful example of the connection between problem-solving and creativity by embracing (and managing) cognitive dissonance is *An Analysis of Leon Festinger's A Theory of Cognitive Dissonance* by Morvan and O'Connor.[2] They make a strong point on how to deal with the paradoxes and dichotomies encountered in real life. From our vantage point, authentic leaders reconcile paradoxes and invite others to explore differing viewpoints in a psychologically safe way. Inviting and fostering dialog to establish solutions to challenges and establish a culture where people want to do good is an act of both authenticity and ethics.

It can be said that authenticity is the reflected, evolving, and internalized (personal) story that is the result of a person's freely triggered appropriation of past, present, and future. From our point of view, a mature person (also in the Jungian sense mentioned above) embraces these different states within and translates them into consistent and hopefully wholesome behaviors that serve the community, company, or family. These behaviors, in turn, promote psychological safety and establish highly engaging environments where people are destined to strive.

What is more, authentic leaders are keenly conscious of their behaviors and display highly developed levels of self-awareness. Inconsistent behavior triggers unease in others. It is a fact that most people do not enjoy cognitive dissonance. When a person does not live up to what he or she preaches, our brains go at full tilt. If something does not match up and paradoxes must be reconciled, irritation and lack of authenticity are the result. Our brain is challenged when exposed to moving targets, apparent inconsistencies, or things that do not make sense at first glance. When interacting with others, preparing and making decisions, reading the room, or giving guidance, conflicting data must be harmonized. In challenging situations, our brains are scanning the room for inconsistencies, which could include something as slight as a micro-expression (for instance, when somebody smiles with their mouth but not with their eyes). Conversely, such inconsistencies may also occur at the macro level. This is the case when a colleague of yours promises to support your case but does not stick to his or her promise during the meeting you both attend. Authenticity is challenging as it can be compromised by situational needs, changing tactics of your counterpart or statements you did not see coming.

When behaviors, statements, or suggestions are made that you did not see coming, a cascade of physiological and psychological processes are triggered. Typically, inconsistencies are interpreted as suspicious, odd, or indicators of something that may be dangerous. We probably all remember the woman in the red dress from *The Matrix*. She symbolizes a red flag and indicates that something is wrong. This is the case for inconsistent information and behavior, too. Why is this an issue? First and foremost, inconsistent information and behaviors keep employees and talents from what they are, in essence, responsible for: their work. All of a sudden, their attention is distracted solely because a leader smiles with his or her mouth but not with the eyes. This will have consequences. Due to a negativity bias, oftentimes people assume the worst and suppress what they think. Many an organization seriously struggles with a lack of authenticity at the cultural level. Lack of authenticity will almost certainly impede psychological safety and be the cause of anxieties. In 2022, Donal Sull, Charles Sull, William Cipolli, and Caio Brighenti wrote an insightful piece on this subject.[3]

Authentic leaders master their own anxieties, as they are highly self-aware, mature and self-controlled. They are well equipped with values - and at their best, these values overarch both their professional and their private lives. These lofty values help them appear natural and personally autonomous, while at the same time showing relationship-orientation and interest in others. In a series of ingenious experiments, Stanford psychologist Carol Dweck has shown that concern about how we will appear to others inhibits learning of new or unfamiliar tasks.[4] Authentic (and by extension, ethical) leaders are autonomous and wholesomely independent. Therefore, they do not rely on the verdict of others, and are protected against possible judgements—and that is why they do not get compromised by anxieties. Their learning agility is, as a consequence, not inhibited by the concern about how they are perceived. As we all know, fear impairs our mental agility, our intelligence, and our capacity to judge. Fear crushes corporate cultures.[5] Authentic leaders have not been inoculated against any kind of fear, obviously. However, authentic leaders have learned to face their fears and take action regardless. As a result, they engender corporate cultures where people strive and flourish.

Authentic leadership is a well-established and researched leadership style. The concept was introduced in the 1960s, and gained prominence between 2003 and 2015 when a plethora of books was published on the subject. Prominent examples might be James Kohnen's article, "Authentic Leadership: Rediscovering the Secret to Creating Lasting Value"[6] or Bill George's *Discover Your True North*.[7] So, the concept has existed for quite a while already. However, this leadership approach is still in its ado-lescence.[8] Researchers are only just beginning to establish common de-nominators and traits such as those mentioned above: ethical perspective, value-orientation, autonomy, self-reflection, consistent behavior (as well as the capacity to deal with a lack thereof), the willingness and competency to establish psychological safety, undisguised openness, and so forth. Still, there are many divergent definitions and approaches to the subject—so if you are a bit confused, you are in good company.

In essence, authentic leadership can only be attained through personal maturation. Authentic leadership includes self-development, working on yourself, being open to criticism and bidding the high chair tyrant farewell.

It is a well-established fact (see Gallup surveys on the matter, for in-stance[9]) that organizations grapple with *brain drain* because of toxic cultures that suppress authenticity. So, we say ethical leaders promote authenticity in self, others, and in the business. This is time-consuming and requires maturity but represents a critical success factor within any organization.

Recipe for Disaster: When Things Go Down the Pipe

If you do not change direction, you may end up where you are heading.
(Siddhārtha Gautama—The Buddha, Founder of Buddhism)

Now, all of this sounds reasonable, and—to go beyond the theoretical discussion—most of us consider ourselves to be authentic, true to ourselves, and largely uninhibited in who we are. This might be a vast generalization but certainly what we have alluded to when stating that authenticity is an ideal we encounter frequently when discussing leadership. Nonetheless, as human beings, we inevitably fail to fully understand who we truly are, how we come across, and how others perceive us (the latter of which, to a certain degree, is none of our business). Positive psychologist Christina R. Wilson, PHD, states that self-knowledge helps when making realistic decisions.[10] Furthermore, it seems obvious that organizations, with their rules, structures, processes, and conventions, are not exactly hotbeds for boundless authenticity.

Authenticity can be seen as a matter of being true to yourself with regard to your avowals and the action you take. Over and above this, it seems that each individual has distinctive feelings, desires, and convictions that are of genuine importance to that person, and that each person ought to ex-press those self-defining attitudes in his or her actions. But what happens if other factors—adverse market conditions, for instance, or lax or ineffective leadership—create an environment ripe for undesirable behaviors? The is-sue at hand is that, in such circumstances, people may grossly overestimate their own authenticity and ethics. And this is where things get even more intricate.

Remember the thought-provoking Greenpeace ad from the 1990s featuring the frog in boiling water?[11] In the ad's first sequence, we see the frog in an empty container, then boiling water is poured in, and the frog jumps out. In the second sequence, the frog begins in a container filled with cool water, which is then slowly heated. This time, the frog does not jump out as the water reaches its boiling point—it just waits, and presumably perishes. If we consider the frog's story as a metaphor, the slowly boiling water can represent a corporate culture characterized by aggressive bottom-line orientation, assertiveness, career-orientation, and competition above all else. In organizations that actively promote such behaviors—even when they do so unwittingly—the danger to the metaphorical frog is even greater.

The irony is that such organizations can survive, and even thrive, despite egregious ethical lapses. Think of the Wirecard, Enron, AIG, Lehman Brothers, Volkswagen, FTX, and the Hertz-Accenture scandals. All these instances raise some intriguing questions: Why do such events keep happening? Why do leaders appear powerless to prevent them? Is it a case of overpaid executives putting profits before people? And why do those in positions of authority ignore ethical concerns despite the risk to their reputation?

Let's take a closer look at corporate cultures that have derailed and promoted unethical behaviors (see Figure 4.1). In most cases, we can observe the following conditions:

1. Unlimited bottom-line orientation: Consider, for instance, the case of the Theranos scandal.[12] In all likelihood, Elizabeth Holmes founded this med-tech giant with the best of intentions. Nonetheless, leaked reports eventually revealed that she had knowingly published exaggerated claims about the accuracy of her technology, prioritizing her company's bottom line over its ethics.
2. Lack of psychological safety: Google conducted an analysis of almost 200 highly effective teams internally in order to derive key success factors from the conditions present in these teams. The pillars thus developed were psychological safety, dependability, structure and clarity, meaning and impact. Psychological safety as a concept has been discussed ever since. A lack of psychological safety is disastrous. In V. Rao Dumpeti's words: "It allows team members to feel comfortable sharing their thoughts, ideas, and concerns without fear of criticism or negative consequences."[13] A lack of psychological safety is a clear recipe for disaster.
3. Dangerously competitive cultures: If a company culture revolves exclusively around market domination and filling the sales funnel, its chances of survival are slim. Think of *The Wolf of Wall Street*, directed by Martin Scorsese, for instance, or the fees-for-no-service scandal at the National

Australia Bank[14]—both illustrations of the dangers a perversely high level of competitiveness can pose for organizations.

4. High-chair tyrants and their license to reign supreme: When workplace bullies and dictatorial types sow a culture of fear and mistrust, brain drain, secrecy, diminishing psychological safety, and self-serving strategies are likely to follow.

5. Unmanageable workload: When professional environments do not allow for creative breaks, employees will burn out, especially if an unmanageable workload is paired with an absence of purpose. This is basically a recipe for disaster, as it perfectly erodes identification and ethical conduct.

6. Carte blanche for unethical behavior: Corporate cultures are bound to deteriorate if blatantly unethical behavior (bullying, noncompliance, gross inequalities in pay, systemic and structural racism, sexism, and so forth) goes unchecked.

7. Toxic positivity: in today's climate where life coaches are omnipresent, people engage in self-optimization, new-age esoteric (as opposed to serious spirituality) is a social distinction, gurus run multi-million businesses, and self-optimization in every regard of our lives (supported by digital solutionism) is a must, there exists a certain inclination toward toxic positivity. Suppressing negative emotions (and being forced to do so by culture) is a recipe for disaster.

From our point of view, the concepts of authenticity and authentic leadership merit a great deal more scrutiny and research. As leadership researchers and consultants ourselves, we embrace the concept and the ideal of authenticity. It is clear, however, that the systems within which we operate—political, social, corporate, and so on—do not necessarily promote expressions of authenticity. Consider the paramount importance of diplomacy, tact, and self-restraint in workplace conversations. Corporate systems, in fact, generally discourage pure expressions of authenticity. It is impossible to develop completely unfettered authenticity within any kind of system determined by power hierarchies, strict standards, economic interests, and competition. Authenticity can be understood as an ideal cultural condition to be approximated. Clearly, economic success is an objective any kind of corporate organism needs to target. However, as numerous Gallup surveys have suggested,[15] motivation purpose and the freedom to unfold authentic potential are equally relevant, and definitely sought by talent considering to change jobs and/or join an organization. Sowing and managing the seeds of authenticity is a good thing, and therefore directly linked to ethical leadership. Ethical leaders are midwives of an authentic culture. Let us now take a closer look at restrictive realities in real life and zoom in on the lessons we can derive from these.

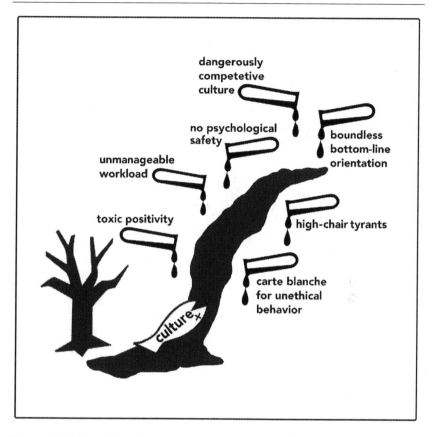

dangerously
competetive
culture

no psychological
safety

boundless
bottom-line
orientation

unmanageable
workload

toxic positivity

high-chair tyrants

carte blanche
for unethical
behavior

culture x

Figure 4.1 Cultural Derailers

Restrictive Realities: The Lessons We Can Derive from Them

> *There are certain life lessons that you can only learn in the struggle.*
> (Idowu Koyenikan—organizational consultant, author)

As has been established above, authenticity seems to be in high demand in our society, and certainly in corporations. We are eager to express ourselves authentically through the clothes we wear, the values we express, the leadership style we promote, or the specialist knowledge we possess. Being true to oneself, however, can conflict with the ethical codes held by others. To illustrate this observation, let us take a closer look at some critical incidents where ostensible authenticity caused severe problems, threatened psychological safety, or chipped away at organizational culture.

The Theranos Scandal

Stanford dropout Elizabeth Holmes founded the biotech startup Theranos in 2003, with the bold vision to develop sophisticated blood analyses from just a few drops. Holmes wholeheartedly contended that accurate blood analyses are a human right. She also cited the widespread fear of needles as an impetus for her less-invasive new method of blood drawing. Young and charismatic, Holmes seemed like a rising star and aspiring Silicon Valley prodigy.

As her company grew in the decade that followed, so did her reputation. Numerous major news outlets published glowing reviews of her work, Pepperdine University awarded her an honorary doctorate,[16] and she was officially declared the world's youngest self-made woman billionaire on the basis of her company's $9 billion valuation. In 2015, however, investigative journalists began to question her technology's effectiveness. A bombshell article in the *Wall Street Journal* revealed that Holmes's blood tests yielded inaccurate results, and that Theranos had actually been using other companies' equipment for most of their testing. In the trial that followed, Holmes was sentenced to more than eleven years in prison for wire fraud and conspiracy.[17]

The most salient detail here is that prior to her conviction, Holmes had been heralded far and wide as a biotech *wunderkind*, a technology genius, a true self-made billionaire, and a heartfelt human rights advocate. In her public appearances, she seemed to exude an effortless confidence, positivity, grit, and authenticity. Much like the visionary Apple founder Steve Jobs, for instance, Holmes dressed almost exclusively in black turtlenecks, the consistency of which may have contributed to her perceived trustworthiness. Another of her trademarks was the deep, sonorous voice she used in public appearances, which has been the subject of extensive scrutiny by body language experts and psychologists.[18] Holmes's natural voice is in fact considerably higher than she pretended it was during interviews and presentations. Perhaps she pretended to have a deeper voice to exude more gravitas, authority, or resolve. Regardless, the sincerity of these carefully crafted elements of her persona was not questioned much if at all before 2015. The interesting thing here, for our purposes, is that while Holmes's leadership was characterized above all by fraud and deception, her *perceived* authenticity played a considerable role in fueling her success—until it all got debunked. Lesson learned: do not mistake oomph, verve, grandeur, and drive for authenticity or ethical leadership.

Trade-Offs in the Realm of Organizational and Human Development

Many companies in the leadership development field claim to advance leadership excellence as a means to help promote a better future. From our point of view, this aspiration is a noble one, an ambitious one, and certainly not a straightforward one. What exactly does a better future mean? Who are the beneficiaries of this better future? What kinds of companies and industries can actually provide the building blocks for it? And should a leadership consulting company seek to take on only these kinds of companies as clients—or where do we draw the line when it comes to declining commissions? Are we as leadership consultants entitled to address or challenge the ethics of a company's practices? Or is it a consultant's duty to remain neutral?

There are no easy answers to such questions. One might argue that turning down potential new business based on ethical or political scruples is unwise, anti-entrepreneurial, and conceited. On the other hand, it could be equally valid for consultancies to accept only the clients whose work aligns with their values. Both perspectives have merit, and both relate to the question of authenticity. Is it authentic to consult an organization you oppose on ethical grounds? And if so, should you enter the project with a clear ethical position or rather be neutral in the positions you hold? Is working on a project you do not support business as usual, or should you take a stand ethically? Do rejection policies make sense, or don't they make a difference at the end of the day? Is it authentic to stay employed at a consultancy that takes on any client without regard for ethical concerns? Just as a doctor is ethically obliged to help any patient, should a consultancy support any business? Is it authentic to refrain from taking a stand? Or should one be picky and challenge policies? If you take these questions seriously, you will understand that there are no easy answers. Lesson learned: leadership implies management of trade-offs. It is worth scrutinizing your personal ethical compass. If this means to welcome discomfort, let go, and sometimes move on, this might be the price of authenticity and integrity.

To Be Vaccinated or Not to Be Vaccinated, That Is the Question!

Vaccines were the subject of aggressively contentious debate in the latter part of 2021. When pharmaceutical giants such as Biontech, Pfizer, and AstraZeneca finally released their COVID-19 antidotes, a sigh of relief echoed through the Western world. However, these companies refused to share their vaccine recipes publicly, triggering a heated debate about vaccination equality. As other parts of the world struggled to access sufficient vaccines for those who wanted them, Western nations plunged into contention over the many companies that began withholding employment and benefits from those who refused the vaccines.

An anecdote reached us about an employee whose CEO had been repeatedly posting his own vaccination pass on LinkedIn. The employee—who deeply identified with his profession—respectfully approached the CEO to ask why he chose to share such private decisions with the general public. As a consequence, the employee was reprimanded and even bullied. Indeed, the latter part of 2021 saw widespread retaliation against those who raised questions related to the vaccines, while those who proudly advertised their vaccinated status could expect to be treated as minor heroes. No matter where one stands on the vaccines themselves, the scenario begs the question: How can a simple, genuine inquiry from an employee like the one discussed above be grounds for reprimanding and even for threats of termination?

To be sure, challenging or even raising questions about the ethical nuances of the vaccine was utterly unacceptable.[19] Those with any dissenting opinions were basically compelled to suppress their concerns and thus to act inauthentically. Did these conditions simply emerge due to the severity and unprecedented nature of the pandemic between 2019 and 2023? Even more to the point, how did these conditions still emerge despite the numerous studies that suggested potential damage the vaccines may cause?

One such study, for instance, explored the approaches to vaccine injury cases in four different European countries (France, Germany, Italy, and the UK).[20] It examined the mechanisms each country was employing to redress vaccine injuries, including specific compensation funds, social security systems, and legislation to hold pharmaceutical companies accountable.[21] Several other analyses, published by physicians, physicists, and psychologists alike, scrutinized whether or not the vaccines actually ended the pandemic.[22] Are these questions subject to the ancient principle of scientific discourse or are these questions only to be raised when things are calm? So, in other words: scientific debate must only be employed when there is not imminent danger. Lesson learned: extreme situations oftentimes distort the scrutinizing of facts and circumstances. There is no discussion without bias and possible marginalization. To safeguard an environment where decisions can be made and matters debated in a well-balanced way is the responsibility of any authentic and ethical leader.

Authenticity and the Career Ladder

Being authentic can be hard. Many of us rarely pause to reflect on whether we are being true to ourselves, or to ponder who we think we are. That is why we were struck by a comment from an individual we were coaching relative to potential promotions. This is what our coachee shared with us:

> "Can I maintain my integrity at the next level? Will I be able to come home to my three young sons and tell them I did the right thing? Will I

be able to lead ethically and with integrity? I hear too many stories about compromises people have made to move up. In addition to this, will I be able to lead ethically once I have advanced to upper management levels?"

We suspect that the fact that our coachee could even ask those questions bodes well for this person's future. At the same time, we are amazed by how rarely we hear questions like these.

In our point of view, the question of authenticity is difficult and—as the title of this section of the book suggests—a dilemma. All too often, leaders may make hollow claims to authenticity when their practices are anything but. Self-understanding and self-realization are already hard enough as it is, without corporate power games thrown into the mix. It is not possible to be perfectly authentic and ethical when holding positions of power. Still, we do not intend to promote a nihilistic view of the matter here—without turning a blind eye to the challenges leaders face in their pursuit of ethical ideals, we do posit that this pursuit is both possible and worthwhile. However, it is key to acknowledge the fact that you cannot be *you* in every respect when climbing up the career ladder. With power comes responsibility. Churchill knew: responsibility is the price of greatness.[23] Greatness necessitates dealing with ethical dilemmas. Dealing with ethical dilemmas requires leaders to regulate (and possibly adjust their desire and aspiration to strive for) authenticity according to situational needs. To share a lesson in humbleness: "To thine own self be true!" cannot and should not be put on a pedestal to be venerated as an axiomatic universal. It is a mature insight to accept the fact that authenticity in positions of power is not possible to its full extent. This does not mean one has to bow down to a lack of authenticity. However, one may come to terms with the fact authenticity is an ideal one will likely never achieve. In other words (and quoting Dr. Ben G. Yakobi):

If life is an art, as in any art form, one can approach perfection, but one can never arrive. As for personal authenticity, some never bother with it, some discover it in certain actions, some strive to approach it in both life and art, but very few ever arrive.[24]

Lesson learned: broadening responsibility and holding positions of power comes at a price. Leaders may want to be authentic, and they can clearly approximate this ideal. Achieving authenticity entirely and still holding a position of power is, in our opinion, utterly impossible. It is key to ponder dichotomies and dilemmas and make conscious, prudent, and sustainable decisions.

Hierarchy of Values: A Possible Way Out of the Maze of Conflicting Viewpoints

Try not to become a person of success. Rather become a person of value.
(Albert Einstein—theoretical physicist)

What can we learn from dilemmas such as the ones outlined above? From our point of view, it is imperative for an ethical leader to be clear about his or her values and rank them in some sort of order. Such a hierarchy of values can serve as a guiding principle in their work. Taking strong ethical stances can produce complexity and conflict, of course, but complexity and conflict are inevitable regardless. Leaders whose decisions are guided by a personal hierarchy of values are the leaders who, in our opinion, will be the best equipped to handle complexity and conflict. We have dedicated an entire chapter to this subject but would like to discuss this interesting question in connection with the dilemma of authenticity as well. We do this based on the assumption that ethical leadership is—amongst other aspects—about dealing with conflicting interests, managing people at differing maturity levels, and reconciling potential personal conflicts. Once a leader has developed a sound way of dealing with such dilemmas this can be categorized as authentic and ethical.

Let us take a look at some hierarchically structured approaches. The first one that comes to mind is Maslow's hierarchy of needs, a ranking of humans' most basic needs according to their importance for survival and personal development, can serve as a model for a leader's hierarchy of personal values. One lesson to draw from Maslow's model is the distinction between *needs* and *wants*. Oxygen and food, for instance, are human needs. According to Rusty Fleischer, program director of Anger Alternatives, needs are fulfilled by wants.[25] So if you are hungry, this is a physiological need. You may satisfy this need by choosing from a wide variety of foods such as noodles, pizza, hummus, or a hot curry dish. These are wants. Such a hierarchically organized system may be extraordinarily helpful for leaders who want to remain true to their own ethical compass while navigating clashes of value systems in the workplace.

Another useful (and hierarchically organized) concept hails from a radically different discipline: the therapeutic treatment of substance abuse. This concept is the hierarchy of values developed by Dr. Joe Gerstein, a nonprofit leader and a pioneer in the field of addiction recovery.[26] Dr. Gerstein used an interview process to help individuals articulate how they rank the things most important to them. For example, an interview subject might come up with the following hierarchy of his or her values:

1. My spouse
2. My siblings

3. My children
4. My health
5. Traveling the world.

Now, one might argue that one's siblings or spouse are not exactly values in the strictest sense. The point here, however, is that any hierarchy of values needs to truly matter to the respective individual, and its elements need to be emotionally charged. The emotional charge is particularly important in the case of the drug addict. For instance, if the above list is what he or she tells you are his or her most important values, he or she may find it striking when you point out to him or her that his or her substance of choice is not among them. This is interesting as it discloses a paradox in the value system and may help in subsequent therapeutic treatment when the patient is reminded of his or her actual personal drivers.

This system also works for groups of people. The tendency here is interesting as, necessarily, values seem to get more abstract and general. Typical hierarchies of values might be:

1. Freedom
2. Authenticity
3. Responsibility
4. (Com)passion
5. Integrity
6. Self-Actualization
7. Autonomy.

It can be a very enlightening exercise to jot down one's own personal hierarchy of values, and really reflect on them for a few days before deciding how you want to rank their importance. Then you can apply your hierarchy of values to specific situations and see how it helps guide your thinking. If you find yourself compromising on one of your values repeatedly, maybe you need to rethink either your behavior or how important that value actually is to you. This can be a painstaking and even painful process, but certainly a rewarding one.

Another approach was developed by the famous philosopher Ayn Rand, who founded the objectivist movement in philosophy. Rand was born in St. Petersburg in 1905 and later emigrated to the United States in 1926. She promoted laissez-faire capitalism, individualism, and objectivism. Ayn Rand's hierarchy of values began with what she called cardinal values (such as reason, purpose, and self-esteem). Rand's most venerated and central value was *productive work*.[27] One might take issue with this as a core value, but this is not our point. The idea here is that it can be helpful to have a core value as a starting point relative to which you organize your other values.

Conclusion

For me, I am driven by two main philosophies: know more today about the world than I knew yesterday and lessen the suffering of others. You'd be surprised how far that gets you.

(Neil deGrasse Tyson—astrophysicist and educator)

This is a highly constructive and loving thought by Neil deGrasse Tyson who is a great educator and scientist. A person who acts with love—even when faced by adversity in, say, discussions about transgenderism with Ben Shapiro. This quality of (unconditional) love and compassion is integral to our understanding of leadership. And that is why deGrasse Tyson rings in these concluding lines. In this chapter, we argue that authenticity is a useful concept in the pursuit of ethical leadership. However, simply acting authentically does not protect a leader from conflict. Quite the opposite, in fact—being true to oneself and expressing one's values authentically is often the reason one clashes with others—and one's own values and ideals. Ethical leaders must develop an aptitude for facilitating respectful conversations about conflicting attitudes. This entails self-criticism, openness to feedback, willingness to compromise, and the capacity to alter one's behavior when necessary. Ethical leaders should be cognizant of their own hierarchy of values, revisiting and updating them on a regular basis—which includes striking a balance between consistency of values and flexible (and vital) adjustment. Authenticity must not be mistaken for a simple, one-and-done ideal, and it must not be invoked in a hollow way without proper reflection.

As we have observed frequently in our leadership consulting work, the concept of authenticity may be somewhat one-sided. Quite often authenticity basically means assertion, being vocal about your viewpoints, and ignoring the fact that there are limitations to authenticity, too. Dr. Ben G. Yakobi correctly points out in his article on authenticity (and its limitations): "it should be emphasized that the individual's freedom is constrained by nature and society, as well as by their own limitations—what Sartre called their 'facticity'."[28] In our point of view, being yourself is inescapable, since whenever you make a choice or act, it is yourself who is doing these things. But on the other hand, we are sometimes inclined to say that some of the thoughts, decisions, and actions that we undertake are not *really* our own and are therefore not genuinely expressive of who we are, but results of roles, conventions, or expectations imposed on us by our circumstances. So, ethical leaders need to incessantly put their values and the way they live by these to the test In order to engender and foster an ethical workplace culture that provides the perfect substrate for authentic unfolding of human potential.

Questions to Ponder

1. What are your particular personal values?
2. What values are upheld by the people you work with on a regular basis?
3. In what way are these group values and the way they influence your life in sync with your personal values? In what ways do you think there are conflicts arising?
4. Try to distinguish between the values most intimate to you personally and those expected from you or imposed on you by your circumstances. Where do you see discrepancies?
5. What values are you willing to compromise on? Which values are absolutely nonnegotiable for you?
6. Who are you? What kind of person are you? How would you describe your authentic self?
7. In which situations would being truthful and authentic support your overarching and most relevant interests? In which situations would a show of authenticity be hampering and foolish?
8. In what way are you surrounded by a culture that rewards authenticity? Are you being asked to compromise on any of your values?
9. In what way do you encourage others to be authentic? Is this something your team or workplace culture would accept?
10. Can you clearly articulate what being authentic means to you? Can you clearly and succinctly explain your most important values?
11. How might clashes and difficult conversations in your workplace be handled more effectively?

Notes

1 Douglas Gillette and Robert B. Moore, *King, Warrior, Magician, Lover: Rediscovering the Archetypes of the Mature Masculine* (San Francisco, CA: University of California, 1990).
2 Camille Morvan and Annette M. O'Connor, *An Analysis of Leon Festinger's A Theory of Cognitive Dissonance*. (New York: Macat Library, 2017, Kindle edition).
3 Donald Sull, Charles Sull, William Cipolli, and Caio Brighenti, "Why Every Leader Needs to Worry About Toxic Culture," *MIT Sloan Management Review*, March 16, 2022. https://sloanreview.mit.edu/article/why-every-leader-needs-to-worry-about-toxic-culture/.
4 Carol Dweck, "The Growth Mindset—What Is Growth Mindset" n.d. https://www.mindsetworks.com/science/.
5 Mary Clare Coghlan, "Why Fear Crushes Your Culture," *IntechOpen*, February, 2023. https://doi.org/10.5772/intechopen.1001049.
6 James Kohnen, "Authentic Leadership: Rediscovering the Secrets to Creating Lasting Value," *The Quality Management Journal* 12, no. 4 (2005): 58–9. https://doi.org/10.1080/10686967.2005.11919272.

7 Bill George, *Discover Your True North* (New York: Wiley, 2015). https://openlibrary.org/books/OL24274767M/True_North.

8 Kelly Labrecque, "What Authentic Leadership Is and Why Showing Up As Yourself Matters," August 4, 2021. www.betterup.com/blog/authentic-leadership.

9 Iseult Morgan, "Employees Want Wellbeing from Their Job, and They'll Leave to Find It." *Gallup.Com*, March 30, 2023. www.gallup.com/workplace/352952/employees-wellbeing-job-leave-find.aspx.

10 Christina R. Wilson, PhD., "What Is Self-Knowledge in Psychology? 8 Examples & Theories," *PositivePsychology.Com*, March, 2023. https://positivepsychology.com/self-knowledge/.

11 "Greenpeace—Frog Advert English," n.d. https://media.greenpeace.org/archive/Frog-Advert-English-27MZIF2T51CF.html

12 EQS Integrity Line, "Elizabeth Holmes & der Fall Theranos: der Betrugsskandal," April 13, 2023. www.integrityline.com/de/knowhow/blog/elizabeth-holmes-theranos/.

13 V. Rao Dumpeti, "5 Key Elements for Building High-Performing Teams from Google's Project Aristotle," *Medium*, March 20, 2023. https://medium.com/my-script/what-i-we-believe-in-5-key-elements-of-high-performing-teams-from-googles-project-aristotle-3ebfb4b1aaf5.

14 Paulina Duran, "Australia's NAB Reveals Anti-Money Laundering Probe, Shares Fall," Reuters, June 7, 2021. www.reuters.com/world/asia-pacific/australias-nab-reveals-anti-money-laundering-probe-shares-fall-2021–06-06/.

15 Jennifer Robison, "The Future of Your Workplace Depends on Your Purpose," *Gallup.Com*, April 19, 2023. www.gallup.com/workplace/257744/future-workplace-depends-purpose.aspx.

16 Jim McDermott, "World's Youngest Female Billionaire at Pepperdine: 'Find Your Non-Negotiable,'" *America Magazine*, May 15, 2015. www.americamagazine.org/content/dispatches/worlds-youngest-female-billionaire-pepperdine-find-your-non-negotiable.

17 Chantal Da Silva, "Elizabeth Holmes Set to Surrender to Start Prison Sentence," July 11, 2023. www.nbcnews.com/news/us-news/disgraced-theranos-founder-elizabeth-holmes-prison-sentence-appears-sh-rcna93593.

18 Jack Brown, "Body Language Analysis No 4195: Elizabeth Holmes, Theranos, and Red Flags—Nonverbal and Emotional Intelligence (VIDEO, PHOTOS)," *Medium*, May 29, 2018. https://medium.com/@DrGJackBrown/body-language-analysis-4195-elizabeth-holmes-theranos-and-red-flags-nonverbal-and-emotional-7a5115e0903f.

19 Alexander Bor, Frederik Jørgensen, and Michael Bang Petersen, "Discriminatory Attitudes against Unvaccinated People during the Pandemic," *Nature* 613, no. 7945 (2022): 704–11. https://doi.org/10.1038/s41586-022-05607-y.

20 "World Health Organization Seeks to Allay Concerns over AstraZeneca Vaccine," 2021. www.nbcnews.com/health/health-news/germany-suspends-astrazeneca-covid-vaccine-amid-blood-clot-worries-n1261097.

21 Jean-Sébastien Borghetti, Eleonora Rajneri, Peter Rott, and Duncan Fairgrieve, *Remedies for Damage Caused by Vaccines: A Comparative Study of Four European Legal Systems* (Alphen aan den Rijn, the Netherlands: Kluwer Law International, 2018).

22 "Will Vaccines Be Able to Eliminate or Eradicate COVID-19?" Centre for Vaccine Safety, n.d. www.covid19infovaccines.com/en-posts/will-vaccines-be-able-to-eliminate-or-eradicate-covid-19.

23 Pixelstorm, "The Price of Greatness." International Churchill Society, May, 2021. https://winstonchurchill.org/old-site/learn/speeches-learn/the-price-of-greatness/

24 Ben G. Yakobi, "The Limits of Authenticity," *Philosophy Now*, Issue 92 (2012). https://philosophynow.org/issues/92/The_Limits_of_Authenticity.

25 Rusty Fleischer, "Needs and Wants—Do You Know the Difference?" Anger Alternatives, n.d. www.anger.org/expectations/needs-and-wants-do-you-know-the-difference.html.

26 Joe Gerstein, "SMART Recovery President Gerstein Responds To New Research Finding That SMART And Other Mutual Support Groups Work as Well as AA," SMART Recovery, March 6, 2018. www.smartrecovery.org/smart-recovery-president-gerstein-responds-new-research-finding-smart-mutual-support-groups-work-well-aa/.

27 Tom Bowden, "Productive Achievement: Man's 'Noblest Activity.'" The Ayn Rand Institute. September 3, 2019. https://ari.aynrand.org/productive-achievement-mans-noblest-activity/.

28 Yakobi, "The Limits of Authenticity."

Chapter 5

Political Leadership

Causal Interdependencies, Archetypal Fountainheads, and Practical Consequences

It is not power that corrupts but fear.

(Aung San Suu Kyi—Nobel Peace Prize laureate)

An Apple of Discord: Can Leadership Be Political?

Aung San Suu Kyi is right when stating that fear corrupts. Fear is a profound force that propels a lot we do—even when we think we are in perfect control. There is always a deeper stratum that determines what we think, feel, and do. Depending on the *Zeitgeist*, national culture, and socio-economic conditions where you live, you may consciously or unconsciously adhere to a certain idea of humankind. Scholars typically differentiate so-called *Menschenbilder* such as *homo ludens* (the playful human), *homo faber* (the dexterous or making human), *homo economicus* (the economic human), *homo sociologicus* (the social, role-oriented human). And there is *the homo politicus* (the political human) which will be scrutinized in this particular chapter on political leadership, and its connection to ethical leadership. If you think sharply and take an overarching view, you may find that there is a certain predominant idea of humankind present in your life—partly personal, partly *suprapersonal*.

This chapter will dwell on the impact of the political sphere on us all, particularly for decision makers and leaders. Everything a leader does can be regarded through a political lens. Naturally, there will be diverging viewpoints and opinions. Some leaders or corporations will clearly embrace the stance that political discussions ought to be banned from the workplace. Think back, for instance, to Google's 2019 decision to issue new company guidelines that ban political debates among employees.[1]

On the other hand, there are entrepreneurs such as Götz Werner. In 1973, Werner co-founded his first drugstore, *DM Drogerie Markt*, in Karlsruhe. By 1978, there were more than a hundred branches in Germany.

DOI: 10.4324/b23260-8

He led the company for thirty-five years, and he also served as the head of the Cross-Department Group for Entrepreneurial Studies at the Karlsruhe Institute of Technology between 2003 and 2010.[2] Until 2018, he was president of the EHI Retail Institute (EHI). Moreover, inspired by Rudolf Steiner's teachings on anthroposophy, Werner was one of the most fervent advocates for basic income in Germany (1,000 euros for each person). He founded the initiative *Unternimm die Zukunft* (*Become an Entrepreneur of the Future*). Before he passed in 2022,[3] he donated his company stakes to charity.[4] His personal fortune amounted to 2 billion euros. As one can see from Werner's example, whether or not one likes his ideas, leadership can be highly political.

Leadership *is* Political

We shall never change our political leaders until we change the people who elect them.

(Mark Skousen—investment expert and economist)

Leadership and political leadership are complex and take place in systems—just like the intriguing quote by Mark Skousen suggests so fittingly. Leadership is political, and ethical leaders should be aware of the political consequences their action (or inaction) will have on their environment. This does not necessarily mean that political discussions must be advocated or banned explicitly (the latter being the case with Google, as indicated above). The point here is a slightly more abstract, fundamental, and subtle one, as we shall explore in this chapter.

Another aspect we will dissect is the nuanced interdependency between the *personal maturity* level of a leader on the one hand and, on the other hand, the maturity level of society, which is—if you will—the playground of each corporation and determined by the overall leadership community's level of maturity. By the end of this chapter, you will have reflected on your personal level of maturity, understood its psychological underpinnings, and come up with a possible action plan. We will discuss the question of personal maturity, which is key for positions of power. Furthermore, we will scrutinize a selection of highly contentious and politically charged situations, and derive some lessons learned from these. Consequently, we will present an integrated system supporting our claim that leadership is and must be political. Finally, we will pose a variety of questions that should be pondered in the context of corporate strategies, departmental principles, and discussion points to be raised in the leadership community.

Let us take a step back and consider the following: if you think carefully about the ordinary activities you take for granted—such as running errands, doing your chores, buying your favorite brand of cereal, going to some

DIY market to purchase some potting soil, or how about investing money in a fund your bank clerk just recommended—you will swiftly realize that virtually everything you do *can* be political. By putting your money in one particular fund, you automatically and oftentimes unsuspectingly comply with investments in industries and sectors you might want to support as a conscious act, or you might reject utterly. Banking can be ethical. Indeed, if you frequent your preferred grocery store on a regular basis, purchasing loaves of bread, meat, vegetables, chocolate, or flour, you will inadvertently exert influence on the food industry, keeping these products in high demand.[5]

Clearly, consumers' decisions have a significant impact on supply and demand and therefore on environmental repercussions.[6] Like it or not, deciding which financial institution, broker, or investment manager you permit to handle your savings is a deeply political act.[7] Furthermore, your decisions about what food you eat, which drugs you take, and so forth are not just health related, they are political as well. Consumption and usage of products—from the pharmaceutical, building, automotive, or food industries, for instance—have an impact.

We do not just live in an interdependent system on the data level,[8] as thinkers have been discussing since the 1970s; we are interconnected as a species, at both a micro and macro level. The perfect analogy: *mycelium fungi* develop, which connects plants and allows them to communicate.[9] Much like a mycelium's fragile, complex, root-like structure with its branching, thread-like connections, we humans are interconnected, and our leaders play a significant role in this interpersonal as well as suprapersonal network. Leaders of global organizations make decisions that leave traces and have consequences. Consequently, it requires maturity and responsibility to think through the potential consequences of every choice.

Personal Maturity as the Key Determinant of Societal Maturity: A Deep Dive into Jungian Archetypes, and Their Leadership Implications

Until you make the unconscious conscious, it will direct your life and you will call it fate.

(Carl Gustav Jung—psychiatrist, psychoanalyst)

At the core of our considerations in this chapter on political leadership, we make use of Carl Jung's archetypes, zooming in on four of them in particular: the King/Queen, the Magician, the Warrior, and the Lover. The number of possible archetypes is endless, but the above four fit our purposes when talking about political leadership. This by no means implies that we deem other Jungian archetypes[10] (such as the Jester, the Mother, the Visionary, the Healer, the Everyman, or the Innocent) unimportant. Furthermore, we do not heed the distinction between male and female archetypes, and we have modified the concept for our purposes. Therefore, we have narrowed the focus of this chapter to a limited number of essential archetypes that are of particular interest when talking about political leadership. In this regard, we will explore the issue of personal maturity, as it is a prerequisite for wholesome leadership (of self *and* others). As is necessary when talking about Jung's archetypes, one needs to take a closer look at the inhibiting and restricting flip side of each archetype as well: its *shadow*. This is key to guard against unwanted behaviors that indicate unfinished business, dangers, pitfalls, and the like.

Leaders exert great influence on their respective corporate cultures. It sounds like a truism that each of a leader's decisions significantly determines the atmosphere, spirit, conventions, values, and motivational fabric of the organization—and for each individual who is part of the organization. As the writer Annie Dillard famously said, "how we spend our days is, of course, how we spend our lives."[11] For many of us, a large portion of our days is spent at work. In fact, the average person will spend 90,000 hours at work over a lifetime.[12] Against this background, leaders have a considerable impact on who they lead. Consequently, the maturity level of leaders does have an impact at the individual level, and when people gather in communities such as corporations, shared values are powerful—and thus must be challenged, scrutinized, and developed. To take a deeper look at individual maturity levels, their flipsides (or, to put it in Jungian terminology, their *shadows*), and their potential political significance, let us proceed to focus on the highest form of self and its destructive undercurrents.

Based on his years of clinical study and his numerous international travels, Jung (and his successors) developed each archetype with a three-part structure. At the top of this structure is the archetype in its perfection, the highest form of *self*. At the bottom lies the bipolar shadow. These shadow aspects are not integrated. Their lack of maturity and cohesion can be observed. In its two dysfunctional poles, the shadow has an active as well as a passive aspect. For the sake of illustration, the King/Queen archetype can have an active (aggressive) shadow side which can be observed in tyrannical or manipulative demeanor (of a leader). The passive side might be observed in behaviors that remind us of a weak puppet (whose strings are pulled) or someone who displays selfish passivity. Let us now consider our selection of archetypes. Toward the end of this chapter, we will turn to the systems determined by individuals and their respective archetypal integration. We will, of course, provide questions for reflection on the lessons you may want to consider and reflect upon as a leader (of self, of your family, or of your department or organization).

The King/Queen

The King/Queen is generous. This archetype can be seen as serving other human beings as well as his or her domain. The King/Queen energy fulfills a structuring purpose; in a way, this archetype orders the chaos, gives (gracious) guidance, provides structure, and manages the paradoxes of reality. Kings and Queens, in their fully actualized form, do not become the royal energy. The do not seek to be this energy and identify with it. They do not act in a way that is arrogant, lofty, domineering or conceited, because they assume they *are* King/Queen energy. Bragging about being this energy is an indicator of the archetype's active and passive shadow aspects. Fully evolved Kings/Queens see themselves as mediums and do not fully identify with their achievements, successes, and positions of power. This is why they remain humble, down-to-earth, and capable of self-reflection. Kings and Queens in their highest forms of self also tend to be thoughtful, creative, gracious, generous, long-term-oriented, and (as mentioned above) humble.

To illustrate this archetype, think of former President of Malawi Joyce Banda, who sold off the presidential jet and the fleet of 60 Mercedes limousines to help her country's faltering economy and to distance herself from predecessors' lavish lifestyle and policies.[13] She was southern Africa's first female president, tackling the toughest jobs in the region and bringing Malawi's failing economy back to normal. Such leadership can be considered to originate from the King/Queen archetype.

The shadow side of the King/Queen archetype consists of the Tyrant as the active aspect of the bipolar dysfunctional understructure, and the Coward, Bystander, or Weakling as the passive function. The Tyrant side of the archetype is malicious, jealous, thin-skinned, and it utterly lacks control of its own destructive impulses (for further discussion, turn to Chapter 6 on the pathology of leadership). The Tyrant indulges in destructive emotions, tends to be vengeful, holds grudges against others, and usually does not show openness to work on herself or himself (Figure 5.1).

Former president Donald J. Trump would be a perfect example for this dysfunctional shadow aspect of the King/Queen. The Coward, Bystander, or Weakling, on the other hand, are rather shy, timid, observant and withdrawn, seem socially insignificant, passive–aggressive, uncertain, and prone to outbursts of aggression that follow lengthy periods of suppression.

Take, for example, Germany's former Minister of Health, Jens Spahn, who served during the outset of the COVID-19 pandemic. Spahn did not admit any wrongdoing when evidence emerged of his ministry's plans to dispose of unusable face masks by handing them out to vulnerable groups amid the coronavirus pandemic.[14] What is more, Spahn came under fire over reports that his husband's company, Burda, sold masks to the ministry

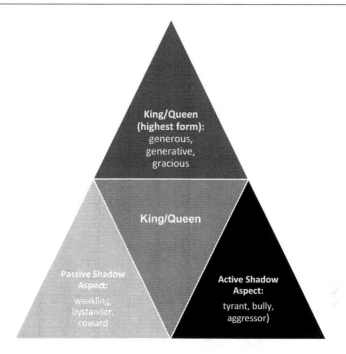

Figure 5.1 King and Queen Archetype

for staggering amounts of money. During the pandemic, Spahn purchased a multi-million-dollar villa in the center of Berlin, even while millions of Germans feared for their jobs, social inequality showed at its starkest, and children were confined to small flats and in many cases exposed to domestic violence. Spahn repeatedly failed to take responsibility for his behavior when confronted about it. This evidently took a toll on his appeal as a minister. Spahn's unscrupulous lack of remorse, especially considering the symbolic significance of his role during the pandemic, also reduced his party's (Christian Democratic Party) popularity and credibility. This could be observed in their landslide defeat during the 2021 elections. On Spahn's part, clearly, exhibiting the immature and underdeveloped aspects of the King and Queen archetype wreaked havoc on his subsequent political career (considering the fact that he has basically vanished from the media).

The Magician

According to Jungian psychology, the Magician (or Mage) is the knower and the master of technology. The Magician archetype possesses the ability to advise, guide, and initiate the process of transition and transformation both structurally and personally. Those who resort to the fully developed potential of the Magician are initiators, thinkers, transformers, and visionaries. Think of Ernest Hemingway's initiation stories[15] (*Indian Camp*, for instance), in which elders initiate adolescents into new spiritual secrets and higher ranks in the tribe. The Magician possesses a certain kind of secret knowledge, if you will, which equips him or her for success as a leader and trainer of others.

The conclusion of contemporary physics, depth psychology, or neuroscientists alike is that things are not what they seem. What we experience as normal reality—about ourselves as well as nature—is only the tip of the proverbial iceberg that arises out of an unfathomable abyss. Knowledge of this hidden domain is the province of the Magician. Take famous astrophysicists such as Michelle Thaller, Stephen Hawking, Cecilia Payne-Gaposchkin, Hisako Koyama, Neil deGrasse, or Michio Kaku. They all represent the Magician in a particularly high form of development, sharing knowledge, exploring the universe to give their knowledge back to others and contribute to a higher level of understanding.

The shadow side of the Magician is the Indifferent Manipulator.[16] People under the sway of this shadow aspect which has not evolved into the highest form of the archetype do not care about others, do not show any empathy, and make decisions without considering possible consequences for others. The Denying Innocent is the passive aspect of the Magician archetype. The active part of this archetype guides others in directions they cannot fathom, understand, or perceive. He or she charges a lot in return for the scarce information he or she shares with others. This little information is usually just enough to demonstrate his or her intelligence, foresight, and ultimately superiority. This shadow side is not just detached; it is downright malicious and cruel. Withholding information or being secretive and making it a mystery is what the active shadow side of the Magician is all about. The passive side is the Innocent One. This archetype claims and deeply enjoys the influence, power, flair, and prestige attached to positions of power. Still, individuals under the power of this archetypal shadow are lazy. They are too entitled and good to undertake any real efforts themselves. Therefore, they slow things down (for instance, decisions, actions taken, or communication) and essentially block others. This archetype is, in a way, scared to death to be unmasked. This dysfunctional form of the Magician archetype is afraid to be discovered as lacking personal integrity, greatness, vital energies, competencies, and wit. There are numerous instances where such weak characters committed unspeakable cruelties under the cloak of feigned naïveté: think of the many cases of high-ranking Nazi officials who were sentenced in the Nuremberg Trials[17] and pretended not to have known anything. In German there is a term for this type: *Schreibtischtäter* (office desk tyrants).

The Lover

The Lover presides over all sorts of love: romantic, passionate, regarding the family, spiritual, and cultural. The Lover archetype in its highest form is geared toward all the nuances of experience that can be captures by the senses. This function appreciates tastes, aesthetics, textures, the arts, sounds, sensations, and perfection. The Nobel laureate, theologian, physician, and musicologist Albert Schweitzer was a paramount example of the Lover archetype. He was an avid reader and worked incessantly to do good; his philosophy of *Ehrfurcht vor dem Leben* (reverence for life) was expressed most notably in the founding and sustaining of the *Albert Schweitzer Hospital in Lambaréné* (then a French colony on the west coast of Central Africa). Schweitzer even used his Nobel Prize to build a leper colony. The Lover in his or her highest form harmonizes, consoles, unites, experiences, feels, and embraces creation, as Dr. Schweitzer did.[18]

As we have seen with the dysfunctional underpinnings of the King/Queen and the Magician, the Lover archetype also has such an understructure. The shadow side of the Lover archetype is divided into an active side as well as a more passive one: the Addicted or Dependent Lover and the Impotent One, respectively. The Dependent Lover is not the master of his or her fate. Individuals under the sway of this shadow aspect are subjected to their own impulses. Their inhibitory apparatus is not strongly developed, and they quickly fall victim to their temporary impulses and destructive emotions. People under the influence of this shadow aspect find it difficult to realize that they are victimized by their own emotions. They find it utterly impossible to accept criticism, reflect on own shortcomings, and self-develop in order to become the best versions of themselves. Conversely, the passive side is that of the Dependent or Impotent Lover. People under the yoke of this shadow aspect will experience life in an emotionally numb way. They try to achieve perfection, claim positions of power and accomplish ambitious objectives. However, they usually fail tragically or develop deficient behaviors. Sadly, they are condemned to feel dissatisfied with what they may have achieved or accomplished. The resulting feelings of impotence and imperfection can lead to self-destructive behaviors. According to K. T. Quill, such a person may be "a collector of possessions, but they never seem to be enough."[19]

The Warrior

One of the central characteristics of the Warrior is aggression. An individual who has developed the highest form of the Warrior makes "judicious use of violence in appropriate situations."[20] This vital energy is a stance toward life that catapults humans into action, movement, and resolve. Aggression usually is associated with acts of (wanton) violence, thin-skinnedness perhaps, and dominance. However, aggression is also a vital force. It propels someone into action and may be lifesaving. It can establish power, influence, and political leeway. In her insightful article on this archetype, Denise Grobbelaar argues that

> the Warrior archetype as expressed in the great Japanese samurai tradition speaks of a sense of duty, loyalty, commitment, discipline, nobility and courage. The Warrior energy embodies the capacity to endure great hardship and personal sacrifice for the sake of a greater good.[21]

Warrior traditions such as those of the Māoris, Ninjas, Samurai, Spartans, fictitious Sith, Zulu, Sikhs, Khutulun, and Mongols all attain clarity of thought by always being aware of the possibility of death. Individuals who have internalized the Warrior archetype and are in connection with the vital energy of aggression are lucid thinkers and great strategists. Indeed, they consistently strive to become the best version of themselves regarding Warrior qualities. They strive toward personal maturity. At the same time, they are cognizant of the fact that they will cease to exist and will perish one day. At some point, they will perish. Life is precious—and fragile. The Warrior archetype is also closely related to the *memento mori* trope in Western culture, which can be translated as *remember that you have to die*. In effect, this awareness makes mature humans humbler, grounded, and dignified.

The Warrior archetype fuels action. It energizes individuals to act in a decisive and bold way. This archetype is concerned with skill, self-regulation, control, asceticism, discipline, and power. As James Luceno put it so beautifully, in his impressive *New York Times* bestseller *Darth Plagueis*, "true power needn't bear claws or fangs or announce itself with snarls and throaty barks .... It can subdue with manacles of shimmersilk, purposeful charisma, and political astuteness."[22] In order to achieve power (as in wholesome influence) over oneself and one's environment, it is key to control one's mind, impulses, and possible shadow. Only then will it be possible to lead in a dignified and wholesome way.

Such integration of the archetype of the Warrior is observable virtually everywhere in life, but especially when it comes to individuals holding positions of power in the corporate world and in politics. To illustrate this, think of Alexander the Great—or rather, the idealized figure that he has become. Born in Pella, Macedonia, around 356 BCE, Alexander is known for his amazing feats, including conquering the Persian empire and his travels to India. Alexander was raised in a strict and disciplined climate to prepare him for leadership. He was thirteen years old when his father, Philip II, King of Macedonia, decided he would need a teacher of high repute to instruct him in various matters. The king chose the philosopher Aristotle, whose father had already acted as a physician in the service of a previous Macedonian king. After inheriting the throne of Macedon at the age of twenty, Alexander embarked on a decade-long conquest, conquering the eastern Mediterranean, Egypt, the Middle East, and parts of Asia in a remarkably short period of time. The idealized figure of Alexander clearly incorporates many of the traits of the Warrior in his or her highest form: dexterity, skill, strategy, discipline, courage, and cunning.

Real problems arise when a person fails to develop his or her Warrior archetype into an integrated inner principle. Consequently, this individual is not guided by self-control, courage, motion, control, reflection, discipline, and, ultimately, love and dignity. Humans can be manipulated by the bipolar shadow strata of the Warrior energy.[23] In essence, this means they fall victim to the energy of the Sadist (active shadow function) or Masochist (passive shadow function).

No matter what your political stance may be: from a strictly psychological vantage point, leaders such as Hitler, Genghis Khan, Himmler, Stalin, Nero, Trump, Mao Zedong, King Leopold II, Ceaușescu, and Idi Amin have certain traits in common: they have shown behaviors that demean others, depreciate, belittle, demonstrate hatred and disgust, inflict cruelty, and reflect an insatiable belief in their personal grandiosity. Such leadership personalities most likely *identified* with their positions of power, as opposed to seeing themselves as fallible servants who have been granted power on a temporary basis. Leaders who find themselves under the yoke of the passive energy of the Warrior shadow experience cowardice within. Such leaders are unable to defend themselves psychologically. Others may exceed their limits. We all may fall under both the active and the passive shadow of the Warrior archetype. Behaviors expressing this may be tendencies to demean others, on the one hand, or on the other hand to suppress our own needs, which creates imbalances within and spontaneous eruptions of rage.

Individual Examples of the Dynamic Interplay of Individual Maturity Levels and Responsibility Borne

The years teach much which the days never know.
(Ralph Waldo Emerson—transcendentalist, philosopher, author)

Now, if one considers the case we have developed at the outset of this chapter on political leadership, it becomes clear that both the responsibility due to positions of power and the respective personal maturity levels of those in power are interdependent. We have established that ethical leadership is political because it generates political repercussions based on decision making. Our brief presentation (and slight modification) of Jungian archetypes, which analyze the level of archetypal integration and maturity in a person, has shown that such aspiration for the highest form of self is key in positions of power. It is abundantly clear that this is a highly complex and charged system under scrutiny.

Let us apply these observations to the individual leadership level now and connect them with our hypothesis that the maturity levels of leaders influence their direct environment and thus are inherently political (according to online encyclopedia, *Wikipedia*, "πολιτικά (*politiká*), *affairs of the cities*; a set of activities that are associated with making decisions in groups, or other forms of power relations among individuals"[24]).

Armin Laschet (German Politician)

Take, for instance, Armin Laschet of the Christian Democratic Party (CDU), who ran for the office of German chancellor in 2022 and lost by a landslide. If one scrutinizes his behavior and media presence during the campaign, one begins to understand why he lost. Take, for instance, the 2021 incident when Laschet visited the Ahrtal Valley, where about 130 people had recently died in a flood. He was caught on camera cracking jokes during the visit, which resulted in a national debate on his fitness for chancellorship.[25] This, of course, is one among many reasons for his defeat, but the Jungian archetype of the addicted Lover may apply here. Laschet's momentary excitement about some humorous element in his environment led to a lapse in decorum, which clearly impacted his public perception tremendously. Our lesson learned here might be that self-control, seriousness, regulation of own (momentary) emotions, and foresight are key. Clearly, in the above case such ethical leadership qualities were lacking.

Jacinda Ardern (New Zealand Politician)

A more positive example may be Jacinda Ardern (who we will mention more than just once due to her exemplary leadership skills). The fortieth prime minister of New Zealand and a member of the Labour Party, Ardern peaked in popularity during the aftermath of the Christchurch massacre,[26] in which a terrorist murdered fifty-one Muslims while they were praying at their local mosques. Ardern asked for pardon from the Muslim community, showing deep and authentic empathy, wearing a head scarf as a gesture of solidarity. *The Guardian* described Ardern's response as an image of hope.[27] Her behavior demonstrates integration of the highest form of the archetype of the Lover: being present, dignified, understanding, and empathetic. Our lesson learned here might be that concern for others, showing of respect, humbleness, tolerance, openness to other cultures and mindsets, and love are ethical leadership behaviors that generate goodness and have a positive political impact as could (mostly) be observed in the aftermath of the incident described above.

Donald J. Trump (Us American Entrepreneur and Politician)

In his book "The Dangerous Case of Donald Trump,"[28] Bandy X. Lee, a forensic psychiatrist, teamed up with twenty-seven colleagues from the field of psychology and related areas of research, focusing on the character of then US President Donald Trump. Essentially, the book emphasized that the mental health of Trump posed a significant threat to the nation—and, in fact, the world. Over his four-year tenure, the Trump team experienced one of the highest personnel turnover rates of an administration in recent history. Prominent departures included former Energy Secretary Rick Perry, former National Security Advisor John Bolton, former Deputy National Intelligence Director Sue Gordon, former FBI director James Comey, and former Department of Homeland Security Secretary Kirstjen Nielsen, to name but a few. For a comprehensive overview, take a look at Brookings overview of the unprecedented (personnel) turnover of the Trump administration.[29] Our lessons learned here might be that consistency, emotional predictability, level-headedness, and long-term orientation are positive political as well as ethical leadership traits.

In our opinion, Trump is clearly a person who feels superior to others and does not accept responsibility for any wrongdoing: consider, for instance, the aftermath of the attack of the Capitol on January 6, 2021. On this fatal day, following Trump's defeat in the 2020 presidential election, a mob of his supporters attacked the Capitol Building in Washington, D.C. It has been established that Trump knew of the planned attacks and had his part in inciting and encouraging the hubbub in one of his speeches on that day.[30]

During the weeks before and after the incident, he continued to exhibit shadow behaviors associated with archetypes such as the Tyrant, the Sadist, and the Denying Innocent One, all underdeveloped strata of the King, Warrior, and Magician archetypes, respectively. The repercussions have included a widespread mistrust in political leaders and the administration. Personal maturity levels are always connected to political repercussions. In Chapter 6 on the pathology of leadership we have also discussed this matter, and derive some valuable lessons learned from this case. The lessons we might want to derive from the above incident are these: taking responsibility, communicating clearly, having the personal dignity to admit—at least in parts—to personal wrongdoing, owning a situation, and showing love, compassion, and empathy. Of course, accepting defeat and showing modesty, humility, consideration, and unpretentiousness are lessons we learn from this Incident as well.

Nelson Mandela (South African Politician)

To conclude, let us consider a prominent figure in politics and political leadership, Nelson Mandela. According to Encyclopaedia Britannica,

Mandela was a South African anti-apartheid activist who served as the first president of South Africa in the years between 1994 to 1999. He was the first head of state elected in a fully representative democratic election.[31] His government consistently dealt with the legacy of apartheid by driving racial reconciliation. Ideologically an African nationalist and politician showing strong inclinations toward socialism, he also served as the president of the African National Congress (ANC) party from 1991 to 1997.[32] Mandela showed perseverance, courage, decisive action, and an inclination to stand up for his ideals, all mature characteristics of the Warrior.

His landmark book, "Nelson Mandela's Favorite African Folktales,"[33] sheds further light on his archetypal qualities. Mandela related his favorite African legends in this subtle and beautifully illustrated anthology. In these tales we meet a Kenyan lion by the name of Simba, a seven-headed snake, and some deceptive characters from Zulu folklore. We hear the voices of the scheming hyena, and we learn from a Khoi fable how animals acquired their tails and horns. If you read carefully, you will sense a loving spirit and a warm-hearted person—the generative and uniting archetype of the Lover becomes visible. Today, Mandela's life continues to serve as a model of dignity, charisma, and unity.

Does this mean Mandela was an immaculate person without any flaws? Most certainly not. The flip side of things is this: Mandela suggested cutting off the noses of persons deemed collaborators of apartheid.[34] His then-wife Winnie advocated *necklacing* instead, placing a burning tire around the neck.[35] "Mandela argued that the apartheid regime left him no option but to fight violence with violence."[36] Thus, the truth is, reality is complex, and one ought to stay vigilant and look at the whole picture, refraining from veneration and oversimplification. Mandela showed great maturity in the archetype of the Lover and the Warrior. At the same time, it is true that he promoted violence for a higher cause, and this shows the shadow side of both King and Warrior. Our lesson learned here may be this: ethical (and politically savvy) leaders show resilience, perseverance, think long term, have vision, direct their ethical attention to a better future, make mistakes and learn from them, and must take responsibility for past actions if necessary. Self-righteousness and conceited (starry-eyed) moralism are ethical vices and must be tackled.

Preliminary Conclusion on the Case of Political Leadership

I would feel no hesitation in saying that it is the responsibility of a decent human being to give assistance to a child who is being attacked by a rabid dog, but I would not intend this to imply that in all imaginable circumstances one must, necessarily, act in accordance with this general responsibility.

(Noam Chomsky—linguist, social critic, cognitive scientist)

Chomsky's observation might indicate that a general sense of responsibility and general goodness must not apply to an individual's totality of her or his deeds. We are faced by complex dilemmas almost daily—and manage these with different levels of maturity. It is a bit of a truism that an individual's economic, educational, and social circumstances influence his or her mindset. Mindset determines behavior, and behavior will most certainly have consequences in interpersonal relationships. Interpersonal relationships will constitute and define the culture of teams, departments, families, and other kinds of groups. Such systems are interconnected with other systems of superstructures such as organizations, corporations, or political environments within a country. These superstructures may form associations, networks, unions, leagues, intergovernmental political forums, or communities of shared values (e.g., the West, the Orient, the First World, Developing Nations, BRIC states, the Western Community of Values, and so forth).

In a globalized world, nations comprise interwoven and interdependent systems. This can be observed when you read the list of ingredients in your favorite snack foods, or when you consider gas price fluctuations in the context of international conflicts.

We have established our belief that no leader can withdraw from the political repercussions of his or her decisions. To put this positively: to truly lead, one ought to embrace the fact that with a broadened leeway and scope of decision making comes greater responsibility. Everything you do as a citizen, and especially one in a position of responsibility—be you a parent, a teacher, a coach, a farmer, or a steel worker—can be political. You will impact the ways people cooperate, conflicts are resolved, and processes are followed. *Polis* is the Greek word for *city*, and politics is the ancient tradition of making sure cities, systems, and peoples can coexist and prosper. As a whole-person leader, you can (and, in in our view, you should) be the gel amalgamating the people you lead into a unified group. In this sense, your leadership is inherently political.

Furthermore, we have examined the multifaceted qualities of Jungian archetypes and their effect on individual behavior. Let us conclude now by moving to a more systemic level, discussing three instances where groups of individuals holding positions of power determined the maturity level of the system which served as their context or, if you will, playground. You may agree or disagree with our interpretation of these contexts. What remains true, however, is the fact that individual maturity levels determine systems and their respective maturity levels.

Circumstantial Examples and the Educational Gifts They Bestow on Us

I never learned from a man who agreed with me.
(Robert A. Heinlein—author, aeronautical engineer, naval officer)

To learn can mean a lot: it can be the inspiring act of instilling ideas into the vessel that is the mind. It can happen through spirited conversations. Learning can also take place through friction and discourse—as the above quote by Robert A. Heinlein suggests. In the following pages, we will take a detailed look at two highly charged and positively contentious situations. When we say *situations*, we mean situational circumstances as opposed to individual characteristics. So, we will *predominantly* focus on the circumstances of each incident and their ethical charge. Furthermore, we will apply the above concept of *shadow aspects* to both these situations (and their protagonists). We would like to emphasize the fact that in the humanities, there are not ultimate truths. Cases such as the role of the National Rifle Association (NRA) in the United States are controversial by nature. Please, bear in mind: our views are strongly determined by our up-bringing, the cultural values surrounding us, our personality, and psychological structure. We have tried to state the facts (if there is such a thing) in the three cases to follow, and do not claim to exhaustively discuss these. It goes without saying, political and societal phenomena are ambiguous to some extent. So let us take a plunge, and we certainly are open to further discuss these matters if you choose to approach us.

The Nra Suing the State of Florida Over Changes to Gun Control Legislation

In the aftermath of the 2018 school shooting in Parkland, Florida, which claimed seventeen lives, authorities arrested a nineteen-year-old suspect, former student Nikolas Cruz. In 2022, Cruz was sentenced to life in prison without parole. His case was highly televised and one of the most emotionally unsettling to date.[37] Cruz was able to legally buy several guns despite having a history of mental illness and making public threats of violence. The NRA sued to block a new gun control law in Florida just hours after Governor Rick Scott signed it.[38]

On a side note: In 1954, Willian Golding published his infamous "Lord of the Flies", a dystopian novel exploring the tension between individuality and groupthink. The book accounts the atrocities children and young people can inflict on one another when left to their own devices. On the desert island Golding depicts, castes evolve, priests rise to power, superstition spreads, and murder is rampant. In 1983, when Golding received the Nobel Prize for literature, the Swedish Academy described his works as "somber moralities and dark myths about evil and treacherous destructive forces."[39] When analyzing the psyche of Cruz, his anti-social tendencies, his fears, his Warrior shadow sides, and immaturity, parallels between Golding's novel and the massacre Cruz created are striking. He justified and glorified his deeds in brief video messages he pre-recorded. He presented himself as entitled to imposing death, and judging others in the most violent way. Dystopia turned reality.

When students at *Stoneman Douglas High School* took to the streets and held their own demonstration against lenient gun-control legislation, they showed mature behavior, courage, dignity, resolve, and a truly generative spirit—an attempt not to maintain things as they are, but to make a difference. In our opinion, all these are mature signs of archetypal integration of the King, Warrior, and Lover energies. The US is characterized by an almost religious veneration of violence, creating ever more advanced weaponry in the name of keeping the peace, and forceful (and oftentimes futile) interference in the politics of other nations. These factors, among others, have triggered a massive and unprecedented wave of mass shootings (i.e., shootings with more than four victims) such as Columbine, Uvalde, Sandy Hook, Sutherland Springs, and the Pittsburgh synagogue shooting. As of August 2022, there have been over 410 mass shootings in the USA.[40]

Clearly, given this context, the NRA, as a system, showed signs of shadow forms of the *Warrior* (i.e., the *Sadist*) when suing the State of Florida in the aftermath of the Parkland Shooting. Strong indicators of the shadow side of the Magician (i.e., the Detached Manipulator) can be observed in their use of women's rights as a pretext to make their case against increased gun regulation. One shadow side of the Lover (the Addicted or Dependent Lover) can be detected here as well, when you consider the NRA's fixation on weapons under the pretext of self-defense. One might venture to ask why humans still haven't outgrown the obsessive urge to make use of tools that kill. In our opinion, individuals such as Wayne Robert LaPierre, CEO of the NRA as of 2018, show strong signs of obsession and shadow aspects of the King. Leaders of this kind, as we have argued, play a considerable role in shaping their culture. This is one of the many reasons why acts of violence are reported on a regular basis in the US.

On a side note: we are perfectly aware of the fact that the above is an exceedingly contentious subject. The owning of weapons is a subject that has been debated for centuries. There are positions such as Burger's, who argues, "second amendment does not guarantee the right to own a gun."[41] *On the other hand, the NRA argues*, "a well regulated Militia, being necessary to the security of a free State, the right of the people to keep and bear Arms, shall not be infringed."[42] This debate is as deep-rooted as bi-partisan politics in the United States, and will not be resolved by this section of our book on ethical leadership. However, the shadow aspects mentioned above are intriguing and, in our opinion, should be considered when discussing the matters of ethical leadership and maintenance of peace.

The Way Individuals, States, and Societies Handled the Sars-Cov-2 Global Pandemic

The COVID-19 pandemic was a rampant global pandemic triggered by a severe acute respiratory syndrome. The pandemic, and the ensuing societal and political crisis, began in late 2019, with its alleged and probable epicenter in Wuhan, China. In this final analysis, we do not intend to delve into any statistics, crunch any numbers, or question the efficacy of rapid tests and so forth. Such a discussion would go beyond the scope of our book on ethical leadership. What we are interested in are the implications for holistic leadership—the kind of leadership that does not turn a blind eye to complexity or ambiguity.

One observation that could be amply made during the pandemic has been an almost compulsory focus on a tried-and-trusted psychological concept: resilience. The Austrian psychiatrist Viktor Frankl established the concept in the twentieth century, scrutinizing the psychological fabric of survivors of Nazi concentration camps.[43] Models focusing on cognitions (motivation, self-belief, humor, self-compassion etc.), environmental factors (social support, purposeful interpersonal relationships, spiritual systems), and behaviors (self-care, sports routines, physical exercise, nutrition, physical awareness) have been widely discussed in the media and in corporate trainings. The concept of resilience is a holistic approach, attempting to capture the complex interplay of energies that keep people and societies wholesome and flexible when difficulties arise. Individuals, organizations, and states alike applied the findings of resilience and derived valuable lessons from it over the pandemic.[44]

When taking a closer look at how societies have handled the COVID-19 crisis, a heterogeneous picture evolves, to say the least. On the one hand, healthcare workers were regularly applauded[45] by grateful citizens at the beginning of 2020. This phenomenon, however, only lasted for a couple of months and was later harshly criticized by upset health workers who got alienated by one-sided discussions and—an almost traditional topic—disastrous working conditions. Furthermore, families supported each other during quarantines when physical contact and gatherings were restricted. In an unprecedented rally, scientists developed a vaccine that promised to end these restrictions and to eradicate, or at least curtail, the pandemic. Many of us experienced an oftentimes exhausting battle with video conferencing tools and connectivity issues—and, eventually, we tamed and mastered these systems, integrating them into new daily routines. Some of us discovered the delights of the home office. Others realized the value of being considerate and respectful when working together in contexts which did not allow virtual approaches, but which had been affected significantly when it comes to accustomed ways of cooperation: *social distancing* being the most prominent measure that was taken.

However, beside the unwitting double-standards alluded to above (applauding health workers for a couple of months only[46]), there were clear *shadow aspects* of the situation as well. Some of us realized them during the pandemic, others only felt comfortable voicing criticism when the thunderstorm had passed.

Let us take a look: One interesting study conducted on the perception of the risks posed by SARS-CoV-2 was Merkley and Loewen's "Anti-intellectualism and the mass public's response to the COVID-19 pandemic," in which they argued that "anti-intellectualism (the generalized distrust of experts and intellectuals)"[47] had played a powerful role in shaping the public's reaction to the COVID-19 pandemic. According to the survey, some people tend to be persuaded by speakers they see as knowledgeable (that is, experts), but only when they perceive the existence of common interests. If this is not the case, these experts may be seen as "threatening to their social identities."[48]

On the other hand, in the wake of COVID-19, communities and nations have exhibited ever more absurd forms of underlying societal ailments and dysfunctions. On social media, conceited hordes of starry-eyed idealists would proudly publish their photographed vaccination certificates. When lawyers, virologists, psychologists, and physicians raised their voices in concern over the disastrous socio-political repercussions[49] that the restrictions could cause, as well as the large-scale adverse health-related ramifications, many were met with accusations of being social-nationalists, conspiracy theorists, esoteric bogeymen, or social parasites. Notions such as democracy, discourse culture, solidarity, and plurality of perspectives were virtually thrown out the window. Prominent political theorists such as Ulrike Guérot[50] and Noam Chomsky have been denounced, as have numerous prominent physicians.[51] Societies around the globe have shown varying levels of readiness to accept one-sided interpretations, and oftentimes worryingly high degrees of willingness to marginalize ordinary people and highly decorated intellectuals, scientists, and politicians alike.

Such traits demonstrate *shadow aspects* of the *King*, the *Warrior*, and the *Magician*. From our point of view, the pandemic has clearly uncovered relatively low levels of societal capacity to handle such a challenge. Make no mistake: the COVID-19 pandemic was an endemo-epidemic, societal, political, economic, and individual precedent. However, it is clear, also, that as citizens and *populus politicus* we are well-advised to reflect on the entire situation, and how we handled it as citizens of the world.

Conclusions and Recommendations: Being Impactful Both Politically and Ethically

In this chapter on political leadership we have basically focused on the following aspects: we believe that leadership is always political—it is strongly influenced by personal maturity levels and integration of archetypal aspects[52] (such as the Lover, Warrior, King/Queen, and Magician), leadership takes place on a personal level, and it is a collective act (leading self, being led by circumstances, biases, and group dynamics[53]). The lessons we derive from the above are manifold. Ideally, an ethical leader who takes his or her political impact into consideration and wants to evolve into the *highest form of self* should work on the following aspects:

1. Compassion and love
2. Trusting self and others
3. Strategy and long-term orientation
4. Openness to others
5. Interest in others/inquisitive mindset
6. Questioning the status quo/driving innovation
7. Mentoring and developing others
8. Reduction of self (as opposed to self-serving interest)
9. Working on self
10. Order and precision
11. Drive, excellence, and target-orientation
12. Showing perseverance
13. Showing non-conformity and driving innovation
14. Establishing community.

These and other aspects can be worked on with a sparring partner, your spouse, another leader, a peer, or a coach.

Furthermore, we believe that leaders can systematically work on their *political impact*. Experience shows that a person's political impact is strongly influenced by his or her personal maturity level. We want to be very clear about this point: if you disagree with the archetypal approach or Jung's take on the matter, this is perfectly fine by us. We are not dogmatic about this in any shape or form. There are numerous models and systems focusing on personal maturity levels. Whether you work with Jung's, Hogan's, Myers-Briggs' (which, of course, is based on Jung), or Belbin's, or prefer the Big Five model, does not matter to us. What does matter is the integration of personality aspects and mature self-conduct.

With this being said: *personal maturity* matters when a leader wants to exert political influence and proceed ethically. Dignity, grace, generosity, an inquisitive mindset, clarity and order, confidence, and so forth should rank at high maturity levels as outlined above. Another key component is *generative will*: a person's urge and desire to create, leave a mark, improve, and serve society and establish community. Communities and cultures can always be improved. Toxic positivity is alien to an agile mindset. If there are conflicts brooding or things get buried under a seemingly smooth surface, things go wrong. On the one hand, politically inclined leaders who

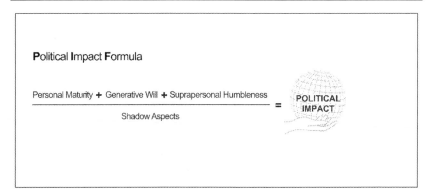

Figure 5.2 Political Impact Formula

care about the right thing will sustain what is right *and* question the status quo at the same time. Finally, a politically inclined and ethical leader must be humble. In essence, hubris suffocates ethical leadership. Ethical leaders are not self-serving: they serve something greater than themselves. As we have seen before, they do not identify with positions of power. They know that they might err, make mistakes, and do not have all the answers. *Suprapersonal humbleness* also means that a leader serves something greater (as in *supra*-). Such leaders apologize and reduce themselves because in the end they do not matter. What matters is the objective of a better world, a better team, a better culture, a better future. As outlined above, *shadow aspects* are driven by anxiety and represent personality aspects that have not yet been integrated. The bottom line here is that any mature ethical leader should work on these shadow aspects—basically to keep the denominator at a low level. What needs to outweigh the *denominator* (= shadow aspects) is the *numerator* (= *personal maturity, generative will*, and *suprapersonal humbleness*) (Figure 5.2). Once these conditions have been fulfilled, political (and ethical impact) is at its highest, and goodness can be pursued.

Questions to Ponder

1. What consequences may your intended decisions have for those around you?
2. In what way do the decisions you make—or the ones you avoid making—trigger consequences on a broader level (interdepartmental or across the organization)?
3. What ideas do you hold about society at a deeper level? In what way does this play into your behavior as a leader?

4. Accepting the fact that, as humans, we are not necessarily made to ascend to the highest levels of self-awareness, what could be challenged about your ordinary way of going about your leadership responsibilities?
5. What societal, environmental, and ethical impacts does your organization have on a larger scale?
6. To what extent is the leadership team attuned to their ethical responsibilities? Is there room for improvement?
7. Assuming you can name a variety of personal values you embrace and cherish, how conscious are you of these when leading?
8. In what way do you contribute or want to contribute to the greater good? Where do you make exceptions? Why?
9. In what way do you contribute to the peaceful coexistence of individuals, teams, departments, and—if your imagination allows it—groups of people beyond your organization? What are you satisfied with? Where do you identify room for improvement?

Notes

1 Annie Palmer, "Google Bans Political Discussion on Internal Mailing Lists," CNBC, August 23, 2019. www.cnbc.com/2019/08/23/google-bans-political-discussion-on-internal-mailing-lists.html.
2 Institute for Entrepreneurship, Technology Management, and Innovation—Homepage. https://etm.entechnon.kit.edu/english/index.php.
3 "On the Death of DM Founder Götz Werner: Why His Entrepreneurial Legacy Is so Important," ACROSS, February, 2022. www.across-magazine.com/on-the-death-of-dm-founder-gotz-werner-why-his-entrepreneurial-legacy-is-so-important/
4 "Imperium gegründet: Milliardär und dm-Gründer verschenkt sein Vermögen," Karlsruhe Insider, December 8, 2021. www.karlsruhe-insider.de/news/imperium-gegruendet-milliardaer-und-dm-gruender-verschenkt-sein-vermoegen-89470.
5 In this regard, consider these greenhouse gas emissions per kilogram of food product. Greenhouse gases are weighted by their global warming potential value (GWP100). GWP100 measures the relative warming impact of one molecule of a greenhouse gas, relative to carbon dioxide, over 100 years: beef herd (99,48 kg), lamb and mutton (39,72 kg), dairy herd (33.3 kg), cheese (23.88 kg), poultry meat (9.87 kg), wheat and rye (1.57 kg) and nuts (0.43 kg).
6 Cf. D. Berki-Kiss, and Klaus Menrad, "Ethical Consumption: Influencing Factors of Consumer´s Intention to Purchase Fairtrade Roses," ScienceDirect 2 (August, 2022): 100008. https://doi.org/10.1016/j.clcb.2022.100008.
7 CFI Team, "Ethical Banking," Corporate Finance Institute, December, 2022. https://corporatefinanceinstitute.com/resources/esg/ethical-banking/.
8 Tyson Macaulay, "Threats and Impacts to the IoT," In RIoT Control. ScienceDirect (2017) 221–78. https://doi.org/10.1016/b978-0-12-419971-2.00012-1.
9 "Materials from Fungal Mycelium," Fraunhofer IAP, n.d. Fraunhofer Institute for Applied Polymer Research IAP. www.iap.fraunhofer.de/en/projects/materials-from-fungal-mycelium.html.
10 Kendra Cherry, "What Are the Jungian Archetypes?" Verywell Mind, March, 2023. www.verywellmind.com/what-are-jungs-4-major-archetypes-2795439.

11 Laura Schadler, "Is How We Spend Our Days How We Spend Our Lives? *KQED*, July 3, 2013. www.kqed.org/pop/6380/what-do-you-plan-to-do-with-your-one-wild-and-precious-life.

12 www.gettysburg.edu/news/stories?id=79db7b34–630c-4f49-ad32–4ab9ea48e72b

13 David Smith, "Malawi's Joyce Banda Discards Presidential Jet and Luxury Car Fleet," *The Guardian*, December 1, 2017. www.theguardian.com/world/2012/jun/01/malawi-joyce-banda-discards-presidential-jet.

14 "Germany's Spahn under Fire for Unfit COVID Mask Plans," Deutsche Welle. Dw.Com, June 6, 2021. www.dw.com/en/germanys-spahn-under-fire-for-unfit-covid-mask-plans/a-57790385.

15 Ernest Hemingway, *The Complete Short Stories of Ernest Hemingway* (New York: Scribner, 1987). http://ci.nii.ac.jp/ncid/BA38237833

16 Scott Jeffrey, "Magician Archetype: The Knower and the Creator of Worlds" (CEOSage, February 18, 2023). https://scottjeffrey.com/magician-archetype/.

17 The Nuremberg Trials, The National WWII Museum, New Orleans, n.d. www.nationalww2museum.org/war/topics/nuremberg-trials.

18 On a side note: The Lover is about connectedness, too. When Obe Wan Kanobe, Darth Plagueis, or Lord Vader referred to the different aspects of the force, this, of course, is reminiscent of Eastern philosophy which sees humankind as waves on the surface of a vast ocean. The lover energy resorts to this oceanic connectedness. The lover archetype in its fullness wants to experience, smell, try out, and sensate everything potentially to be experienced.

19 K. T. Quill, "Four Archetypes of Masculine Maturity Series: The Lover." *Medium*, August 9, 2022. https://ktquill.medium.com/four-archetypes-of-masculine-maturity-series-the-lover-2c9ad8424c5d.

20 Denise Grobbelaar, "The Warrior Archetype." 2020. www.denisegrobbelaar.com/blog/the-warrior-archetype.

21 Grobbelaar, "The Warrior Archetype."

22 James Luceno, *Star Wars: Darth Plagueis* (New York: Arrow, 2020).

23 Mr. Purrington, "Carl Jung Never Said: 'Shadow Work Is the Path of the Heart Warrior' but He Did Say ...." Carl Jung Depth Psychology, September 13, 2022. https://carljungdepthpsychologysite.blog/2020/06/05/carl-jung-never-said-shadow-work-is-the-path-of-the-heart-warrior-but-he-did-say/.

24 Wikipedia contributors, *Wikipedia*, July, 2023. https://en.wikipedia.org/wiki/Wikipedia.

25 Deutschland, RedaktionsNetzwerk, "Hochwasser: Laschet lacht während Ansprache von Steinmeier," RND.de, February 25, 2022. www.rnd.de/politik/hochwasser-laschet-lacht-waehrend-ansprache-von-steinmeier-DCWRLX2X2NEP7D6ITVDZM6JDOU.html.

26 "New Zealand Mosque Shooting in Christchurch," NBC News. September 16, 2021. www.nbcnews.com/news/world/new-zealand-mosque-shootings.

27 Nesrine Malik, "With Respect: How Jacinda Ardern Showed the World What a Leader Should Be," *The Guardian*, March 28, 2019. www.theguardian.com/world/2019/mar/28/with-respect-how-jacinda-ardern-showed-the-world-what-a-leader-should-be.

28 Bandy X. Lee, *The Dangerous Case of Donald Trump: 27 Psychiatrists and Mental Health Experts Assess a President*, 2917. https://openlibrary.org/books/OL27759971M/The_Dangerous_Case_of_Donald_Trump.

29 "Tracking Turnover in the Trump Administration," Brookings, February 14, 2023. www.brookings.edu/articles/tracking-turnover-in-the-trump-administration/.

30 Zengerle, Patricia, Richard Cowan, and Doina Chiacu. 2022. "Trump Incited Jan. 6 Attack after 'unhinged' White House Meeting, Panel Told." Reuters, July 13, 2022. www.reuters.com/legal/government/us-capitol-riot-probe-turns-focus-trump-allies-extremist-groups-2022–07–12/.
31 The Editors of Encyclopaedia Britannica, "Nelson Mandela," *Encyclopedia Britannica, History and Society*, July 14, 2023. www.britannica.com/biography/Nelson-Mandela.
32 "Nelson Mandela," We Are Family Foundation, April 28, 2017. www.wearefamilyfoundation.org/nelson-mandela.
33 Nelson Mandela, *Nelson Mandela's Favorite African Folktales* (New York: W.W. Norton, 2002).
34 Andrew Bolt, "The Dark Side of Nelson Mandela," *Herald Sun*, December 8, 2013. www.heraldsun.com.au/news/opinion/the-dark-side-of-nelson-mandela/news-story/68f4acdbf2b0b4e6c799e458a55e6cb2.
35 Alex Perry, "Fire and Forgiveness: How Apartheid Left Its Mark on Winnie and Nelson Mandela," TIME.Com. December 14, 2013. https://world.time.com/2013/12/14/fire-and-forgiveness-how-apartheid-left-its-mark-on-winnie-and-nelson-mandela/.
36 Bolt, "The Dark Side of Nelson Mandela."
37 CBS News. 2022. "Parkland Shooting Gunman Nikolas Cruz Sentenced to Life in Prison, Called a 'Monster' by Victims' Family Members," CBS News, November 2, 2022. www.cbsnews.com/live-updates/parkland-shooting-nikolas-cruz-sentence-watch-live-stream-today-2022-11-02/.
38 "NRA Files Lawsuit over Florida Gun Control Bill," PBS NewsHour, March 9, 2018. www.pbs.org/newshour/politics/nra-files-lawsuit-over-florida-gun-control-bill.
39 James M. Markham, "Briton Wins the Nobel Literature Prize," *The New York Times*, October 7, 1983. www.nytimes.com/1983/10/07/books/briton-wins-the-nobel-literature-prize.html.
40 John Woodrow Cox, Steven Rich, Linda Chong, Lucas Trevor, John Muyskens, and Monica Ulmanu, "There Have Been 386 School Shootings since Columbine," *Washington Post*, April 3, 2023. www.washingtonpost.com/education/interactive/school-shootings-database/.
41 W. E. Burger, "Second Amendment Does Not Guarantee the Right To Own a Gun (From Gun Control, P 99–102, 1992, Charles P. Cozic, Ed.—See NCJ-160164)," Office of Justice Programs, 1992. www.ojp.gov/ncjrs/virtual-library/abstracts/second-amendment-does-not-guarantee-right-own-gun-gun-control-p-99.
42 "What Is The Second Amendment and How Is It Defined." NRA-ILA, n.d. www.nraila.org/what-is-the-second-amendment-and-how-is-it-defined/.
43 Viktor E. Frankl, *Yes to Life: In Spite of Everything* (Boston, MA: Beacon Press, 2020).
44 Zhishen Wu, Mohammad Noori, and Xilin Lu, *Resilience of Critical Infrastructure Systems: Emerging Developments and Future Challenges* (Boca Raton, FL: CRC Press, 1920).
45 Luke Hurst, "Coronavirus: Health Workers Clapped across the World for Battling on the COVID-19 Frontline," *Euronews*, March 24, 2020. www.euronews.com/2020/03/24/coronavirus-health-workers-clapped-across-the-world-for-battling-on-the-covid-19-frontline.
46 Grzegorz Szymanowski, "Nursing Staff Demand More than Applause," DW.com, April 2, 2020. www.dw.com/en/coronavirus-crisis-underpaid-overstretched-nursing-staff-demand-more-than-applause/a-52995776.

47 Eric Merkley and Peter John Loewen, "Anti-Intellectualism and the Mass Public's Response to the COVID-19 Pandemic," *Nature Human Behaviour* 5, no. 6 (2021): 706–15. https://doi.org/10.1038/s41562-021-01112-w.

48 Merkley and Loewen, "Anti-Intellectualism and the Mass Public's Response to the COVID-19 Pandemic."

49 Matteo Bonotti and Steven T. Zech, "The Human, Economic, Social, and Political Costs of COVID-19," In *Springer EBooks*, 1–36 (2021). https://doi.org/10.1007/978–981-33–6706-7_1.

50 deutschlandfunk.de, "Debatte um #allesdichtmachen—Guérot: 'Es gibt keinen Raum mehr für legitime Kritik'." Deutschlandfunk, n.d. www.deutschlandfunk.de/debatte-um-allesdichtmachen-guerot-es-gibt-keinen-raum-mehr-100.html.

51 Andreas Speit, "Umstrittener Rechtsmediziner Püschel: Zu Besuch bei den Braunburschen," TAZ Verlags- Und Vertriebs GmbH, November 2, 2021. https://taz.de/Umstrittener-Rechtsmediziner-Pueschel/!5812018/.

52 On a side note: it does not really matter which system of personality typology or personality analysis you prefer. The essential point is, to us, that there are maturity levels in people. Self-development, dealing with personal trauma, and evolving to a well-levelled stage is a life's journey and may be approached from different directions when it comes to psychological tradition.

53 Gustave Le Bon, *The Crowd: A Study of the Popular Mind* (New York: Ballantine Books, 1968).

Chapter 6

A Pathology of Leadership

Expressions of Mis-Leadership, and the Lessons It Harbors

Preliminary Thoughts on Mishaps, Divergence, and the Aspiration of This Chapter

Nature is as well adapted to our weakness as to our strength. The incessant anxiety and strain of some is a well nigh incurable form of disease.
(Henry Thoreau—essayist, poet, philosopher)

In this chapter we will delve into some unfavorable or destructive leadership behaviors. This is important because by examining these negative behaviors which we refer to as *mis-leadership*—we can refine our positive sense of what just and ethical leadership looks like. Such insights are inspired by instances where things went wrong, or where it became abundantly clear that positions of power potentially elicit negative tendencies in those who occupy them. Studying pathological forms of leadership can teach us a great deal about where to look closely, be cautious, self-reflect, and possibly change course.

The first step involves looking at examples of narcissism, self-centeredness, surpluses of certain traits that are usually deemed strengths, and mandatory prerequisites for leaders. We will scrutinize some well-known examples of corporate scandals (and keep doing so in order to derive lessons from these instances) and zoom in on the phenomenon of corporate psychopathy. Our aim is to construct a portrait of the ethical leader *ex negativo* from these instances of derailed ambition.

This inspection also serves as a reminder of the pitfalls that positions of power hold by nature, something that no one is charmed against. To attain true maturity as a leader and—first and foremost—as a human being, you need to be aware of your own inclinations, patterns, and prejudices. Only then is it possible to unfetter yourself and rise to wisdom, peace of mind, and maturity. We also believe that the privileges that come with positions of power, unconscious routines, and hierarchical structures can potentially

DOI: 10.4324/b23260-9

engender narcissism. Biases tied to your perception bubble, one-sided focuses dictated by the system you are part of, and peer pressure are factors
that can hamper the blossoming of true greatness and mature leadership.
Such phenomena have been exhaustively explored by psychologist Rainer
Mausfeld in *Angst und Macht*[1] ("Fear and Power"), as well as *Warum schweigen die Lämmer?*[2] ("Why the lambs keep silent").

Make no mistake: the ultimate goal of this chapter, and of this book, is
to inspire you to think critically about yourself, the structures you have left
behind, the structures you are rooted in, your management style, your ambitions, and the culture you establish around yourself. In the short article
on the psychology of erring, "Intelligent People Learn from the Mistakes of
Others", a blog on psychology and philosophy, Shaydon Raney expounded
the matter:

Someone once said that all people can be divided into three big groups:
one that assimilates their mistakes; another that in addition to their own,
also does this with the mistakes of others; and a final group that does neither of these. It is good to belong to this second group, especially because
doing so reduces our probability of falling into a well just to prove that it is
there. Staying aware of what is happening around us is a defensive weapon
to prevent avoidable injuries.[3]

So learning from own mistakes and those from others is the first premise
we would like to highlight here.

The second premise is inspired by the following: a two-part townhall
discussion at the District Six Museum in Cape Town, South Africa. Arch-
bishop Desmond Tutu, former secretary general of the UN, Kofi Annan,
Hina Jilani, a well-known Pakistani human rights lawyer and activist, and
former prime minister of Norway, Dr. Gro Harlem Brundtland, at the po-
dium, addressed the relevancy of ethical leadership, critical thinking, and
peaceful coexistence. The event also brought to light some sad truths of
geopolitics: the so-called African World War that was caused over the conflict about natural resources in the Democratic Republic of Congo in 1998
and dragged eight countries into the belligerent turmoil of the situation.
During the insightful discussion, in the words of Dr. Gro Harlem Brundtland, "to be bold, to have the courage of your convictions and to think long
term, not short term or for political expedience: those are characteristics
common to good leaders."[4] Maybe, paradoxically, this is exactly the spirit
we have in mind when pondering the divergent behavior every leader must
be vigilant against. So, it is our second premise not to brush off negativity
and situations where *things went down the tubes*. Rather the opposite: engaging in dialectic analysis of deviant behavior or situations can be a most
inspiring experience and source of knowledge. This is the second premise
determining the motivation of the chapter on pathological leadership, or
mis-leadership.

When Things Go Wrong

Never interrupt your enemy when he is making a mistake.

Napoleon Bonaparte

Let us begin our dive into this subject by looking at some well-known and some lesser-known instances of *misleadership*. We will scrutinize these four instances where leadership went awry. In a perfect world, healthy and dignified culture fosters morale, motivation, and accountability. The exact opposite—we may refer to this kind of circumstance as *wickedness* or *immorality*—sows the seeds of fear, hatred, divisiveness, and ultimately, destruction. As author Frank Herbert wrote in his beautiful book *Dune*: "Fear is the mindkiller."[5] We believe that this is true. However, overcoming fear is an act of courage. Willpower and perseverance are beautiful qualities of living beings. Love is the exact opposite of fear. That is why we dedicated one entire chapter to leadership that stems from love. Let us now, however, zoom in on divergent behaviors and see what lessons we can extract from these.

Donald J. Trump, Forty-Fifth President of the United States of America

In December 2020, then US president Donald J. Trump pardoned four former *Blackwater* contractors, a company founded by Erik Prince, brother of then Secretary of Education, Betsy DeVos.[6] It took a drawn-out and intricate judicial process for these contractors—later operating under the name Academi[7]—to be convicted for killing fourteen Iraqi citizens in 2007. According to US prosecutors, this carnage was not without precedent: Blackwater was notorious at the time for disregarding the rules of engagement in Iraq, frequently using heavy artillery to fire indiscriminately at civilians. Blackwater contractors routinely do not follow the rules of engagement in Iraq, shooting indiscriminately into cars and buildings and frequently disrespecting locals. US prosecutors stated that, in 2007, the heavily armed Blackwater contractors made use of sniper weapons, automatic guns, and grenade launchers to fire at civilians in the crowded traffic circle, causing considerable carnage and the killing of two children.

Trump's pardon of these four contractors followed an array of questionable leadership decisions on his part, such as his handling of the George Floyd protests, his public promotion of various controversial conspiracy theories, and, consequently, a dramatic exacerbation of the US American national divide. For the sake of illustration, let us name some such divisive actions, behaviors, and questionable narratives supported: Executive Order 13769, President Trump's promotion of conspiracy theories such as the Joe Scarborough Murder Conspiracy Theory, Biden–Ukraine Conspiracy

Theory, Climate Change Denial, the (irrelevant) Birther Controversy, the Global Warming Conspiracy Theory, the White Genocide Conspiracy Theory, his recommendation to utilize detergent against COVID-19 (and his adamant subsequent assertion that these were humorous remarks misrepresented by the media), and his withdrawal from the Paris Agreement in June 2017.[8]

Against this backdrop, when Trump pardoned the Blackwater contractors, the decision met with international condemnation and moral outrage. "President Trump's decision to pardon four mass murderers shows just how little respect he has for both our legal system and the sanctity of human life, especially the lives of Muslims and people of color,"[9] Nihad Awad, executive director of the Council on American–Islamic Relations, announced in a statement. "These Blackwater mercenaries were convicted of perpetrating one of the most infamous war crimes of the American occupation of Iraq," Awad went on. "Pardoning them is an unconscionable act of moral insanity."[10] Only two weeks later, on January 6, 2021, the departing president played a role in inciting violent protests by making largely falsified claims about irregularities in the 2020 presidential election. In all fairness, it must be noted that Trump still has not been charged for initiating the January 6 insurrection. However, with a bit of common sense, one must acknowledge he played a role and certainly wasn't innocent. His inflammatory language most probably played a role regarding the brief invasion of the Capitol in Washington, DC. Later that day, then-President-elect Joe Biden urged Trump to make a public statement, which he did. However, this statement presented some mixed messages: on the one hand telling the mob to go home, and on the other empathizing with their sentiments, stating that they were very special and that he loved them. An interesting observation in this regard: even though most Americans reject the attack on the Capitol in 2021, millions seem to empathize with the mob.[11]

The FIFA Scandal

Let us take a look at another instance where leadership went wrong. On May 27, 2015, the US Department of Justice indicted fourteen Fédération Internationale de Football Association (FIFA) executives and officials on charges of racketeering, wire fraud, and money laundering. The Department of Justice's 164-page indictment details over $150 million in bribes taken by FIFA executives for providing advertisers with marketing rights, over a period dating as far back as 1991. Switzerland opened parallel probes around the same time, including one investigation that confirmed FIFA executives enriched each other with as much as $80 million.

While FIFA president Sepp Blatter was not charged in the indictment, he resigned shortly thereafter.[12] In their scathing article on this and other scandals of the 2010s, journalists Evan Comen and Thomas C. Frohlich commented: "Due in part to the legal costs and loss of sponsors incurred in the wake of the scandal, FIFA reported net losses of $122.4 million in 2015, $368.8 million in 2016, and $191.5 million in 2017."[13] For the Justice Department, the next steps were to extradite the indicted men back to the United States of America and enact harsh punishments to deter future corruption. But it should be noted that the United States of America is not the only country that has been investigating FIFA: Swiss officials raided FIFA's headquarters as part of an investigation into how the 2018 and 2022 World Cups were awarded. Furthermore, the clamor continued for FIFA to do something about the alleged human rights violations swirling around Qatar's World Cup construction efforts. In 2022, Human Rights Watch observed and demanded:

> *Since Qatar was selected as World Cup host, many migrant workers have faced serious abuses including illegal recruitment fees, wage theft, injuries and unexplained deaths. Human Rights Watch calls on FIFA and Qatar to remedy these historic abuses, including by providing financial compensation to victims who made the tournament possible.*[14]

The Volkswagen or Dieselgate Scandal

News of one of the largest corporate scandals in years broke on September 18, 2015, when the Environmental Protection Agency ordered the German car manufacturer Volkswagen to recall some 482,000 diesel passenger cars sold in the United States. Researchers had discovered that a number of Volkswagen models were emitting illegally high levels of poisonous nitrogen oxides, and that these vehicles contained illegal software that could detect when the cars were being tested and change the performance to pass the emissions tests. It has since been revealed that 11 million vehicles contained the software. Volkswagen was ordered to pay more than $25 billion in fines to the United States and reported an operating loss of $1.77 billion in 2015. According to a study published in *Environmental Research Letters*, fifty-nine premature deaths resulted from the excess pollution of illegal Volkswagen cars in the United States alone. Clean Energy Wire, a platform dedicated to journalism for the energy transition, reported:

> *The German Federal Court of Justice (Bundesgerichtshof—BGH) ruled on 25 May that Volkswagen car owners are entitled to damages in the emissions scandal. The court said that owners could return their car and receive the price paid minus a share for using the car in the meantime. The ruling will likely shape many other current court cases on the issue in Germany.*[15]

Humongous Prices for Life-Saving Drugs: The Turing Pharmaceuticals Scandal

The final example of leadership gone awry concerns Turing Pharmaceuticals. In 2015, former Turing CEO, Martin Shkreli, increased the cost of the life-saving drug *Daraprim* by 5,000%, driving the price of the drug from $13.50 to $750 per pill. *Daraprim*, which costs less than a dollar to manufacture, is a medicine for toxoplasmosis, which can lead to deadly infections in people with HIV and affects about 2,000 Americans per year. The price hike caused widespread outrage.

Shkreli was required to testify in front of Congress over the company's pricing tactics and was eventually convicted of securities fraud, for which he is currently serving a seven-year prison sentence. According to KFF Health News, "Shkreli, 35, is now serving a seven-year prison term for securities fraud (unrelated to Daraprim). Turing has renamed itself Vyera Pharmaceuticals."[16]

The Martin Shkreli scandal was big news on its own, but it was by no means an isolated problem. To give another example (in the same vein, and showing striking similarities), it was just one year later that pharmaceutical company Mylan boosted prices by 400% for its EpiPen auto-injector, a life-saving medicine for cases of severe allergic reactions. In his 2016 article on the matter, journalist Phil McCausland explained that "Mylan didn't invent nor does it produce the EpiPen. The company bought the rights to the EpiPen in 2007, which received approval in 1987 and has dominated 90 percent of the market."[17]

Another such example of corporate greed (in stark contrast to the values proclaimed by the respective organization) would be this: during the COVID-19 pandemic, Israel paid a premium price for the millions of COVID-19 vaccines it ordered from the US-based pharmaceutical company Pfizer, over 40% more than the US and European Union nations paid for it. In their insightful article on this incident, journalists Stuart Winer and Toi Staff stated: "Israel will pay a premium price for the millions of COVID-19 vaccines it has ordered from US-based pharmaceutical company Pfizer, over 40 percent more than the US government or the European Union, Channel 13 news reported Sunday."[18]

Conclusions from *Mis-Leadership*

A persons character is shown through their actions in life NOT where they sit on Sunday.

(John Navone—Jesuit priest)

John Navone is right in this observation: a polished surface does not mean anything. Abiding by the rules and acting meek and mild does not shield someone from committing atrocious acts. The history books overbrim with ample evidence. Even though the above instances of *misleadership* have occurred in different organizations with quite distinct track records and serving different markets, the commonalities here are striking. So, let us take a closer look.

There is a plethora of publications dedicated to the behaviors of Donald J. Trump, be it former FBI director James Comey's scathing critique of both Trump's demeanor and the culture he instilled in the White House,[19] or the ground-breaking analysis of Trump's mental health published by thirty-seven psychiatrists and mental health experts. *The Dangerous Case of Donald Trump*[20] elaborated on Trump's fundamental lack of trust, paranoia, extreme hedonism, narcissism, and sociopathy. When scrutinizing interviews conducted by *Vice News* with Martin Shkreli,[21] it is not difficult to realize the high level of conceit, self-righteousness, utter lack of remorse and personal responsibility he shows. A closer look at FIFA's corporate structure reveals how toxic and non-transparent such payment and bonus systems can be. Furthermore, a brief visit at VW's Wolfsburg headquarters will instantly instill a feeling of hierarchy and consequential leadership culture into the visitor—a culture that nurtures a lack of ethical conscience and discourages speaking up. On a side note: in their interesting article "I office, therefore I am", architects CSMM state that "if new office environments and coworking spaces are to be more than a pretty place, they need depth: company culture and corporate DNA must be reflected in facility design. Poor design threatens businesses with identity."[22] There is a plethora of analyses scrutinizing how the effects of architectural design affect human emotions. Just think of the nudity of materials of brutalist architecture or the architecture of governmental buildings, which, oftentimes, is anything but inviting. The Volkswagen headquarters in Wolfsburg are a prime example of just that. The connection of shape and form on the one hand and corporate culture on the other is a fascinating one. However, discussing this matter would go beyond the scope of our chapter here whose prime focus is on *mis-leadership*.

From the above analyses we catch a first glimpse of where things may go wrong: if an individual (or entire organizational system) is mainly driven by the question of how he or she is perceived on the one hand and unlimited bottom-line orientation on the other. In our chapter on the dilemma of authenticity (in connection with ethical leadership), we will scrutinize *boundless bottom-line orientation* as a toxic cultural determinant in some detail. If values like care for others, sacrifice, questioning oneself, humility, and sustainability are not heeded, the probability is high that leadership may inadvertently turn into *mis-leadership*. Analyzing the above cases yields a number of behaviors that can be labelled unethical, as we must always bear in mind that ethics generally raises the question of goodness and how to attain goodness.

Mis-leadership utterly lacking ethical direction may thus be character-ized by the following aspects (see Figure 6.1):

1. A lack of accountability and, essentially, love
2. Discrepancies in the faculty of embracing or developing *Ehrfurcht vor dem Leben* (i.e. lack of *reverence for life* a notion coined by French–Germany physician, theologian and musician, Albert Schweitzer)
3. A diminished ability to experience fear and learn from it
4. An inability to develop *moral emotions* like empathy, compassion, altru-ism, remorse, or guilt
5. A strong inclination toward narcissism and self-centeredness
6. A strong focus on personal gain and a disregard for long-term consequences
7. A lack of systemic reasoning as well as a disregard for the interdepend-encies within systems; in other words, simplistic thinking
8. The incapacity to observe oneself critically in the context of the systems one determines and influences; in other words, a lack of meta-analysis
9. Psychopathic tendencies: essentially, a lack of conscience, stimulus orientation, emotion-processing problems, an inability to bond, and a pathological preoccupation with power and control (as described in the *Diagnostic and Statistical Manual of Mental Disorders (DSM)*[23]).

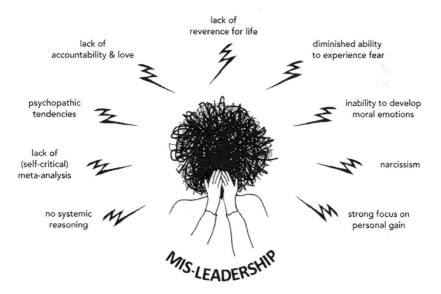

Figure 6.1 Mis-leadership

Peeking into the Rabbit Hole and Staring into the Abyss

I'm sorry for the rabbit hole I'm about to introduce you to.

(Cat Voleur—author)

This quote is in line with Nietzsche's thoughts on abyss-staring. To fathom yourself as a human being, you must concern yourself with traumas, disappointment, and your own destructivity. This is what Cat Voleur may indicate in the above preliminary apology. In our previous list, we have basically described some defining characteristics of what makes a psychopath. The question, however, remains why we choose to discuss psychopathy in a book on leadership. Our answer to the question refers to one of the two premises we introduced at the outset of this chapter: intelligent people clearly learn from the mistakes of others *and* their own. In our opinion, the stance *in order to understand health, one must study sickness* (pathogenesis) is as true *as in order to understand health, one must study the resources that keep us healthy* (salutogenesis). As counterintuitive as the answer may be, studies describing effective leadership traits and styles—and how they may be associated with psychopathic traits—are not hard to come by. For instance, it was found that boldness (an amalgam of adaptive traits, such as immunity to stress, emotional resilience, adventuresomeness, social poise, and charisma) associated with psychopathy was positively correlated with a host of good presidential leadership indicators, such as positive congressional relations, crisis management skills, tendency to initiate new projects, and being viewed as a figure of worldwide significance.[24] Corporate leaders with psychopathic traits are the subject of a growing scientific literature. Here, we relate psychopathic leaders to research on toxic and destructive leadership, leader personality disorder, and the dark triad/tetrad of psychopathic, narcissistic, Machiavellian, and sadistic personalities.

While psychopathy may be a term more often associated with film industry depictions of knife-wielding killers like Hannibal Lecter, Michael Myers, John Bates, Norman Bates, or the Zodiac killer, there is definitive evidence that suggests psychopaths are surprisingly common in the business environment. Intriguing research conducted by Sophia Wellons of Western Oregon University concludes that

> with enhanced executive cognitive functioning as well as lack of empathy and remorse, successful psychopaths are able to hide very well within society and businesses. Interested in self-gratification, personal success, money, and power, the Corporate Psychopath may perhaps care little for the success of others in the company or even the company itself (Clarke, 2007).[25]

Furthermore, research on the matter suggests that approximately one in five filling senior management positions display psychopathic patterns in their behavior, charming their way through the workplace. A perfect (and at the same time frightening) parody of this psychopathic type was impersonated by actor Christian Bale in *American Psycho*, directed by Mary Harron in 2000. The movie is based on the 1991 novel by Bret Easton Ellis and describes the unnerving double life of a well-off, highly successful, vain, and narcissistic investment banker, Patrick Bateman. Bateman leads the life of a driven, smart, and ambitious banker who goes on a killing spree in his secret life. The trope is a decidedly traditional one. Novelists like Robert Louis Stevenson in his 1886 book *The Strange Case of Dr. Jekyll and Mr. Hyde*[26] put it at the very center of their story or the double mask representing the Roman god of beginnings, transition, and gateways, Janus (name giver of the first month in the year, January), expressed evolution, ambiguity, polyvalence, and, to some extent, uncertainty. So, two-facedness and psychopathy in connection with positions of power represent an ancient subject indeed. Research conducted by psychologist Paul Babiak suggests that about 4% of powerful people in the US could be deemed psychopaths by definition.[27] Another long-term study on supply chain managers concluded that between 3% and 21% displayed clinically relevant traits of psychopathy.[28] This number has been compared to the normal distribution within the psychologically general population where psychopathy occurred in 1% of the cases. The American Psychological Association (APA) found that

> *The seemingly never-ending stream of corporate scandals over the past decades, from Enron to Theranos, suggests that something is rotten in corporate leaders. Many place the blame on psychopaths, who are characteristically superficially charming but lack empathy, anxiety, or any sense of blame or guilt.*[29]

To some extent, psychopathic traits may come in handy for people in positions of power. They may exude boldness, drive, ambition, territorial behavior, and perseverance. However, psychopathy will most certainly hinder establishment of ethical culture. In our experience, the mix of these traits is decisive. Indeed, an unfavorable combination of these traits, however, will have dire consequences. At some point, these individuals may tip from being assertive to becoming a bully. In this regard, take a look at, for example, the plethora of anecdotes found in Mary Trump's "Too Much and Never Enough"[30] where she shares stories of greed, bullying, recklessness, and other rather unpleasant behaviors in the 45th president of the United States of America.

It is an interesting fact that individuals who display psychopathic behavioral patters are way more likely to climb up the corporate ladder and fill positions of power. It is also true that subordinates will not regard them as likeable, trustworthy, empathetic, and effective leaders. When, for instance, 360-degree-feedbacks are carried out, subordinates are likely to evaluate their leaders in a way that does not confirm or praise their leadership qualities. Thus, they are not seen as effective leaders. Furthermore, studies suggest that males displaying psychopathic traits are more likely to fill upper management positions. They are also more likely to be rated as more effective when it comes to achieving targets, showing bottom-line orientation, and the capacity to make bold decisions. Females showing psychopathic behavioral patters are less likely to be promoted to top jobs. When it comes to rating their leadership efficacy, they would also score lower evaluations. To wrap things up, the results of the research we have screened over the years suggest that it might be a bit of a cliché that C-Suite leaders display higher levels of psychopathy. However, psychopathic behavioral patterns such as boldness, manipulativeness, lack of remorse, (aggressive) charisma, impulsiveness, need for power, sadistic enjoyment of pain and suffering, bending the rules, callousness, exploitation of others, exceedingly political behaviors, deception, or exaggeration may provide a minor advantage in attaining upper management positions.

To do some more reading, we highly recommend *Snakes in Suits: When Psychopaths Go to Work*[31] by Babiak and Hare, "Is boldness relevant to psychopathic personality? Meta-analytic relations with non-psychopathy checklist-based measures of psychopathy"[32] by Lilienfeld, Smith, Sauvigné, Patrick, Drislane, Latzman and Krueger, and "Triarchic model of psychopathy: Origins, operationalizations, and observed linkages with personality and general psychopathology"[33] by Patrick and Drislane.

Psychopathy can be fully described by a single model: the triarchic model of psychopathy. This proposes that psychopathy consists of three intersecting, but distinct, symptomatic (phenotypic) constructs:

1. Boldness
2. Disinhibition
3. Meanness.

Boldness is ultimately about taking action and being outgoing. It is a collection of largely adaptive traits, such as immunity to stress, absence of anxiety or reduced risk perception, emotional resilience, venturesomeness, social ease, and charismatic demeanor. Disinhibition is a collection of largely maladaptive traits such as lack of inhibitory control resulting in difficulties in regulating emotions. This affects instinctual, emotional, cognitive, perceptive, and even motor aspects, leading to weak restraint, impulsiveness, open aggression, and mistrust and hostility towards others. Thirdly, meanness is a collection of largely socially harmful traits. This results in conceitedness, a sense of entitlement, self-gratification, self-empowerment through destructiveness or cruelty, predatory and exploitative behavior, contempt toward others, lack of an affiliative pro-social capacity, and certainly lack of empathy. Psychopathic tendencies are deeply rooted in the dysfunctional ability to perceive fear and derive lessons from it. It clearly inhibits development of *moral emotions* such as shame, guilt, gratitude, empathy, altruism, disgust, or compassion. Consequently, according to this group of models, an absence of fear and remorse leads to disinhibited behaviors, which characterize many psychopaths (see Figure 6.2).

We have dedicated one entire chapter to leadership that is fueled by love. Love is also an emotion, and, from the vantage point of this book on ethical leadership, the exact opposite of fear. Psychopaths are a lot less likely to develop loving bonds with others (research suggest, however, they may want to be loved). So, in a way, we posit that in psychopaths the

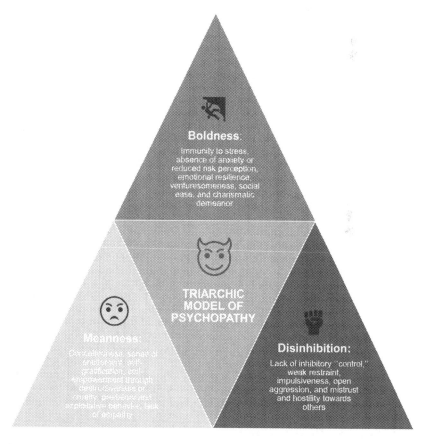

Figure 6.2 Triarchic Model of Psychopathy

capacity to love is not given. In our opinion, love is the very foundation for inspiring, inclusive, meaningful, and sustainable leadership. Hence follows, personalities who display psychopathic tendencies will never be truly convincing leaders.

What Can We Learn *Ex Negativo* from Scandals, Mis-leadership, and Psychopathy?

God turns you from one feeling to another and teaches by means of opposites so that you will have two wings to fly, not one.

(Rumi—Persian poet)

In light of the derailing behaviors both on the personal and the corporate (and more systemic level), what can we learn from these deviations? We believe that ethical leaders have the obligation, mission, and sense of personal destiny to inspire credibility from their *followers*. They seek to understand the abilities, potentials, goals, needs, and desires of their followers—not just to make them perform at their best, but to serve goodness and act as eliciting servants when it comes to self-actualization. In our opinion, ethical leaders are *advocates of becoming*: they are midwives to strategy, develop people, seek to drive change that matters, care about others, display a generative mindset, establish community, and always think beyond their immediate interests. In a sense, they gravitate toward objectives that must be described as transcendent. They reach for the stars, follow an ethical north star, and never focus merely on momentary, materialistic gains. Ethical leaders focus on developing their followers to the highest standards. They consistently question themselves to avoid falling into the traps of self-centeredness and self-righteousness. Hence it follows that ethical leaders are *followers* at the same time, realizing when they err and allowing others to inspire them as well when they go astray. An ethical leader must develop the capacity to be very much aware of personal values. At the same time, these values are a very personal and subjective matter. Values differ across cultures[34] and therefore must be negotiated with care. As counterintuitive as it may sound, ethical leaders must avoid artificial harmony, and instead establish a culture in which values can be discussed, challenged, and dissected.

Furthermore, artificial harmony must be replaced with genuine *psychological safety*,[35] a fascinating concept developed by the Harvard scholar Amy Edmondson.[36] Edmonson defines psychological safety as the "belief that one will not be punished or humiliated for speaking up with ideas, questions, concerns or mistakes."[37] To the leader who values genuine harmony and psychological safety, status is secondary. Mission, purpose, and the pursuit of goodness are key. Goodness, however, must not be self-righteous or self-centered. It must be challenged, checked, re-checked, and incessantly pursued. Status does not matter to the ethical leader. What matters is truth-seeking, dignity, self-reflection, and, ultimately, love. Leaders showing pathological tendencies as those detailed above cannot generate such conditions. That is the most commanding lesson we have extracted from the discussion of *mis-leadership*.

Do you remember the 2019 Christchurch killings, when a gunman massacred fifty-one people ranging from children to octogenarians? It wasn't the heated debates over New Zealand's gun laws, nor the trial of the shooter, that drew the most media attention. One picture went viral in the aftermath of the attacks: that of Jacinda Ardern, then Prime Minister of New Zealand, embracing a veiled woman at Kilbirnie Mosque and asking for forgiveness.[38] Symbolically, she wore a headscarf. Just take a moment and ask yourself—withholding all possible judgment, rejection, and intellectualization for a moment—what would a less culturally and emotionally sensitive leader have done at that moment? We believe this was ethical leadership in its purest form.

Questions to Ponder

1. Where do you possibly accept compromises when it comes to your own set of values?
2. In what way do you potentially observe unfavorable behavior in your direct or indirect environment that you deem unfair or dangerous? What could you do about it?
3. When was the last time you witnessed questionable behaviors in your environment? Did you stand up for what you strongly believe to be good and fair? Why or why not?
4. In what way could you contribute to your environment's culture to approximate more of an ethical ideal? What could you tangibly change about yourself and your actions in order to strive for such an ideal state?
5. In your opinion, what might be an advisable and appropriate strategy for approaching someone showing questionable (or possibly divergent) behavior as described in this chapter?
6. What might be implicit or unchallenged assumptions in your own mindset that you may want to change or reflect upon? Who could you talk to as a sparring partner?
7. What inclinations have you observed in yourself that might have a destructive effect on others? Why is that? What could you do about this?
8. Without a doubt: we all know what techniques of cognitive dissonance reduction there are (distractions, over-simplification, putting yourself on a pedestal, externalization, and so forth). What might be areas where you do this? What might be areas where you are a little vain, overly confident, lazy, or self-righteous? What do you want to do about it?

Notes

1 Rainer Mausfeld, *Angst Und Macht: Herrschaftstechniken Der Angsterzeugung in Kapitalistischen Demokratien* (Munich: ABOD Verlag, 2019).

2 Rainer Mausfeld, *Warum Schweigen Die Lämmer?: Wie Elitendemokratie Und Neoliberalismus Unsere Gesellschaft Und Unsere Lebensgrundlagen Bedrohen*, 3rd edn (Frankfurt: Westend Verlag, 2018).

3 Shaydon Ramey, "Intelligent People Learn from the Mistakes Others Make," *Exploring Your Mind*, July 28, 2022. https://exploringyourmind.com/intelligent-people-learn-mistakes-others-make/.

4 "Elders in South Africa for Ethical Leadership Debate," October 30, 2013. https://theelders.org/news/elders-south-africa-ethical-leadership-debate.

5 Frank Herbert, *Dune* (Philadelphia, PA: Chilton Books, 1965).

6 Zoe Christen Jones, "Trump Pardons Security Contractors Involved in Baghdad Massacre," *CBS News*, December 23, 2020. www.cbsnews.com/news/trump-pardons-security-contractors-involved-in-baghdad-massacre/.

7 Lorenz Hemicker, "Söldnerfirma Blackwater: Eine Ansammlung zweifelhafter Charaktere," *FAZ.NET*, n.d. www.faz.net/aktuell/politik/ausland/amerika/black water-der-schlechte-ruf-von-amerikas-soeldnerfirma-bleibt-13226392.html.

8 Matt McGrath, "Climate Change: US Formally Withdraws from Paris Agreement," *BBC News*, November 4, 2020. www.bbc.com/news/science-environment-54797743.

9 Jihan Abdalla, "Trump Pardons of Blackwater Contractors an 'Insult to Justice,'" *Al Jazeera*, December 26, 2020. www.aljazeera.com/news/2020/12/25/trump-pardons-blackwater-contractors-insult-to-justice.

10 Abdalla, "Trump Pardons of Blackwater Contractors an 'Insult to Justice.'"

11 Philip Bump, "Most Americans Reject the Attack on the Capitol— but Millions Empathize with the Mob." *Washington Post*, January 9, 2021. www.washingtonpost.com/politics/2021/01/09/most-americans-reject-attack-capitol-but-millions-empathize-with-mob/.

12 Nick Gass, "FIFA President Sepp Blatter Resigns," *POLITICO*, June 2, 2015. www.politico.eu/article/fifa-president-sepp-blatter-resigns/.

13 Evan Comen and Thomas C. Frohlich, "The Biggest Corporate Scandals of the Decade," *247wallst.Com*, July, 2021. https://247wallst.com/special-report/2019/12/20/the-biggest-corporate-scandals-of-the-decade/2/.

14 "FIFA World Cup Qatar 2022," Human Rights Watch, October 20, 2022. www.hrw.org/tag/fifa-world-cup-qatar-2022.

15 Sören Amelang and Benjamin Wehrmann, "'Dieselgate'—a Timeline of the Car Emissions Fraud Scandal in Germany," *Clean Energy Wire*. May 25, 2020. www.cleanenergywire.org/factsheets/dieselgate-timeline-car-emissions-fraud-scandal-germany.

16 Shefali Luthra, "'Pharma Bro' Shkreli Is in Prison, but Daraprim's Price Is Still High," KFF Health News. May 4, 2018. https://kffhealthnews.org/news/for-shame-pharma-bro-shkreli-is-in-prison-but-daraprims-price-is-still-high/.

17 "Mylan CEO Excoriated in Congressional Hearing," September 21, 2016. www.nbcnews.com/health/health-news/mylan-releases-300-generic-epipen-after-price-hike-outrage-n697181.

18 Stuart Winer and Toi Staff, "Israel Will Reportedly Pay Much More than US, EU for Pfizer Coronavirus Vaccine," *Times of Israel*, November 16, 2020. www.timesofisrael.com/israel-will-reportedly-pay-more-than-us-eu-for-pfizer-coronavirus-vaccine/.

19 James B. Comey, *A Higher Loyalty: Truth, Lies, and Leadership* (New York: Macmillan, 2018).

20 Bandy X. Lee, *The Dangerous Case of Donald Trump: 27 Psychiatrists and Mental Health Experts Assess a President* (New York: Thomas Dunne Books, 2017). https://openlibrary.org/books/OL27759971M/The_Dangerous_Case_of_Donald_Trump.

21 "Martin Shkreli—Vice Video: Documentaries, Films, News Videos." n.d. *Video*. https://video.vice.com/en_us/topic/martin-shkreli.

22 "I Office, Therefore I Am: How a Lack of Corporate Architecture Shakes up a Business's Identity," CSMM—Architecture Matters, n.d. www.cs-mm.com/en/journal/i-office-therefore-i-am-how-lack-corporate-architecture-shakes-business-identity.

23 *Diagnostic and Statistical Manual of Mental Disorders, Fourth Edition, Text Revision (DSM-IV-TR)*. 2000. *American Psychiatric Association eBooks*. https://doi.org/10.1176/appi.books.9780890423349.

24 Scott O. Lilienfeld, Irwin D. Waldman, Kristin Landfield, Ashley L. Watts, Steven Rubenzer, and Thomas R. Faschingbauer, "Fearless Dominance and the U.S. Presidency: Implications of Psychopathic Personality Traits for Successful and Unsuccessful Political Leadership," *Journal of Personality and Social Psychology* 103, no. 3 (2012): 489–505. https://doi.org/10.1037/a0029392.

25 Sophia Wellons, "The Devil in the Boardroom: Corporate Psychopaths and Their Impact on Business," *Pure Insights* 1, article 9, Western Oregon University, 2012.

26 Robert Louis Stevenson, *The Strange Case of Dr Jekyll and Mr Hyde* (NewYork: Addison-Wesley Longman, 1978).

27 Cynthia Mathieu, Craig S. Neumann, Robert D. Hare, and Paul Babiak. 2014. "A Dark Side of Leadership: Corporate Psychopathy and Its Influence on Employee Well-Being and Job Satisfaction," *Personality and Individual Differences* 59 (March 2014): 83–8. https://doi.org/10.1016/j.paid.2013.11.010.

28 Simon Evans, "Why Supply Chain Managers Are Psychopaths," *Australian Financial Review*, September 13, 2016. www.afr.com/companies/retail/why-supply-chain-managers-are-psychopaths-20160913-grevxs.

29 American Psychological Association, "Psychopaths in the C-Suite?" October 15, 2018. www.apa.org/pubs/highlights/spotlight/issue-123.

30 Mary L. Trump, *Too Much and Never Enough: How My Family Created the World's Most Dangerous Man* (New York: Simon & Schuster, 2020).

31 Paul Babiak and Robert D. Hare, *Snakes in Suits: When Psychopaths Go to Work* (New York: HarperCollins, 2006).

32 S. O. Lilienfeld, S. F. Smith, K. C. Sauvigné, C. J. Patrick, L. E. Drislane, R. D. Latzman, and R. F. Krueger, "Is boldness relevant to psychopathic personality? Meta-analytic relations with non-psychopathy checklist-based measures of psychopathy," *APA PsycNet*, 2015. http://dx.doi.org/10.1037/pas0000244.

33 C. J. Patrick and L. E. Drislane, "Triarchic model of psychopathy: Origins, operationalizations, and observed linkages with personality and general psychopathology," *Journal of Personality* 83, no. 6 (2015): 627–43. https://doi.org/10.1111/jopy.12119.

34 Stephan Dahl, "Intercultural Research: The Current State of Knowledge," *Social Science Research Network*, January 2004. https://doi.org/10.2139/ssrn.658202.

35 Amy Gallo, "What Is Psychological Safety?" *Harvard Business Review*. February 15, 2023. https://hbr.org/2023/02/what-is-psychological-safety.

36 Amy C. Edmondson, *The Fearless Organization: Creating Psychological Safety in the Workplace for Learning, Innovation, and Growth* (Hoboken, NJ: Wiley, 2018). https://ci.nii.ac.jp/ncid/BB2750129X.
37 Michael Boykin, "An Introduction to Psychological Safety," *Range* January 24, 2022. www.range.co/blog/introduction-to-psychological-safety.
38 Nesrine Malik, "With Respect: How Jacinda Ardern Showed the World What a Leader Should Be," *The Guardian*, March 28, 2019. www.theguardian.com/world/2019/mar/28/with-respect-how-jacinda-ardern-showed-the-world-what-a-leader-should-be.

Section III

Practical Applications of Ethical Leadership

Chapter 7

Competencies and Ethical Leadership

Ethics is nothing more than reverence for life.

(Albert Schweitzer)

Developing as a leader is a journey. Becoming an ethical leader takes that journey even further. No one is the same leader or same person at age fifty that they were at twenty. Experiences, failures, successes, and maturation make you a different and, hopefully, more effective leader as your gifts evolve over time. The same can be true of your approach to ethics, as it can shift over time due to experience and growth. At the core, however, as Schweitzer notes, reverence for life should dominate all else and we suspect this is the bedrock of ethical leadership that is surrounded by additional skills.

While most people are raised with a basic sense of right and wrong, how one reasons and acts on moral issues changes over time. The same goes for life as for leadership: the more experience you gain, the more your opinions will evolve. When you are a child, you act with a defined set of assumptions based on right and wrong as defined by your parents or older adults. As you get older, right and wrong may be defined by your peer group—a broader group than your parents, but still a group with specific norms for behavior. Later, in adulthood, your view of ethical behavior may be shaped by the laws of the larger community, the norms of your employer, or your religious affiliation. In this chapter and the one that follows, we explore how leaders' approaches to ethics and moral issues evolve over time, drawing on both traditional psychological approaches and newer models for the development of ethical leaders.

As we have noted previously, most models of ethical leadership propose either a series of traits that ethical leaders possess or, alternatively, a competency or behavior-based model. Most definitions of ethical leadership suggest that the ethical leader acts in a manner that is consistent with a moral structure or a moral belief system. If we accept this premise, then

DOI: 10.4324/b23260-11

we can consider someone an ethical leader as long as they are behaving in a manner consistent with their organization's values. As long as the leader's behavior aligns with the morals and norms appropriate for their environment—whatever those may be—they are leading ethically. While we do agree with the premise, we believe that definition is only applicable to a hierarchical view of ethics. A leader may have a moral structure that they act on, but that moral structure itself may have an underlying unethical motivation—perhaps an unhealthy degree of self-interest, outright greed, or false viewpoints such as white supremacy. We will explore this at greater length in the next chapter.

For the moment, let us look at trait models versus competency models of ethical leadership. Trait-based models tend to be descriptive and linked to an individual. Often these models will identify a person who is presumed to be an ethical leader and then describe the characteristics of that person. If one were to use Gandhi as an example, you might hear him portrayed with characteristics such as visionary, courageous, oriented toward justice, and fair. These are all certainly wonderful characteristics to have. However, if one aspires to be an ethical leadership these trait descriptors quickly prove insufficient. Look at the following list of traits that the Western Governors University (USA)[1] uses in its description of the ethical leader:

- Leads by example
- Willing to evolve
- Respects everyone equally
- Communicates openly
- Manages stress effectively
- Mediates fairly.

If I am a new leader, or I want to hire ethical leaders, the above list of traits is extremely attractive, but it tells me nothing about *how* one can attain those traits. Trait models are analogous to descriptions of great athletes such as Messi, Ronaldo, or Mbappé. You can describe their skills, flair, and innate athletic ability all you want—but those descriptors ignore the countless hours they devoted to practicing their craft, and they fail to provide a roadmap for others to follow.

Consequently, we are much more aligned with behavior-based competency models, which account for the specific behaviors an ethical leader needs to demonstrate or practice on a regular basis. One's ethics as a leader can be evaluated by observing the objective presence or absence of specific behaviors. This is not to say, of course, that competency models are perfect. We'll come back to practical applications of competencies later in this chapter.

Let's begin our discussion of competencies with a discussion of competencies for leadership in general. There are countless models espoused by different organizations and consulting firms. A very typical model, in our experience, is the one proposed by the widely respected Center for Creative Leadership (CCL).[2] The CCL model—based on decades of research using their statistically valid, 360-degree feedback instruments—suggests that the sixteen most important leadership competencies[3] are as follows.

The Most Important Leadership Competencies for Those Leading the Organization

1. **Strategic Perspective:** Understands the viewpoint of higher management and effectively analyzes complex problems.
2. **Being a Quick Study:** Quickly masters new technical and business knowledge.
3. **Decisiveness:** Prefers quick and approximate actions in many management situations.
4. **Change Management:** Uses effective strategies to facilitate organizational change initiatives and overcome resistance to change.

The Most Important Leadership Competencies for Those Leading Others

5. **Leading Employees:** Attracts, motivates, and develops employees.
6. **Confronting Problem Employees:** Acts decisively and with fairness when dealing with problem employees.
7. **Participative Management:** Involves others, listens, and builds commitment.
8. **Building Collaborative Relationships:** Builds productive working relationships with coworkers and external parties.
9. **Compassion and Sensitivity:** Shows genuine interest in others and sensitivity to employees' needs.
10. **Putting People at Ease:** Displays warmth and a good sense of humor.
11. **Respect for Differences:** Values people of different backgrounds, cultures, or demographics.

The Most Important Leadership Competencies for Leading Yourself

12. **Taking Initiative:** Takes charge and capitalizes on opportunities.
13. **Composure:** Demonstrates self-control in difficult situations.
14. **Work–Life Balance:** Balances work priorities with personal life.
15. **Self-Awareness:** Has an accurate picture of strengths and weaknesses and is willing to improve.
16. **Career Management:** Uses effective career management tactics, including mentoring, professional relationships, and feedback channels.

Based on our decades of experience helping our clients hire, promote, and develop leaders, the above list of competencies is fairly standard. While there may be some variance depending on the organization or the level of the leader, the list is very thorough and basically comprehensive. Except for one thing: upon closer scrutiny, we believe the existing leadership models and definitions are incomplete. These general leadership models effectively describe leadership overall, but they only give brief acknowledgment to the ethical component of leadership competency, often phrasing it as some variation on integrity. Most of the competency work that we are familiar with is generated by psychologists or human resources professionals, not philosophers, and consequently the models tend to be practical and focused.

Interestingly, in a study conducted by Dr. Sunnie Giles in 2016, out of 195 leaders from around the world, 67% identified "strong ethics and safety" as the top-priority competency area for leaders and leadership development programs. As Sunnie notes, "A leader with high ethical standards conveys a commitment to fairness, instilling confidence that both they and their employees will honor the rules of the game."[4] We find it remarkable that most leaders around the world see ethics and safety as the most critical priority for leaders, and yet most competency models and selection systems fail to sufficiently address ethics, honesty, integrity, or any other aspect of ethical leadership.

There are competency models focusing on ethical leadership, but those we have seen thus far have tended to be more trait based than behavior based. We believe a hybrid, dynamic model of ethical leadership is more appropriate. Simply put, our model looks at three components, each of which will be discussed at greater length as we proceed through this chapter and the next one:

1. The competencies of an ethical leader
2. The issues ethical leaders focus their attention on
3. The progression one makes (or fails to make) as leader, coupled with the leadership stages of an ethical leader.

The Competencies of an Ethical Leader

To our knowledge, there are no competency-based models of leadership that focus specifically on the ethical aspects of leadership. Most leadership competency models (e.g., Lomminger, etc.) cover a variety of behaviors germane to leadership, with perhaps one competency area that addresses ethics or integrity.

These models do have their place; in fact, we have both used them extensively in our own consulting work. They provide a general framework for exploring an individual's abilities and behaviors in areas such as technical skills, leadership skills, communication skills, and analytical skills. What is missing, however, is the ability to differentiate between leaders based on ethical behaviors or moral choices. Carried to the extreme, looking only at general competencies when selecting leaders might make it difficult to differentiate between a tyrannical leader and a benevolent one if each demonstrated the same basic leadership behaviors. We see nothing inherently wrong with the common broad frameworks that exist to define leadership competencies, but an ethical framework can offer deeper insight into a leader's potential. Put another way, we would re-slice the competency pie to include a large piece that focuses on ethical leadership behaviors.

To be absolutely clear as we transition to ethical leadership competencies, we do not think one can be an effective ethical leader without being an effective leader. Ergo, as we discuss developing ethical leaders later in this book, we clearly believe standard leadership competencies are important. Any effective leader needs to be able to lead his or her organization to accomplish its goals. However, the ethical leader needs to be effective with an enhanced set of ethical competencies.

What might that slice of ethical pie look like? Below is a list of competencies that constitute the meaningful behaviors an ethical leader must exhibit. There may be others, but we would suggest these serve as a core that can be used in conjunction with other leadership competencies to hire, promote, and develop ethical leaders:

Integrity. We define integrity as Zenger and Folkman do.[5] It is honesty combined with assertiveness. Integrity means that an individual must not only be able to speak the truth, but also be willing to do so in situations where he or she may be challenged. Integrity means speaking the truth without regard for consequences.
Behaviors:

- Speaks up when others remain silent
- Holds to his or her position in the face of opposition
- Speaks even when he or she knows there will be opposition or knows his or her position will be unpopular.

Moral Courage/Willpower. Courage is a willingness to act on one's beliefs and values, and to stand up to others when one believes a decision or action is ethically or morally wrong. Courage is the strength of conviction to act regardless of the potential outcome or consequences. Moral courage may also be notable in its absence, as in, "he failed to stand up for what was right and allowed the group to rule unchecked." Behaviors:

- Makes his or her beliefs public and transparent
- Supports others who speak up or share thoughts that oppose the views of others
- Is willing to challenge the moral or ethical aspects of proposed decisions

Trust. Trust speaks to the ability to act in a consistent, predictable manner. Others can rely on your consistency of action and thought. Others can rely on you to honor commitments and promises. It also means taking personal accountability for mistakes and errors without blaming others.

- Builds positive relationships with individuals and groups
- Acts in a consistent, predictable manner
- Walks the talk. Lives up to commitments and takes accountability for his/her actions.

Treats Others with Concern and Fairness. Fairness focuses leaders' decisions on their impact on others. Fair leaders treat others with justice and balance. They do not play favorites; they apply a consistent, caring manner to all. Fairness places people above profits. In the literature this concept is often referred to as procedural justice.

Behaviors:

- Applies organizational standards of fairness and justice to members of the organization equally
- Does not "play favorites" in making decisions
- Within the limits of confidentiality, explains the rationale for decisions that are made about individuals or groups.

Empathy. Demonstrating empathy shows that an individual understands the concerns and feelings of others and anticipates how they will respond to your actions and decisions. It takes that into account and prepares for it. This shows up frequently in models of emotional intelligence.[6]

Behaviors:

- Adapts his/her messages to the needs and concerns of others
- Actively anticipates how others will respond to issues and acknowledges their concerns
- Actively listens to others and reflects back both the content and feelings behind the statements of others; often summarizes what he/she to check for understanding.

Moral Mindset/Moral Competence. Moral mindset demonstrates curiosity about the nature of right, wrong, and fairness. It goes beyond rules and procedures to ask, "What is right?" and acts on that view. It is aware of how others may perceive and judge the nature of right and wrong, and is not limited to organizational norms, going beyond those norms to ask, "What is just?"

- The concept is similar to the "moral mindset" discussed by Heres and Lasthuizen,[7] among others, where they suggest that moral competence is a necessary but not sufficient pre-condition for ethical leadership.

Behaviors:

- Engages others in discussions of right and wrong
- Is constantly curious about ethical issues when making decisions
- Acts on his or her values and applies those values to decision making
- Refuses to act on decisions he or she believes are unethical, immoral, or illegal.

Acts with Transparency. Transparent leaders share their thinking and the reasoning behind their decisions openly with others. They share relevant information that does not violate any personnel privacy issues or concerns. Transparency builds trust and reliability in the eyes of others. It's a willingness to share personal feelings and reactions as well.
Behaviors:

- Shares his or her thinking and rationale behind decisions
- Provides data that supports the decision-making process
- Share personal feelings about the decisions being made, including doubts and fears
- Is willing to listen to and hear contrary opinions.

Critical Reasoning. Critical reasoning can be defined as the logical processes one uses to sort through data and arrive at a final decision. In the context of ethical leadership, critical reasoning also applies to the analysis of right and wrong relative to the decision being made and incorporating ethical considerations into the final decision.
Behaviors:

- Can sort through the assumptions that others are using relative to decision making
- Will evaluate various options by considering both traditional and ethical factors
- Makes decisions that are ethical, moral, and legal.

In a simplistic way, you can self-test these behaviors. Think about someone you consider, by your own definition, to be an ethical leader. Think about your experience with that person. Did they exhibit the behaviors or competencies mentioned? If the answer is yes, there may be points where you have questions or disagreements. And that is fine, as debate and democratic discussion on a topic is valuable and meaningful.

Discussion

Two additional comments regarding competencies are worth making before moving on to other points. First, any list of competencies that are going to be used in an organization needs to be validated within that organization. Not all of the above competencies are applicable to every job or organization. The competencies need to be customized to each organization's language, norms, and culture assuming the organization wants ethical leaders.

Second, as mentioned earlier, we support a hybrid model. We believe a valid competency model needs to be a blend of traditional leadership competencies and ethical leadership competencies. One needs both an ethical core and the ability to use that ethical core in combination with more traditional measures of influence and leadership.

To look at competencies from a real-life perspective, consider Donald Trump, the 45th President of the United States. Does he pass the competency test relative to integrity, trust, fairness, and moral curiosity? While such a comparison is fraught with political peril, even his most ardent supporters are far from universally positive in evaluating his performance against ethical leadership competences. Misuse of presidential powers, chauvinism, and berating those that oppose him can be seen by many as inappropriate.[8] There is an adage in US politics that "character counts." When people use that phrase in conjunction with a politician or leader, they are essentially referring to ethical competencies. President Trump may be an extreme example for many reasons. However, if you have doubts about the concept, do the same exercise regarding a current political leader or one from history that you admire.

Using competencies, we can observe behavior, provide coaching, or even create simulations that allow for observation. In short, competencies provide a platform for many of the activities human resource professionals use to select and develop organizational talent. While no competency model is perfect, basing decisions on observable behaviors is arguably the most objective means available.

Still, the perspective that competencies provide is a limited and incomplete one in describing ethical leaders. To fully understand the ethical leader, we also need to understand the issues he or she engages with and how those change over time.

Ethical Issues

An ethical leader engages with issues that may not be found in a job description or easily measured by traditional metrics. That is not to say that the traditional measures of leadership effectiveness are inappropriate or meaningless. It is to say that engaging in ethical issues is a changing realm for leaders. For our purposes, we define an ethical issue as a problem that requires a choice between two or more options where the ethical answers are unclear—in other words, a moral dilemma. Ethical issues often bring into play personal values, organizational values, and professional standards. They are situations that require the most thought, involvement of others, and potential risk. And these issues often occur when a potential decision conflicts with ethical standards.

Let us look at a specific example based on the pandemic in 2020 and 2021. We assume that concern for safety is an ethical issue for most leaders, but how one engages with the safety issue will vary by the nature of one's leadership role. If you are a first-line supervisor in a manufacturing facility, your safety concern is largely focused on those individuals directly under your span of control, including both your direct reports and those you interact with on a regular basis in the plant. Your span of ethical control is relatively narrow, and an evaluation of your ethics as a leader would focus on how you lead and manage relative to those safety issues imposed by the pandemic. We will talk more about this later, but this illustrates that how one is judged as an ethical leader will vary by role and, even for each individual leader, will change over time.

This point can be further illustrated by looking at another leadership role in the same plant: the plant manager. During the pandemic, the plant manager's span of ethical control is much broader and involves not just the plant but the broader community as well. It does not take much effort to think of the myriad of concerns the plant manager has to consider. Not only does the plant manager have to consider safety—which may include access, scheduling, quarantines, social distancing, and more—he or she also must potentially weigh safety concerns against financial concerns and the future of the plant. Of course, none of these are one-time issues. In many ways, safety concerns become an even greater issue if the plant has been shut down and is then given the chance to re-open. To illustrate this, one need only look at the very real dilemma created by the meatpacking plants in largely rural areas in the USA that had major outbreaks of COVID-19 among their employees.[9]

Several authors/researchers have considered ethical issues for leadership, and there does not appear to be a general consensus on the matter. Some point to racial and gender equality, overpromising, health and safety, accounting practices, privacy, fraud, and accountability as top-priority business concerns. Others focus on toxic leaders, discrimination, conflicting goals, or questionable use of company technology. We suspect other non-business organizations face a similar array of ethical concerns.

We have also looked at attempts to provide guiding principles for ethical decision making. Too often, the response to ethical issues is "contact human resources with your concerns" or something similar. We have found the most promise in those professions that try to codify guiding principles. For example, Beauchamp and Childress[10] provide a framework for biomedical ethics that includes:

- *Respect for Autonomy*: respect for individual patients and their ability to make decisions about their own health and future; respect for patients' right to self-determination.
- *Beneficence:* Doing and promoting good; preventing and removing evil or harm.
- *Nonmaleficence:* Doing no harm; avoiding harming.
- *Justice:* Maximizing benefits to patients and society while emphasizing equality, fairness, and impartiality.

There is no way to develop an exhaustive list of the ethical issues leaders may encounter during their career. As witnessed by the pandemic, the world can change overnight for a wide variety of reasons, each of which brings new challenges, new dilemmas, and new choices that must be made. Still, there is a general trend line of issues that we believe encompass most of the ethical challenges leaders encounter. Among these are:

- **Safety.** Ethical leaders grapple with safety daily by considering whether they have done everything they could have to minimize risk to their employees. Safety can include psychological safety, not just physical safety. Safety takes into account of discrimination, harassment, and other concepts that leaders often deal with. Keeping people safe in the broadest sense of the word becomes a guiding concern. Our own experience supports this, as we have heard numerous senior leaders report going home at the end of the day and asking themselves, "Have I done everything I could have to keep people safe?"
- **Fairness and Justice.** Leaders who are concerned with fairness ask themselves questions such as, "Is the way I treat people consistent, fair, and just? Do I set reasonable, clear expectations, and provide appropriate feedback to all? Am I concerned about the well-being of the people around me, both on and off the job?" Being fair does not mean that an ethical leader avoids holding people accountable; in fact, consistent accountability is an essential part of fairness.
- **Normative Standards.** This refers to the defined values and ethical standards that are part of an organization's culture. The ethical leader operates in a transparent and consistent manner in accordance with the values and beliefs of the organization. Such leaders are open and provide reasons if they make choices that seemingly contradict organizational values.

- **Societal Concerns.** This refers to those issues that an organization may affect—including community, climate change, environmental issues, and so on—which are broader than the organization itself. Most organizational values that address sustainability, environmental concerns, or the broader community would fall in this area.

Every leader should grapple with the above concerns to some degree, no matter where they are in an organization's hierarchy. However, the ethical leadership competencies we have proposed in this chapter can be difficult to self-evaluate. Consequently, the competencies can best be used in two forms: multi-rater feedback, and more traditional forms of assessment. In the case of multi-rater feedback (360), we think feedback from others can be a valuable form of measurement for developmental purposes, particularly when it can identify the blind spots that might impede self-analysis. We also believe that traditional assessment tools—in the form of carefully crafted integrated case studies, simulations, and role plays—can provide accurate evaluations that could be used for both selection and development (see Chapter 10 for further discussion).

Application

Clearly, we believe that behavior-based competencies are the foundation of any ethical leadership program—whether that is selecting leaders, developing leaders, evaluating potential, or ensuring that the culture supports ethical leadership. Likewise, at the individual level, an aspiring ethical leader needs to know where he or she needs to develop or reinforce existing skills. To that end, we suggest the following:

1. *Develop a clear list of ethical leadership competencies with behavioral anchors.* There are multiple methods for doing this, including focus groups, interviews, and surveys. Typically, a human resources department would have this capability. In conducting an analysis of competencies, there are several issues to consider:

    a. Are you creating overall competencies for the organization, or are there differences in the expected behaviors at different levels of leadership? Many organizations we are familiar with produce organizational competencies; however, they will also look at subsets or differences in expected behavior at different levels.

    b. Do the competencies describe existing behaviors or are they aspirational? Particularly if your organization is attempting to change the culture or changing the business model, the organization will need to focus on the competencies desired in its future leaders. If this is the case, senior leaders who have a vision of the organization's future will need to be involved in determining the competencies and related behaviors.

2. *Integrate competencies into ongoing practice.* While ethical leadership competencies may not apply to all processes or systems, they should serve as the underpinning of numerous processes. Development, selection, and promotion are addressed in later chapters, so we will defer discussion of those areas for the moment. There are several other areas where competencies should be applied, however. These include:

   a. *Performance Management.* Many performance management systems include a section beyond key performance indicators (KPIs) that discusses "how" a person achieves each objective. These sections usually include observations from both the employee and the manager and should be based on the key competencies of each employee's job.

   b. *360-Degree Feedback.* Customized multi-rater feedback based on employee competencies is an invaluable tool for development. Open-ended questions about strengths and development needs are important add-on tools.

   c. *Coaching.* When an employee is being coached by a manager, outside coach, or peer, discussion of behavioral competencies should be incorporated. Coaching provides a structured approach to development where individuals are given assignments, practice new skills, and receive feedback.

   d. *Peer Group Discussion.* While peer group discussions are not a typical process, we recommend them in the context of ethical leadership. Conducting discussions about real-life dilemmas your organization faces helps both to develop leaders and to foster a great ethical awareness for all employees.

Questions to Ponder

1. While accuracy in self-assessing personal performance against competencies may be difficult, it is an exercise that can be valuable. Go back through the list of ethical leadership competencies and identify three things you do well and three you could improve upon. Or, alternatively, ask you team for their feedback on you relative to the competencies.

2. Get together with some colleagues from your organization and rank the competencies from most important to least important. Discuss why you made the decisions you did. Is your ranking actually reflected in the everyday world of your organization?

3. Pick a leader you admire and evaluate their performance against the competencies. What do they do that makes them an ethical trustworthy leader?
4. Do the same thing with a leader you do not respect.

Notes

1 "What Is Ethical Leadership?" *Western Governors University* (blog), February 4, 2020. www.wgu.edu/blog/what-is-ethical-leadership2001.html#openSubscriberModal.

2 Leading Effectively Staff, "The Most Important Leadership Competencies," CCL, September 15, 2022. www.ccl.org/articles/leading-effectively-articles/most-important-leadership-competencies/.

3 We would hasten to note that 16 competencies is a lot if you are using competencies for selection or other HR processes. In our experience, most organizations will reduce that number down to the 8–10 competencies most important to them.

4 Sunnie Giles, "The Most Important Leadership Competencies, According to Leaders Around the World," *Harvard Business Review*, October 25, 2017. https://hbr.org/2016/03/the-most-important-leadership-competencies-according-to-leaders-around-the-world.

5 Zenger Folkman, "Honesty and Integrity—Establishing Character That Transforms Workforces," October 27, 2022. https://zengerfolkman.com/webinars/honesty-and-integrity-establishing-character-that-transforms-workforces/.

6 Chris Westfall, "Understanding Empathy: How EQ Can Improve Your Career Impact," Forbes, January 15, 2021. www.forbes.com/sites/chriswestfall/2021/01/15/understanding-empathy-how-eq-can-improve-your-career-impact/?sh=d2b904a400b2.

7 L. Heres and Karin Lasthuizen, "What's the Difference? Ethical Leadership in Public, Hybrid and Private Sector Organizations," *Journal of Change Management* 12, no. 4 (December 4, 2012): 441–66. https://doi.org/10.1080/14697017.2012.728768

8 Paul Waldman, "All the Trump Books Agree: He's Just as Bad as You Think," *Washington Post*, September 7, 2020. www.washingtonpost.com/opinions/2020/09/07/all-trump-books-agree-hes-just-bad-you-think/.

9 Alvin Chang, Michael Sainato, Nina Lakhani, Rashida Kamal, and Aliya Uteuova, "The Pandemic Exposed the Human Cost of the Meatpacking Industry's Power: 'It's Enormously Frightening.'" *The Guardian*, November 16, 2021. www.theguardian.com/environment/2021/nov/16/meatpacking-industry-covid-outbreaks-workers#:~:text=In%20the%20first%20four%20months,least%20298%20meat%20plant%20workers.

10 Katie Page, "The Four Principles: Can They Be Measured and Do They Predict Ethical Decision Making?" *BMC Medical Ethics* 13, no. 1 (May 20, 2012). https://doi.org/10.1186/1472-6939-13-10.

Chapter 8

Toward a Stage Model of Ethical Leadership

You will never regret doing the right thing.

(Antique sign)

For a moment, put yourself in the position of leading a team in your organization. It doesn't matter what level the team is in the organization, but assume there are five or six members of the team who report to you. The team is grappling with an issue that does not suggest clear-cut answers, particularly as it relates to right and wrong. Regardless of what decision is made, the decision will affect the lives of others—positively or negatively. The team has been wrestling with the issue for some time, and positions have been staked out by members of the team along the following lines:

- Some members of the team want to make a decision based on the impact on the people in the organization. It is a relatively small organization, and these team members want to meet the needs of their friends and colleagues.
- Some want to make a decision based on what would be legally correct. The potential decision puts the organization in a "grey area," and these team members want to be sure they are following the letter of the law.
- One person wants to make a decision that takes into account the broader community, providing the greatest good for the greatest number.
- And at least one member of the team will make the decision that the majority of the team supports.

Positions have begun to harden, and tempers have risen, as team members have begun making accusations about the reasoning behind the positions of others. The team appears bogged down in arguments about the reasoning behind choices and a lack of understanding of the reasoning of others.

As the leader, what would you do in this situation?

DOI: 10.4324/b23260-12

We started this chapter with this short scenario for several reasons. In the previous chapter, we introduced behavior-based competencies as one framework for looking at ethical leadership. We believe that is a practical framework for looking at ethical leadership, but that it is incomplete, as a leader could exhibit most of those competencies and still behave immorally. We think a hierarchy of moral reasoning is an appropriate add-on to competencies to present a complete picture, which in turn leads us to the axiom on the sign which started this chapter.

Also, we wanted to reflect the reality of organizational life. People do reason about issues in different ways, people may disagree with the reasoning of others, and people often misunderstand the reasoning of others through no fault of their own.

This makes being an ethical leader even more complex—hence the need to look at a hierarchy of reasoning, or, as we call it, a stage model of moral reasoning.

Overview of Stage Theory

As we move toward a description of our ethical leadership stage model, providing some clarity on our underlying assumptions is crucial. We have drawn from a variety of development psychologists (Piaget, Kohlberg, Gilligan,[1] and others) to provide a framework for looking at ethical leadership. We have drawn most heavily from Kohlberg's work, as his approach to moral reasoning closely parallels our approach to ethical leadership.[2] In doing so, we have relied on some key beliefs as follows:

- Individuals move through predictable stages of life, and their thinking and cognitive processing about morality changes in defined stages.
- These stages imply a hierarchy of thinking and reasoning. In Piaget's case, it is a progression toward more abstract, conceptual thinking, while in Kohlberg's model it is a progression toward a more principled approach to moral reasoning.[3]
- Not all people move through all stages of development. For a variety of reasons, an individual may stay at a certain stage of development. Some people may not enter a stage that involves abstract reasoning, or others may remain in a moral reasoning stage that is oriented toward small-group norms and standards.
- People at lower stages of reasoning may not understand the reasoning or thinking of someone at a higher stage. In other words, there may be dissonance between people simply because they do not understand how the higher-order person is reasoning.
- Actions or behavior may not be consistent with reasoning. A person may be capable of using principled reasoning but still act in ways that are immoral or inappropriate.

Kohlberg's research was based on structured interviews with individuals, exploring the reasoning participants would use to make decisions in ambiguous moral dilemmas. Over time, Kohlberg developed a systematic typology of moral reasoning, which we will explore in the following pages.

Below is a brief synopsis of Kohlberg's theory of moral reasoning. Note that Kohlberg describes six stages, but for simplicity's sake we will condense them into three stages, remembering that Kohlberg's focus is on how individuals' reason through moral dilemmas.[4]

Stages 1 and 2: Typically, but not always, these stages are associated with younger children, whose reasoning is based largely on right and wrong as defined by someone who is bigger or stronger and possesses the authority to tell them how to act. In this stage, reasoning is based on pleasing the person who is bigger or stronger and avoiding their displeasure. Oftentimes this bigger person may be a parent(s), but it may also be a boss or some other authority figure.

Stages 3 and 4: These are the classic "law and order" stages, and probably the highest level of reasoning most of the adult population attains. At the lower end, reasoning about moral issues is based on the norms and expectations of a small group—a peer group, religious organization, or ethnic group, for instance. As a person's moral reasoning advances, he or she becomes more focused on broader societal norms, with a strong law-and-order orientation. Right behavior is defined by codified laws, standards, and rules. That is not to imply that this stage is necessarily rigid. What is legal, i.e. abortion or gay marriage, may change over time. The higher end law and order individuals will adapt to the laws of a country, while those at a lower stage (peer group orientation) may not adapt and instead cling to the norms of their particular peer group.

As an aside, this differentiation along with the following stage, may explain some of the political polarization that is occurring in many countries. Simply put, people may be making arguments and holding discussions that others do not understand. You may hear this stated as "they live in a completely different world" or "it is like we are talking two different languages.

Stages 5 and 6: Reasoning at this level goes beyond codified laws to general principles. Principles such as the "golden rule" or achieving the greatest good for the greatest number dominate reasoning on moral dilemmas, and principles are applied to determine what is right even if it represents a violation of the law. At the highest level, principles like social justice become paramount.[5]

We are fully aware that Kohlberg's theory of moral development is open to legitimate criticism on a variety of fronts—gender, culture, and hierarchy, to name just a few. Our intent here is not to suggest that his theory is perfect. Rather, it is to suggest that Kohlberg's theoretical framework offers two important takeaways for ethical leadership: it provides a framework for the consideration of right and wrong, and it provides a basis for a stage model of ethical development.[6,7]

Before moving on to discuss our approach to a stage model of ethical leadership, we suggest that you pause and consider the following questions:

- Is there a difference between how an entry-level leader looks at ethical dilemmas and how a more experienced leader looks at the same issues?
- What is the difference between how Nelson Mandela thought about issues facing South Africa and how the previous apartheid regimes considered the direction of the country?
- Think of leaders you admire. Have they changed over time, have their positions become more nuanced, and have they grown as human beings?
- Think about leaders you know in your organization. What is the difference between those you respect and those you have less regard for?

We think that when most people step back and consider the above questions, they will intuitively arrive at the same conclusions we have reached: that different leaders think about ethical issues in very different ways, and that those differences are especially pronounced when you consider the differences between entry-level and more experienced leaders. As one matures and develops as a leader, a progression occurs.

The Developmental Stages of Ethical Leaders

In the following pages, we will provide a specific description of our stage model for ethical leaders. Before going into detail, we want to start with a high-level overview to provide a frame of reference as you progress through the more detailed proposal.

Fundamentally, we believe leaders may progress through four stages on their ethical journey. Remember that we are not suggesting that all leaders progress through all stages, just that there are stages in existence. Also, as you will note below, we hypothesize the existence of a rare fourth stage. Note that we use both numbers and names for each stage for ease of reference and to reflect movement and hierarchy. The stages are as follows:

Stage One: Sub-Group Focus

Consider this stage as a leader's first leadership role. Titles may vary, but assume this is the first time you are leading others, whether it be in a factory, insurance company, church, or any other kind of organization or institution. At this stage, your focus is relatively narrow: getting the job done, producing a high-quality product, and maintaining a positive work environment for those working for you. The ethical issues you engage with typically include safety, fairness, and consistency with organizational standards. Success is measured in how these issues play out daily within the work group and by the reactions of your immediate supervisor. There is little awareness or appreciation for how your actions are viewed by other leaders or other departments.

Stage Two: Systems Focus

Organizationally, this stage coincides with a shift to leading other leaders or a broader scope of control. Typically, this also means increased interaction with other departments, other areas of responsibility, and other collaborators outside of your immediate span of control. At this point, knowledge of the larger organization, how departments interact with one another, and the overall flow of work becomes crucial to success. Ethically, the issues you grapple with are not significantly different, but awareness of the impact of your decisions on others becomes much broader. You tend to look at issues more systematically as well. You now consider the long-term implications of your actions and act with a broader end goal in mind.

Stage Three: Ecosystem Orientation

A leader's view of his or her organization expands even further in stage three. Now the view expands to include the broader community and systems. While continuing to grapple with the issues addressed in stages one and two, the orientation expands to include the safety of the community and a more pronounced view of societal concerns. Questions of right and wrong take on a more extensive, complex framework. Likewise, the proper course of action is less defined, and the leader is probably more vulnerable to criticism from a wide variety of stakeholders. Ethical decisions take on a more principled orientation and are less reliant on rules and regulations, although those are certainly considered when making decisions.

Stage Four: Moral and Social-Justice Orientation

As noted earlier, this is a hypothetical stage, and if it exists, people who achieve it are probably rare. A leader at this stage has a broader view of society and culture that is rooted in concerns for justice, particularly social justice. It is roughly analogous to Kohlberg's sixth stage, which concerns itself with social welfare and social justice based on principles. These leaders transcend ethical systems to become a moral force for what is right and good. Leaders such as Martin Luther King, Jr., Gandhi, Mandela, or the Dalai Lama may fall into this small, select group. Kohlberg suggests, and we would agree, that the scarcity of leaders at this level may be due to the discomfort of challenging the norms and beliefs held by most of one's contemporaries.

Commentary

Before moving into a more detailed description of our proposed stages, let us digress for a moment. We tend to think of leadership as a metrics-driven, bottom-line process. While this is plainly stated in business terms, it also applies to other types of organizations, institutions, or governments. Success as a leader is typically measurable, black-and-white, and clear. A leader either succeeds or fails based on quantitative measures. And we are not ignoring that. Successful ethical leaders, almost by definition, must be successful leaders in the conventional sense first. If a leader is not successful in reaching a profitable bottom line, however that is defined in the organization, no one will care if he or she is an ethical leader. Being an effective leader is a necessary precondition for being an ethical leader.

At the same time, the path to the bottom line is strewn with a barrage of ethical choices that a leader must make on a constant basis. Think of some of the following for a moment:

- Is the job safe?
- Are we following procedures, or do we allow variance?
- How high do we set the quality bar?
- Can I pass/approve some items that may not be perfect?
- Are people working too hard?
- Are our expectations and standards clear?
- How will others feel if I allow Joe to attend his son's soccer game during work hours?
- Do I stop production to perform maintenance?

And the list could go on. Leaders do not operate in a moral vacuum, devoid of consideration of right and wrong. In fact, it is just the opposite. As leaders work within their organizations or work unit, striving to reach or improve the bottom line, they are constantly making moral decisions and judgments. Organizations inherently make it necessary to balance contrasting needs—for example, between budget constraints and safety. This suggests that the workplace should be filled with both effective and ethical leaders. We make a distinction between the two because historically the emphasis has been on leadership, without much emphasis on ethics; as we have argued in previous chapters, we believe there is a growing desire to create a synergy between the two concepts.

And that leads us back to our proposed stage theory of ethical leadership:

Stage One: Sub-Group Focus

Before diving into the stages, we would ask you to stop and think for a moment about your first leadership job (or perhaps you are in your first leadership role, or thinking about taking on a leadership role). What were your worries? What did you look forward to? What skills did you have and what skills needed improvement? What concerns did you have about the people you would be leading?

There is clearly no right or wrong answer to any of the above, but it is important to reflect on that first leadership experience as you progress. So, take a few minutes to think back or and reflect.

In the first stage of ethical leadership, the primary focus relative to ethical issues and standards of right and wrong is a narrow one. The leader is primarily focused on those who report to him or her, and if they have peers at the same level in their department, they may focus on them as well. In other words, the leader is concerned with how the employees under him or her will respond to decisions and actions, while having an awareness of how the decision may affect peers. This is not a negative judgment; it is the reality of a new leader's position.

Likewise, a stage one leader's ethical framework and attention will be narrow. At stage one, the ethical focus is on the work group and organizational policies and procedures. In that sense, ethical thinking is largely about adherence to rules and regulations, with group norms being a major concern as well.

Note: Our intent in proposing a stage model is both theoretical and practical. It is theoretical in the traditional sense that the stages offer an accurate description of reality; it is practical in the sense that if an organization needs entry-level leaders who are also ethical leaders, it should be able to select individuals against ethical leadership characteristics. Discussing the first stage relative to new leaders and their focus creates clarity. We do not mean to imply that all entry-level leaders remain at stage one ethically. Nor does it imply that if someone remains in an entry-level position, they are somehow ethically inferior. Far from it. Individuals make career and lifestyle choices that don't necessarily reflect their ability to process complex ethical issues.

The vantage point of processing the general ethical issues that leaders face at this stage is as follows:

- **Safety.** The focus on safety at this stage is on the work group. Does the leader plan in such a way as to minimize risks to the work team? Do they have the skills and tools necessary to carry out the work? Will they follow standard procedures and policies in completing the task? The focus is on basic safety, and leaders will typically express this as "making sure everyone goes home in the same condition as they came to work." Safety is tangible and expressed in terms of no one getting injured or dying on the job.

- **Fairness and Justice.** The issue here is fairness and consistency in the treatment of the work group. Do they think you are fair? Do they trust you? Fairness is largely local, although the leader may pay some attention to the impact of his or her decisions on other peer leaders. Fairness also applies to job performance and holding people accountable. Consistency is crucial. For the new leader, this may be the first area where you are tested, as skills, motivation, and performance can vary widely from individual to individual, which may necessitate differences in treatment.
- **Normative Standards.** At this stage of leadership, norms are largely focused on obeying the rules and regulations of the organization. For the new leader, this is about holding others to the standards and policies, using appropriate forms of discipline, and providing feedback to others on their behavior. This also may require confronting the difference between the stated normative standards and the cultural norms that have arisen over time. New leaders may encounter this when change occurs and the response is, "That's not the way we do things," or, "We tried that before and it didn't work."
- **Societal Concerns.** Unless it is part of the organization's stated mission or values, the broader world has little impact on the ethical decisions a stage one leader makes.

Stage Two: Systems Focus

At some point, for many leaders, the world broadens. You may be leading other leaders, you may have more diverse groups under you, or you may no longer be the subject-matter expert.

How does that move feel? What are your concerns? What do you worry about?

In the traditional view of organizations and career advancement, at some point in your leadership journey, your span of control increases. You may now be a manager, director, or some other title that rises above entry-level leadership. At least three things also occur. The first is that a leader may no longer be the immediate subject-matter expert and/or may not actually have expertise in the area(s) they are leading. Second, the leader is now leading through and with other leaders. Different skills may be required to be successful at this point, and abilities like delegation become more critical to long-term success. Third, work and success may be more influenced by other parts of the organizational system. An ability to work with others outside of one's own span of control becomes essential.

In other words, the role of the leader becomes more complicated, and so do the ethical issues the leader faces. At a minimum, the ethical issues involve more complicated variables and, typically, the rules and standards for action become more nuanced. Where once rules provided answers, now the leader becomes the judge, balancing shades of grey and weighing multiple options.

- *Safety.* Where previously the focus on safety was limited to the work group, now safety concerns have become broader and more complex. At this point, the leader may be doing more balancing between safety and budget, and there is certainly more awareness of the impact of safety decisions on other people and systems in the organization. In short, there is a great deal more emphasis on the implications and consequences of decisions related to safety. For example, a controller may make decisions about spending costs that consciously or unconsciously have an impact on safety.
- *Fairness and Justice.* For the leader at this level, fairness and consistent justice become wider and more visible. Where previously the leader had to be primarily concerned with individuals and job performance, now those individuals and their job performance become part of a broader system, in which no decision exists in a vacuum. The way the leader treats one person has a ripple effect in the organization. Each decision a leader makes has the potential to set a precedent or draw criticism. The consequences and implications of individual decisions percolate through the organization. While procedures and standards may govern some decisions, there is much greater room for judgment, fewer black-and-white decisions, and fewer guidelines for action.
- *Normative Standards.* At this level, the leader becomes less the enforcer of organizational norms and standards, and more the interpreter of those standards. What such leaders prioritize, what they choose to speak to and reinforce, and what they choose to ignore all play a key role in shaping organizational culture (see Chapter 7). The standards that one must pay attention to may also broaden in this stage, as external regulations, governmental constraints, and compliance become more significant. Decisions become even more complex, and the implications of individual ethical decisions become even more far-reaching.

- *Societal Concerns.* Where before the external world was largely sepa-
rate, leaders at this level begin to encounter the world outside the organization more directly. Now the actions a leader takes may reverberate in
the external community; for instance, terminations or layoffs are bound
to have an impact on families and communities. Likewise, social issues
can affect ethical decisions in the workplace. Laws designed to protect
individual rights and freedoms become a matter of much greater concern. External political events or turmoil may have repercussions within
the organization, and the leader may have to deal with the on-the-job
consequences of those events.

Before moving on from the first two stages of ethical leadership, several
comments are in order. From a moral reasoning perspective, our stage one
and stage two are roughly equivalent to Kohlberg's stage three and stage
four. That is, they involve a strong orientation toward following organizational norms and maintaining law and order. Rules provide some of the
organizational glue that is necessary for any entity to function well. This
structure is important, as it provides parameters for behavior, clarifies expectations, and offers some sense of direction. If you are creating an organization or hiring and promoting leaders, you want your leaders to be at
stage two—able to make nuanced ethical decisions within the boundaries
of policies and procedures. In other words, you want assurance that your
leaders will do the right thing, particularly in those situations where the
answers are ambiguous.

So, in short, much of an organization's hiring and development efforts
should be on ensuring that its leaders are functioning at stage two. Which
leads us, in turn, to the discussion of stage three and beyond.

Stage Three: Ecosystem Orientation

Just as we started our discussion of stage one with the premise (for discussion purposes) that it might be the typical stage of a new leader, we begin
our discussion of stage three from the opposite end of the spectrum. To
illustrate, let us assume that stage three ethical leaders, by and large, are
leaders of organizations, institutions, or businesses. That is not to suggest
that all business leaders are at stage three ethically or that leaders at lower
levels cannot be at stage three. We are using the organization leader for
illustrative purposes.

When you take on the role of organization leader, the ethical leadership
world becomes infinitely more complex. Not only do the decisions you
make about the organization's future have broader implications, but the
world of stakeholders also expands dramatically. You may now report to
an external board or serve as the public voice of the company, and every

decision you make affects every portion of the organization. As an example of this complexity, consider the scenario below:

> In 2020, the United States experienced a series of protests, some of them violent or destructive, in the wake of the murder of George Floyd.
>
> As part of larger communities or organizations with concerned members or organizations that employed concerned citizens, many leaders were called upon to make statements on behalf of their organization in response to the protests.
>
> What would you have done in response to those requests?
>
> What would you do if some of your employers staged a protest in the workplace in solidarity?

As this example illustrates, leading an organization can be extremely complicated, often with no clear-cut guidelines for action. Likewise, while the issues a stage three ethical leader confronts are the same as those faced by a stage one leader, the balance tends to skew more toward the broader societal concerns for the organizational leader. And, as we will further explain, many of these complex decisions reflect the contradictions between the financial bottom line and the moral bottom line.

- *Safety.* Safety remains a paramount concern, but the focus at this stage may become more long term than short term. At this level, you are asking yourself the simple question of whether you did everything in your power to keep people safe today. But you are also balancing safety needs against budget concerns. Risks associated with your safety decisions become greater, as a poor decision may have a significant impact on your employees and/or the larger community. Likewise, safety becomes more of a long-term strategic decision than a day-to-day focus.
- *Fairness and Justice.* Fairness and justice become less about the needs of an individual and more about the broad needs of all. In that sense, the utilitarian principle of the greatest good for the greatest number becomes the standard for what is fair. While ethical leaders at this stage place a great deal of value on fairness, they recognize that not every decision they make will be seen as fair by all. To maintain trust, the ethical leader needs to be open and transparent about decisions and acknowledge that the decision might not be perfect for all concerned.
- *Normative Standards.* A leader at this level can define and shape the normative standards of the organization. The leader must work with a variety of stakeholders to fashion the organization's mission, objectives, and values, while still being the final authority on most policy and

procedures. As a stage three leader, you have the means to shape both concrete norms (policies and procedures) and implicit norms of behavior that you model and reinforce.

- *Societal Concerns.* As implied in the question box above, the organization leader becomes not only the face of the organization but also its voice in the community, professional associations, and the world at large. Whether responding to social-justice issues on behalf of the organization or dealing with the local community's environmental concerns, the ethical leader walks a fine line of balancing organizational needs (i.e., profit) with the well-being of society at large. At this level, the range of stakeholders has expanded beyond employees, customers, and shareholders to include the wider community and political structures. Moving beyond the traditional areas of focus requires not just thought but also the moral courage to take action.

At this level, being an ethical leader is multifaceted, to say the least. While complex and often convoluted, there are a few virtually foolproof rules for action.

Commentary

Before moving on to a discussion of the final hypothetical stage, several comments are in order:

- First, not all leaders who have become stage three ethical leaders can remain successful. One can be a successful leader and also be considered ethical by remaining in stage two. Is it desirable to have ethical stage three leaders in charge of an organization? We think so, particularly given the complex, diverse, and chaotic world we live in. Chapter 2 makes the argument in favor of higher-level ethical leadership and higher-order moral principles. We believe in that and think the world values that.
- Most studies of leadership tend to focus on "big" leaders: prominent historical figures and contemporary leaders who have achieved widespread fame (or infamy, as the case may be). Because of the richness of their lives or the amount that has been written about them, such figures tend to be great sources of information and stories on leadership. This approach does have its place, but it is somewhat limited.
- Try a quick experiment: ask some of your friends to list ten ethical leaders they admire and respect. We suspect, when all is said and done, that there will be considerable overlap between your friends' lists. To some extent, this is probably a reflection of the fact that fewer and fewer leaders advance to higher stages of ethical leadership, so there are fewer and fewer of them to observe.

- We also suspect that there are probably many stage three ethical leaders who never get or want large-scale recognition. We believe that there are numerous small-business owners, social workers, philanthropists, teachers, parents, religious leaders, and others who serve their communities as ethical leaders in the fullest sense of the term. They are out there; they are just not seen. Test this for yourself and do the same exercise that started this paragraph, but confine your list to ethical leaders in your local community. See what you come up with then.

Stage Four: Moral and Social-Justice Orientation

Stage four ethical leaders focus on societal change, social justice, and moral leadership. The list of names associated with this stage (Mandela, King, and Gandhi, for example) tends to be short and generally lacking in leaders from the business world. It is worth noting that none of the people commonly named as moral leaders are perfect human beings. One can be an effective moral leader and still exhibit human flaws. While there may be exceptions to this, most business leaders' attention is elsewhere, and amid the day-to-day challenges of running their organizations, they have little time to contemplate more sweeping changes. Most of the individuals we identify as moral leaders come from the non-business realm, and, even outside the business world, there are very few of them. Even Kohlberg acknowledges the scarcity of leaders or individuals at this level, which tends to suggest that its attainment may be more of a chance occurrence than a natural progression. See the historical example below to gain greater understanding.[8]

William Lloyd Garrison (1805–1879)

Garrison was the foremost white abolitionist in the United States prior to the Civil War. He edited and published a newspaper, *The Liberator*, which advocated for the immediate emancipation of slaves, he formed the American Anti-Slavery Society, and he advocated for the rights of women. He believed that owning another human being was an abomination, speaking throughout the country on the topic. He was a moral force in the US from the early 1830s through the Civil War, consistently espousing his cause and advocating for the rights of the oppressed.

In addition to his anti-slavery work, he supported nonviolent protest as a means of action in opposing injustice. Both King and Gandhi later cited his thinking as crucial to their own approaches.

If stage four ethical leaders exist, they exist on the fringes. They are advocates for change, whether that be climate change, social change, or any other form of change. They are the advocate for others and serve as a conscience in the face of moral failures, speaking hard truths often at great personal risk. Leaders at this level are prone to being shunned or reviled by others, making their work grueling and often lonely. Calling for courage in the face of physical harm and modeling a principled way of approaching the world and others, such leaders are as exceptional as shooting stars.

Do these mythical, heroic ethical leaders exist? We think so, and we think they have a critical role to play in moving our world forward. Is it possible to identify what exactly causes these leaders to develop their unique passion and selflessness? We are skeptical about that. Certainly, when you look at King or Mandela or Gandhi, you can see some trends, such as a strong aversion to injustice. But many others have faced the same injustices without rising to the level of greatness. There are multiple factors involved in the formation of an exceptional leader that extend far beyond an aversion to social injustice.

Application

Up next, we will focus our attention on identifying and developing ethical leaders, but before moving on, we want to provide some brief comments on the topic.

Developing ethical leadership behavior is a complex topic that is subject to frequent debate. To be sure, one can train people on do's and don'ts relative to compliance and behavior. For example, in the US, there are many workplace training programs on sexual harassment. These trainings clearly define what constitutes harassment, what is and isn't allowed, and what consequences one may face for violating the policy. But the question is: Does taking training like this really result in a change in behavior? That is debatable. The same may be true of training in ethics. Does training on ethics that involves guidelines, moral dilemmas, and discussion change behavior? The research on this question appears to be divided.

As we noted in the previous chapter, we think there are ways to assess competencies, and the same is true of the stage model, particularly when hiring entry-level supervisors or when making hiring decisions at more senior levels of an organization. Providing a candidate with a series of scenarios regarding safety, fairness, values, and how to strike a balance between all of these factors could provide a valuable glimpse of the candidate's qualities as an ethical leader and as a leader in general. Seeing how people reason about moral dilemmas can provide significant insight into how they will approach their responsibilities.

Recognizing that leading an organization is complex under the best of circumstances, and even more so when your organization is debating moral and ethical issues, we think aspiring ethical leaders need to recognize the diversity of reasoning that exists in their organization and do the following:

- Acknowledge the concerns of others. When you are sharing a decision, it is important that you acknowledge the concerns and reasoning of others who may see the world from a different perspective. Let people know you understand their concerns, why they may disagree, and what impact your decision will have on them.
- Provide a clear rationale for the course of action or decision. Share the reasons for your decision in ways that go beyond the bottom line. Talk about what you wrestled with, the pros and cons, and the impact on individuals.
- Be transparent. People trust leaders who are transparent. Transparency is a theme that runs through this book. We think effective transparency provides insight into not only what you think about a decision, but also how you feel about a decision. Here is what we mean by that.

> We had the experience several years ago of working with a family-owned business that made the difficult decision to close one of its plants, which was located in a small town. The decision affected many people, their families, and the community at large.
> The owners of the company visited the plant in person and made the announcement. They shared the reasons for it, expressed their personal anguish over the decision, and gave people the opportunity to share their concerns and questions.

- Take the time to answer questions and listen to concerns. Too often leaders announce difficult decisions, even decisions that are potentially gut wrenching for them, and then end the conversation without allowing questions. Painful as it may be, it is imperative to take the time to listen to people's questions and answer them thoughtfully.

Questions and Activities to Consider

1. Find and read biographies of significant moral leaders or leaders you admire. Google lists of great leaders, find people who interest you, and read about them. Pay particular attention to how they deal with moral dilemmas or challenges in their lives. Ask yourself how you would handle those situations and why.

2. Create a lunch group to discuss the ethical issues individuals face on the job. Discuss the pros and cons of various approaches to challenges that you face on a daily basis. This is a sharing activity geared toward people who are concerned with ethical challenges. You may want to select participants carefully, as not everyone will be concerned about ethical issues or ethical leadership.

3. Ask a mentor how they handled significant ethical challenges in their career. How did they make decisions? What worked well and what would they have done differently?

Notes

1 Cynthia Vinney, "Gilligan's Theory of Moral Development," *Verywell Mind*, March 20, 2023. www.verywellmind.com/the-carol-gilligan-theory-and-a-| woman-s-sense-of-self-5198408.

2 Saul Mcleod, "Kohlberg's Stages of Moral Development," *Simply Psychology*, June 8, 2023. www.simplypsychology.org/kohlberg.html.

3 Rick Ansorge, "Piaget Stages of Development," WebMD, October 14, 2010. www.webmd.com/children/piaget-stages-of-development.

4 Lawrence Kohlberg, "FROM IS TO OUGHT: How to Commit the Naturalistic Fallacy and Get Away with It in the Study of Moral Development," *Cognitive Development and Epistemology*, ed. Theodore Mischel (New York: Academic Press, 1971), 151–235. https://doi.org/10.1016/b978-0-12-498640-4.50011-1.

5 "Kohlberg's Stages of Moral Development," *Education, Society & the K-12 Learner*, n.d. www.coursehero.com/study-guides/teachereducationx92x1/kohlbergs-stages-of-moral-development/.

6 Kendra Cherry, "Kohlberg's Theory of Moral Development," *Verywell Mind*, November 7, 2022. www.verywellmind.com/kohlbergs-theory-of-moral-development-2795071.

7 "Criticisms of Kohlberg's Theory," n.d. https://web.cortland.edu/andersmd/kohl/kohlcrit.html.

8 Henry Mayer, *All on Fire: William Lloyd Garrison and the Abolition of Slavery* (New York: W.W. Norton). www.amazon.com/All-Fire-William-Garrison-Abolition/dp/0393332365.

Chapter 9

Toward a Hierarchy of Values

Tell me what you pay attention to, and I will tell you who you are.
(José Ortega y Gasset)

In Chapter 8, we began to explore a hierarchy of ethical leadership based on how one reasons about ethical and moral issues. In this chapter, we add to that concept by exploring the idea of a hierarchy of guiding principles. In other words, we suggest that in considering ethical leadership—which is closely connected to values—some guiding principles are "better" or stronger than others. As Ortega y Gasset implies in the introductory quote, the choices we make define who we are and what we value. We make this suggestion because several of the definitions of ethical leadership that we have run across in our research define an ethical leader as one who acts in a manner that is consistent with the values of his or her organization. That definition is fine, but it begs the obvious question of how one distinguishes among guiding principles in complicated situations.

Note: We think the term "guiding principles" is a better descriptor than "values." Principles provide a framework for action and decision making without providing absolute, black-and-white answers. They provide, as the term implies, guidance, without being overly directive. In that sense, the Golden Rule or Kant's categorical imperative are guiding principles which require thought and discussion. Hence, we believe that guiding principles are a better term than values, although we will use both terms for the remainder of this chapter, as much of the literature on the overall topic references values.

Take, for example, two guiding principles that we see often in corporate settings: integrity and concern for people. Some decisions may bring these two guiding principles into conflict. It is entirely possible for a leader to make a high-integrity decision that also appears to cause harm. Think about the need to downsize due to a change in business conditions. The decision to downsize may be necessary, responsible, and in every way the "right" decision, yet it still hurts people.

DOI: 10.4324/b23260-13

That is not to say that integrity and concern for people cannot be combined in making decisions. Recall the leaders of the firm we mentioned in Chapter 8, who made the hard decision to eliminate a plant and all of the associated jobs. These leaders believed it was also their responsibility to provide as much support as possible to the people involved and to deliver the news in person, even though they knew it would not be a pleasant discussion.

Before diving into a discussion of guiding principles, we want to share what we think is a rather remarkable letter. The letter was written by Chip Bergh, who was at the time the CEO of Levi Strauss, the apparel company. Most of the letter is self-explanatory, although it was written in response to a specific event: Donald Trump's 2017 ban on immigration to the USA by citizens from a number of Muslim-majority countries. Bergh's letter to the employees of Levi Straus reads as follows:

This past Friday, President Trump issued an executive order banning people from seven Muslim-majority countries, including a permanent ban on Syrian refugees, from entering the United States. Like many of you, I've been watching the news and wondering what this means for our employees and our business; but even more, what these new policies mean for our country and for the world.

For generations, the United States has played such an important role in being a safe haven from oppression and wars, and for openly receiving immigrants. Our country has benefited immensely from those who have come to the U.S. to make a better life for themselves and their families, and we would not be the country we are today were it not for immigration. In fact, we would not be the company we are today if it weren't for Levi Strauss, who was himself an immigrant. He instilled a sense of doing what's right, and our company values of empathy, originality, integrity and courage are perhaps even more meaningful today than they were 163 years ago.

It's because of these values that we have never been afraid of diversity and inclusion or speaking up about it. We desegregated our factories in the U.S. 10 years before it became the law of the land. We were one of the first companies to offer domestic partner healthcare benefits, long before it was popular. We have been a strong voice for inclusion, diversity and giving everyone an opportunity to achieve their fullest potential at LS&Co. regardless of race, gender, sexual orientation, nationality or religious preference. We know, deep in our soul, that diversity of all kinds is good for business and that a diverse organization will outperform a homogeneous one every time.

It is, in fact, our values that are guiding our perspective with respect to the executive order on immigration. Any policy that seeks to restrict or limit immigration based on race, nationality or religion is antithetical to what we believe as a company. Our success has been based on our ability to attract and retain the very best talent from all backgrounds, to embrace diversity, to be inclusive and benefit from different perspectives. Restricting the flow of talented individuals will, over time, impact the competitiveness of the country and the companies based here in the U.S.

We will not sit idly by. Because our employees are our first priority, we are reaching out to any employee who may be directly affected. We will stand by our colleagues and their families and offer support to any employee or family member directly affected by the ban. Looking back on the history of this company, we are not afraid to take a stand on important issues of our day, and I believe this is one of those moments. If we stay true to our values and support those who champion equality and justice while working with policymakers to ensure our voice is heard, I'm confident our business and our communities will be stronger as a result.[1]

We find this letter striking for a number of reasons: first, Bergh is writing about a political issue that potentially affects Levi Strauss employees, not a typical business issue. He also explicitly disagrees with the leader of his country in very specific ways, running the risk of backlash from the president and his supporters, many of whom may also be Levi Strauss customers. Second, he specifically references the historical values of Levi Strauss and how those guiding principles played out in previous generations. In doing so, he also makes a strong statement about what the culture of Levi Strauss has been and will continue to be. In short, he is "taking a stand on an issue of the day." He goes on to reiterate the values of the company and issue a call to action in defense of those guiding principles. We think the letter is remarkable given the coherence of its stance on the company's guiding principles, and the relative rarity with which business leaders espouse such moral stances.

Guiding Principles

There are multiple definitions of values and different typologies of guiding principles. For our purposes, we will use a definition provided by the Mc-Combs School of Business at the University of Texas, which states, "Values are the beliefs that motivate people to act one way or another. They serve as a guide for human behavior."[2] While this definition applies to individual or personal values, we believe it also applies to organizational guiding principles, as organizations define their guiding principles to drive behavior and decision making.

Philosophers and other researchers look at different types of values. For example, Everett defines different categories of values including economic, bodily, recreational, character, aesthetic, intellectual, and religious guiding principles.[3] Others have added to that list legal, industrial, value-of-life, and emotional guiding principles—and the list could go on. More and more organizations now include their core guiding principles on their websites and on display in their offices. These core guiding principles typically align with the organization's mission and usually represent a broad array of principles that define the organization. Although organizations typically name five to seven core guiding principles, Firstup[4] provides a list of ten potential core values. Others provide longer lists, but the Firstup list will serve for discussion purposes.

1. Integrity
2. Honesty
3. Fairness
4. Accountability
5. Promise to the Customer
6. Diversity and Inclusion
7. Learning
8. Passion
9. Teamwork
10. Quality.

As another example, recall the Levi Strauss letter quoted at the beginning of this chapter, in which Bergh states the following about the company's values:

It's our values: **empathy, originality, integrity and courage**. These guide every decision we make and every action we take. And they fuel our commitment to drive profits through principles.

Notice the careful wording as well around profits. There is nothing wrong—in fact, there is a lot right—with linking guiding principles to the mission of the organization. One can be ethical while making money or achieving some other goal at the same time.

For any organization—whether it be corporate, educational, non-profit, or volunteer—the intent of a value statement is to define expected behavior and to guide decisions. As such, we believe guiding principles play an important role in ethical behavior, leadership, and the culture of an organization. However, value statements also raise questions, notably:

- How does our organization determine our guiding principles?
- How does our organization define our guiding principles and the behaviors associated with those guiding principles? As noted elsewhere, we feel it is imperative to provide specific examples of the expected behaviors linked to guiding principles, in order to codify concrete expectations and avoid confusion.
- Are our guiding principles ranked in a particular order? Are some of our guiding principles more important than others?
- How do we communicate our guiding principles and reinforce their use on a daily basis?

Defining Organizational Guiding Principles

The practice of developing corporate core guiding principles is considered by some to have started with Collins and Porras's 1994 book *Built to Last*, which argued that the best companies have a set of core guiding principles.[5] Since that time, it appears that naming core guiding principles has become quite common, with many prominent CEOs embracing it and business schools teaching it. Check out any organization you frequent; chances are, it has a set of core values or guiding principles.

In Chapter 7, we discussed the basics of developing competencies and the application of competencies to ethical leadership. Some of the same concepts apply when developing guiding principles, especially the notion that guiding principles need to be defined in behavioral terms that can be understood by everyone in the organization. A behavior-based approach may be even more important for guiding principles than for competencies. Too often, guiding principles are described in single words and short definitions which, while meaningful, do not provide direction or expectations relative to how one should behave. What, for example, does teamwork, integrity, or innovation mean exactly? Without specific behavioral examples showing how they can be implemented, concepts like these are little more than platitudes.

To put it simply, we think there are three approaches to developing core guiding principles which may function as standalone processes or function in combination. These are:

1. A bottom-up process, which can include interviews, focus groups, sorting activities, and consensus seeking, to develop guiding principles

across the organization. This approach is analogous to the way an individual may identify his or her personal guiding principles, applying a similar approach to the organization. Typically, this kind of process is driven by the HR department and has the advantage of gaining high buy-in from employees, as they have been involved every step of the way and had ample opportunities to offer their input. The disadvantage is that the perspective is limited to the current situation, as this approach may not include senior leaders, who tend to have a broader vision of what the organization needs now and what it will need in the future.

2. A top-down process, often facilitated by an external consultant or HR, which focuses on executives' views of what the organization should be now and in the future. The advantage of this approach is that it is driven by people who have a view of what the organization needs to be and what needs to change. They can link guiding principles to the future. The disadvantage is that this approach often results in a wish list of guiding principles that may or not reflect the current reality of the organization. Furthermore, employees may not be as enthused about guiding principles when they have not been granted the opportunity to contribute to them; however, this can be mitigated with an effective communication process.

3. The *shining star* approach can be used when one is establishing core guiding principles related to a desired organizational change or change in the business model. This approach is best used when an organization is *not* demonstrating certain guiding principles that leadership wants to prioritize. The idea is to find the few employees who *are* exhibiting the desired guiding principles and behaviors, and to build the core guiding principles around their actions. The advantage of this approach is that the future-oriented guiding principles are grounded in reality and not just a wish list from senior leaders. The disadvantage is similar to that of other approaches: there may not be organizational buy-in and, as in any change effort, there will inevitably be some resistance.

We favor a blended approach to determining core guiding principles, particularly when the expected core guiding principles are designed to change behavior or to reflect a change in the direction of the business. In these cases, we think the following should occur:

1. Senior leadership needs to be heavily involved. Changing core guiding principles, particularly those that are aspirational, is changing the culture of the organization. Culture change is the responsibility of senior leaders, and they are the key players who communicate, reinforce, and

model the expected change in guiding principles and behavior. It is also vitally important that senior leadership is aligned at a personal level with the core guiding principles. No one wants to be in a situation where the organization names teamwork as a core guiding principle and yet senior leaders neither believe in nor practice teamwork.

2. Use interviews of "shining star" employees to obtain behavioral data. Identify what these employees do on a regular basis to manifest the potential core guiding principles. Articulating these behaviors serves as the foundation for descriptions of the core guiding principles and provides concrete examples that leaders and others can use in describing expectations.

3. Use survey data to gain insight on employees' agreement with the core guiding principles and how employees rank them in order of importance. The ranking step can reveal a hierarchy of importance among the guiding principles, as well as providing the opportunity for more employee involvement and buy-in.

In the end you need core guiding principles that include a definition, behavioral anchors, examples of how the principles should be put into practice, and a hierarchy of importance among the guiding principles.

Before proceeding, we want to issue one note of caution. Values are typically associated with strong feelings and can be deeply personal. There can and will be emotion associated with developing guiding principles, as individuals at all levels of the organization will have strong opinions on them. Therefore, in many cases (and we are not hunting for business here), it may be advisable to bring in a third party who can remain objective during the process of developing values. This may be a trusted advisor, some board members, or an outside consultant. Someone with an external perspective can provide a less biased view of potential decisions about guiding principles.

Pairing Guiding Principles

Certain philosophers have addressed the relative strength of guiding principles, particularly as it pertains to decision making. They suggest a pairing process in which two guiding principles are brought together, and decisions are made about which value is stronger, more important, or of a higher order. For those who suggest this process, it is a somewhat abstract concept, usually rooted in esoteric discussions of the meaning and importance of different guiding principles. However, we believe the approach has utility for organizations as they look at which guiding principles are central to their mission.[6] Let us look at an example to see how this might work. In response to worldwide events, recent years have seen a rise in organizations prioritizing diversity, inclusion, and equity. Many organizations have hired diversity officers and made diversity a specific organizational value. While diversity is important for many reasons, both practical and philosophical, is diversity a more important guiding principle than fairness? Or is it more important than justice for all? We suspect not, and we believe that the higher-order value—the more inclusive value, that is—is one that addresses fundamental fairness, equality, or social justice. While some organizations may choose to emphasize diversity to address flaws in their organization or omissions based on the prejudices of the past, the long-term guiding principles should be based on fairness for all.

Guiding principles need to be clustered or ranked in order of importance, and this can be accomplished through surveys. After initial ranking, we recommend using a pairing process to confirm that the order works when making decisions and that one value supersedes all others.

Aspirational vs. Descriptive Guiding Principles

Most of us have been in numerous offices or establishments that post their guiding principles on a wall for all to see. Many, including employees, may walk past those signs and posters every day without really seeing the words or processing their meaning. However, we think those value statements deserve more scrutiny. Based on a list of the twenty-five top workplaces and their core guiding principles provided by Wishlist[7] and our own examination of additional value statements, we think most guiding principles can be divided into two categories. Some guiding principles are descriptive. That is, they describe the current culture—how we behave toward one another—while conveying to outsiders what it is like to work in the organization. In this category, you will see guiding principles such as fun, work–life balance, teamwork, and going the extra mile, to name just a few.

Other guiding principles are aspirational. They speak to a future state or an expectation and tend to have more of a decision-making orientation. In this category, you will see guiding principles such as integrity, entrepreneurial orientation, doing the right thing, or being extraordinary.

Lencioni suggests a similar typology in a *Harvard Business Review* essay, in which he divides guiding principles into aspirational, permission-to-play, and accidental vales, with accidental guiding principles arising out of the culture, which suggests a similar approach.[8]

Let us pose a short question before moving on.[9]

Congruence Between Values and Action

Elsewhere (Chapter 1) we provided a short moral dilemma based on the tobacco industry and the oil industry. We asked readers to reflect on how they would have reacted or felt if they knew they and their company were knowingly involved in unethical activities.

That same analysis applies to your own company and the congruence between its stated values and its actions. There is more and more data to suggest that employees want their employer to "walk the talk," so to speak, and this is especially true relative to ethical and moral issues.

While employees certainly take note of the degree to which their employer puts its guiding principles into action, there is an additional level of congruence that is crucial for ethical leaders. This level has to do with a more personal congruence between individual and organizational values. Are your personal guiding principles congruent with those of your organization, and do you act in a manner that is consistent with those guiding principles?

A Proposed Hierarchy

Value Analysis by Biography. Before moving on to discuss a hierarchy of guiding principles, we want to analyze a handful of individuals we consider to be ethical leaders. Looking at what motivates people is a revealing exercise, and we would encourage you to undertake the same exercise with leaders you admire, living or dead. We have provided very short overviews of a few leaders here and have cited additional reference material for your own review, although generally Wikipedia provides a reasonable summary of each person (with one exception) on our list.

Albert Schweitzer. Theologian, musician, physician whose work as a medical missionary was built around the principle of "reverence for life." Committed his life and energy to providing medical care for the less fortunate.[10]

Mohandas Gandhi. Leader of the Indian independence movement. Espoused militant non-violence as a means of attaining social justice. Led a mass movement to throw off the yoke of British colonial rule, resulting in the independence of India.[11]

Benazir Bhutto. Liberal prime minister of Pakistan. First woman leader of a Muslim-majority country, who attempted to enact numerous reforms. A passionate advocate for women and other minorities in her home country.[12]

Nelson Mandela. Prisoner of conscience and president of South Africa. A moral force in his country and the world. Led the drive to abolish apartheid in South Africa and the subsequent reconciliation efforts.[13]

Rev. Thomas Johnson. Co-founder of college preparatory school for minority youth. Promotes accountability, cultural awareness, and non-violence in a spiritual environment.[14]

Jacinda Ahern. Former prime minister of New Zealand. Notable for her handling of a mass shooting in her country, her approach to the COVID pandemic, and her overall leadership. Consistently demonstrated empathy for all citizen of New Zealand.[15]

Thich Nhat Hanh. A Buddhist monk and activist from Vietnam. Protested the Vietnam War and was exiled from Vietnam as a result. Promoted engaged Buddhism and mindfulness around the world.[16]

Chip Bergh. Former CEO[17] of Levi Strauss, who has consistently supported the values of his organization and taken public stands on a number of political issues facing the company and the US. Puts the values of the organization into play internally and with suppliers.[18]

Hamdi Ulukaya. An immigrant to the United States who started Chobani, a yogurt company, that has grown dramatically in a short period of time. Gave his employees 10% of the company, and 30% of his workforce consist of immigrants and refugees.[19]

There are central themes associated with these leaders and, we think, with most ethical leaders. While opinions and wording may vary, the following appear to cut across the lives of all of the ethical leaders with have used as examples.

- To use Schweitzer's phrase, each has a reverence for life. While they may have differences of opinions with those they encounter, they respect and honor the sanctity of each individual. For some, that may mean a reverence for potential, for others the sanctity of life on the shop floor, and for others care for the less fortunate. Meanings may vary, but the core reverence remains a driving force for action.
- They have a strong orientation toward justice and fairness. Perhaps following from a reverence for life each one attempts to treat every individual—regardless of culture, country, religion, or race—as equal and entitled to the same basic dignity and rights.
- Each appears to shun violence. While there may be some variation on this issue (one could argue, for instance, that Mandela proposed revolutionary violence at early points in his life), fundamentally they suggest through their actions that violence toward others is abhorrent.
- They work to make their country or community a better place for all concerned. Combined with the above, there is an action orientation to take the principles they live by and put those principles into action.

- Underlying the above is the moral courage to go forth at personal risk and against potentially great odds. While courage is not necessarily a value, without the moral courage to act, words become empty and meaningless.

You may be asking what all the above means in the context of a discussion of guiding principles for organizations. These leaders are individuals who are acting on their personal values, not some set of corporate principles. We would argue that these examples are relevant and applicable in the corporate context, for several reasons. First, these leaders are or were able to influence others to their way of thinking. People followed or follow them precisely because of the moral heroism they convey. Second, at a simplistic level, what is the difference? Organizations are collections of individual people, and if an organization does not have principles that motivate and guide its employees, it may not be built to last.

Ordering of Guiding Principles

As referenced earlier in this chapter, we believe there is an order of importance among values or guiding principles for organizations. When guiding behavior and providing a decision-making framework, some values are better than others. We make this claim recognizing that others will disagree with us. Indeed, we hope they do. At its core, effective ethical leadership is rooted in dialogue, discussion, and the seeking of consensus. No one likes to have their guiding principles dictated by others. People want to be involved, people want to have input, and people want something to which they can commit.

Before presenting our perspective, a quick suggestion or two. We think an organization should have no more than five to seven guiding principles. Most of us have a limited ability to process more than five to seven, and the more you have, the more potential there is for conflict or contradictions among the values. The values chosen for your organization should cut across the hierarchy spectrum. That is, you should have one or two principles at each level of the hierarchy (Figure 9.1).

The broadest range of values, and those most critical to the operation of an organization on a daily basis, are those that govern behavior within the organization, which we call maintenance principles. Maintenance principles serve as the backbone of an organization and describe how people are expected to interact with one another, treat one another, and approach their work. Principles based on teamwork, innovation, quality, entrepreneurship, and concern for the customer would be examples of the values that would rank at this level. Maintenance principles are crucial to day-to-day activity and provide an underlying structure to the organization.

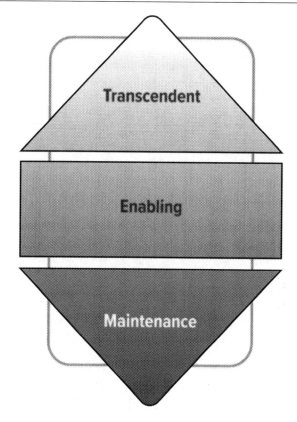

Figure 9.1 Guiding Principles Hierarchy

If I am an employee of an organization, its maintenance principles underly my assumptions about how I should be treated and how I treat others. On a daily basis, these are the core guiding principles.

The second level of principles are those that enable other action or encourage more in-depth analysis. They offer a degree of freedom from maintenance values and provide a safety cushion for those who take risks within an organization or venture beyond the prescribed boundaries of their roles. Enabling principles would include such values as integrity, courage, transparency, and empathy. The Chip Bergh letter quoted at the beginning of this chapter illustrates the importance of enabling principles. Because Levi Strauss has integrity and courage among its core values, Bergh had both the permission to speak up and the mandate to do so. We suspect, as well, that enabling values can also give lower-level employees the confidence to "speak truth to power" without fear of retaliation.

Last, most important, are what we call transcendent principles. These are the often aspirational, perhaps universal, values that speak to a higher purpose. Each of the leaders cited in this section lives according to their transcendent principles in one form or another. The well-being of people, the environment, the community, or justice and fairness, for example, are higher-order values that should transcend all others when describing the behaviors and actions expected from members of an organization. These values provide the ultimate framework for a decision by asking whether it is right for the company, for the environment, and for the community at large.

Reinforcing Guiding Principles

An organization can select the best guiding principles in existence that fit its culture and mission perfectly, and still fail miserably at nurturing, sustaining, and acting on those values (see Enron[20]). Reinforcing guiding principle on a consistent basis is crucial for their long-term comprehension and use. Much has been written about this process, and there appear to be common trends. Among these are:

- Integrate guiding principles into every process. Constantly checking decisions and actions against their alignment with guiding principles is crucial.
- Practice what you preach. Senior leaders, in particular, need to regularly talk about the guiding principles and model the expected behavior in action.

At this point in our discussion of how guiding principles for ethical leadership can be modeled and applied, it is worth touching on the distinction between ethical leadership and sainthood. We think this can be a very fine line. As an example, think of the Reverend Dr. Martin Luther King, Jr., the American civil rights leader, who is often cited as an example of ethical leadership. His leadership of the American civil rights movement is legendary, but he was far from a saint in his personal life. Does that make him less of an ethical leader? We think not.

While congruence between one's leadership role and personal life is certainly desirable, having personal flaws or lapses does not necessarily reflect on one's leadership. Certainly, in some situations it can be a deterrent to success, but not in all cases. Even the most ethical leaders are humans with flaws, and lapses can be forgiven by followers.

- Recognize individuals at all levels of the organization who practice the guiding principles frequently and publicly.
- Make the guiding principles part of traditional HR processes such as hiring, promotion, and performance management.
- Keep people who get results and live the values. Let people go who do not or will not live the values.
- Celebrate individuals who demonstrate the organization's values both regularly and in an exemplary fashion.
- Be transparent about failures if leaders take action that is inconsistent with the organization's values.
- Make the guiding principles come alive by constant reference to them in public forums and in writing.
- Just as many organizations begin every meeting with a safety briefing, begin each meeting with a discussion of a value and how people can live that value each day.

Questions to Ponder

1. Do you apply your organization's guiding principles on a daily basis? Do the guiding principles affect the decisions you make?
2. Does your leadership model use the guiding principles?
3. Are the guiding principles reflective of the actual culture of the organization?
4. Are people rewarded or promoted who do not use the guiding principles?

Notes

1 Chip Bergh, "Our Values in Action," *Levi Strauss & Co.*, January 31, 2017. www.levistrauss.com/2017/01/31/our-values-in-action/.
2 Ethics Unwrapped. "Values: Values Are Society's Shared Beliefs about What Is Good or Bad and How People Should Act," November 5, 2022. https://ethicsunwrapped.utexas.edu/glossary/values#.
3 Tong Keun-Min, "A Study on the Hierarchy of Values," 20th WCP, n.d. www.bu.edu/wcp/Papers/Valu/ValuMin.htm#:~:text=Walter%20Goodnow%20Everett%20classified%20values,%2C%20(8)%20religious%20values.
4 Firstup, "Communicating Company Core Values: Definition, Examples, and Why It Matters," *Firstup*, May 4, 2023. https://firstup.io/blog/communicating-company-core-values/.
5 James C. Collins and Jerry I. Porras, *Built to Last: Successful Habits of Visionary Companies* (New York: Harper, 1994). Book review: *Competitive Intelligence Review* 6, no. 3 (January 1, 1995): 84. https://doi.org/10.1002/cir.3880060321.
6 Tong Keun-Min, "A Study on the Hierarchy of Values."
7 Wishlist. "25 Top Workplaces and Their Core Values," *Wishlist*, March 7, 2022. https://enjoywishlist.com/25-top-workplaces-and-their-core-values/.

8 Patrick Lencioni, "Make Your Values Mean Something," *PubMed* 80, no. 7 (July 1, 2002): 113–17, 126. https://pubmed.ncbi.nlm.nih.gov/12140851.

9 Relative to the moral dilemma referenced in this example. Our cursory review of the cited industries (Tobacco and Petroleum) suggests that they have made substantive changes in their core values or guiding principle as result of those ethical lapses. See Phillip Morris or ExxonMobile websites as examples.

10 "Albert Schweitzer," *New World Encyclopedia*, n.d. www.newworldencyclopedia. org/entry/Albert_Schweitzer.

11 Leonard Gordon, "*Gandhi's Truth: On the Origins of Militant Nonviolence.* By Erik H. Erikson (New York: Norton, 1969)." *Journal of Social History* 4, no. 4 (July 1, 1971): 420–33. https://doi.org/10.1353/jsh/4.4.420.

12 "Benazir Bhutto," *Biography*, May 4, 2023. www.biography.com/political-figures/benazir-bhutto.

13 Nelson Mandela, *Long Walk to Freedom* (Boston, MA: Little, Brown & Co., 1994). https://en.wikipedia.org/wiki/Long_Walk_to_Freedom.

14 Thomas Johnson, Personal Interview, 2022.

15 Jeff Wallenfeldt, "Jacinda Ardern," *Encyclopedia Britannica*, History & Society, June 4, 2023. www.britannica.com/biography/Jacinda-Ardern.

16 Seth Mydans, "Thich Nhat Hanh, Monk, Zen Master and Activist, Dies at 95," *The New York Times*, January 29, 2022. www.nytimes.com/2022/01/21/world/asia/thich-nhat-hanh-dead.html.

17 "Chip Bergh, American Businessman," *Encyclopedia Britannica*, n.d. www.britannica.com/biography/Chip-Bergh.

18 Ibid.

19 "Hamdi Ulukaya," n.d. www.forbes.com/profile/hamdi-ulukaya/?sh=5ca753cc1405.

20 Bethany McLean and Peter Elkind, *The Smartest Guys in the Room: The Amazing Rise and Scandalous Fall of Enron* (New York: Penguin, 2013).

Chapter 10

Can you Identify, Select, and Develop Ethical Leaders?

Educating the mind without educating the heart is no education at all.

(Aristotle)

At various points throughout this book we discuss positive and negative examples of ethical or unethical leaders. For the sake of argument, let's take two examples: Rev. Dr. Martin Luther King Jr., the American civil rights leader, as a positive example, and Josef Stalin, the Russian despot, as a negative example. Further, let's assume you work for an organization that wants to hire leaders who will be ethical, and let us assume that King and Stalin both work for your organization. Could your talent identification system pick up differences between the two? Or, assuming both were candidates for a leadership position, could your selection system predict who would likely be the more ethical leader?

Can You Identify and Select Ethical Leaders?

As Aristotle notes and we discuss later in this chapter, developing ethical leaders and instilling ethical behavior is tricky—to put it mildly. Predicting that someone will be an ethical leader may be even more complex. The literature is replete with studies that strongly suggest that how one tests on matters of integrity or ethical behavior is not actually predictive of how one will behave on the job. A simple example probably proves the point. To become a member of the clergy in most, if not all, faith traditions, one must first pass a series of hurdles in which one's faith, beliefs, integrity, personality, and other factors are evaluated. It is a rigorous vetting by almost every measure. And yet, almost every faith can find instances of misbehavior among its clergy. While sexual misbehavior seems to make the news most frequently, there are numerous other examples of embezzlement, financial impropriety, etc.

DOI: 10.4324/b23260-14

Consequently, there are two critical questions that need to be attended to:

1. Can an organization of any type identify potential ethical leaders? Just as many business organizations have talent identification programs, typically to identify individuals with the potential to assume leadership roles in the organization, can an organization identify ethical leaders to assume positions of major responsibility?
2. Can an organization predict in their selection process who will be ethical leaders?

The answer to the above is a qualified "yes," in the sense that you can do both things—identify and select—but the outcome may be dependent on the organizational culture. We have made this point previously, but it bears repeating: to paraphrase Peter Drucker, "Culture will eat ethics for lunch." In simpler terms, I can be the most ethical leader in my organization, but if the culture does not support ethical behavior, then I probably fail as an ethical leader, unless I am able to shape the culture and change it. More on this in Chapter 11 which is devoted to culture.[1]

So, if the answer to the above questions is yes, how do we proceed?

Identifying Ethical Leaders

Identifying and selecting ethical leaders are built on the same premise: observing the behaviors ethical leaders exhibit. In Chapter 7, we suggested the following as the competencies or traits of an ethical leader, with an example of a behavioral anchor for each:

1. *Integrity.* We define integrity as Zenger and Folkman do. It is honesty combined with assertiveness. Integrity means that an individual must not only be able to speak the truth but is willing to do so in situations where he or she may be challenged. Integrity is speaking the truth without regard for consequences.

    1.1 Behavioral anchor: Supports his or her position on matters of right and wrong even when challenged by others.

2. *Courage/Willpower.* Willing to act on beliefs and values. Will stand up to authority or others when he or she believes a decision is ethically or morally wrong. Has the strength of conviction to act regardless of the potential consequences.

    2.1 Behavioral anchor: Stands up to leaders above him/her when they are ethically wrong.

3. *Trust.* Trust speaks to the ability to act in a consistent, predictable manner. Others can rely on your consistency of action and thought. Others can rely on you to honor commitments and promises. It also means taking personal accountability for mistakes and errors without blaming others.

   3.1 Behavioral anchor: Acknowledges when a mistake has been made either as an individual or as an organization.

4. *Fairness.* Treats others with concern and fairness. Focuses his/her thinking about decisions by strongly considering the impact of decisions on others to include all stakeholders. Treats others with fairness and balance. Does not play favorites but treats others in a consistent, caring manner. Places people above profits.

   4.1 Behavioral anchor: Treats everyone in a consistent, caring manner. Applies the same standards to all.

5. *Empathy.* Understands the concerns and feelings of others. Anticipates how they will respond to actions and decisions. Takes that into account and prepares for it.

   5.1 Behavioral anchor: Demonstrates an understanding of the concerns of others. Anticipates how they will respond.

6. *Moral mindset.* Demonstrates curiosity about the nature of right, wrong, and fairness. Goes beyond rules and procedures to ask, "What is right?" Acts on his/her view of what is right. Is aware of how others may perceive and judge the nature of right and wrong. Is not limited to organizational norms.

   6.1 Behavioral anchor: Provides a rationale for decisions and is curious about how others arrived at their decisions.

7. *Acts with transparency.* Shares his/her thinking, reasoning, and rationale for decisions openly with others. Shares factual data and information that does not violate any personnel privacy issues or concerns. Transparency builds trust and reliability in the eyes of others. Willing to share personal feelings and reactions as well.

   7.1 Behavioral anchor: Discloses his or her thoughts, rationale, and feelings in an open manner.

Notice in the above list that we are not listing beliefs, explicit creeds, or a definitive ethical code of behavior. Rather, we are focused on competencies that can be observed. We are looking at competencies based on what an ethical leader does, not what he or she believes. We also recognize that additional research may refine and add to this list of competencies.

We are focusing on the ethical factor in leadership. To truly identify and select ethical leaders, we would also have to look at some of the traditional competencies associated with leadership—you may be the most ethical person in the world, but you'll probably have minimal impact if you cannot influence or lead others effectively. Former US president Jimmy Carter might fall into this camp. By all accounts, he is a fine, ethical person, but he is generally considered an ineffective president due to his inability to inspire, motivate, and influence others. As we discuss various selection tools and approaches in the following pages, we are assuming that organizations are evaluating overall leadership potential while they are searching for ethical leaders.[2]

Intuitively, most of us use past behavior as a predictor daily. We shop at stores that have provided good service or products in the past, we eat at restaurants where we have had good experiences, and we probably stay friends with people who have in the past proven themselves to be fun, loyal, caring, etc. We also gain insight from past experiences friends and family have had.

In short, we all use this approach multiple times a day, on an almost unconscious basis.

In short—and this is used in many identification and selection systems—we believe past behavior or observed behavior in real time is the best predictor of who will or will not be an ethical leader.

Is past or observed behavior a perfect predictor? No—if there was a perfect predictor of success in any future endeavor, we would not be writing this book, as we would living off the royalties from our perfect prediction formula. Psychometric tests are imperfect no matter how statistically valid they are, interviews are imperfect predictors, and while past behavior is also imperfect, it is the most objective method available.

Put another way, if you were hiring someone to work for you, which would you prefer: to hear how someone *might* handle a situation, to hear how they *did* handle a situation, or to *see* them handle a situation in real time? Would you rather have someone tell you how fast they planned to run a marathon, learn about how fast they ran in previous marathons, or actually see them run one? Most people we know would opt for the latter two options as the best predictors of success.

We think you can identify and select ethical leaders using behaviors that are based on the competencies associated with ethical leadership.

How?

Many organizations around the world use some form of what is known as the "9 block" or some other matrix method for evaluating and identifying talent. While not a perfect process, the matrix approaches provide the ability to look at an individual's current performance and compare that to perceived potential. Most matrix models use some form of evaluating performance on one axis and evaluating potential on the other with the assumption being that those with the greatest potential and performance are the future leaders of the organization.[3]

With the matrix method as a framework, organizations use a range of tools to evaluate current performance and future potential, including:

- performance review data
- evaluations by department heads
- engagement surveys or 360 feedback
- development centers to obtain examples of observed behavior (you can find additional information on this concept in our discussion of selecting ethical leaders beginning on page xx).

Typically, the resulting data is presented to a group of senior leaders with a recommendation and discussion to confirm the evaluation. The amount of effort put into this process and the range of tools used vary widely, from an informal discussion to a sophisticated, extensive, and time-consuming process.

The new approach we are suggesting here is to add the element of ethical leadership explicitly to this process. The observed data may be imprecise at this point, as you may be dealing with younger people who are not as advanced in their careers. Still, simply making the question of ethics an overt part of the process can alter the mindset of the participants and the focus of the organization.

Let's explore this concept in a slightly different way. In the US, gun ownership is a right protected by the Constitution. However, with the dramatic upsurge in gun ownership (estimates suggest that there is at least one gun in circulation for every man, woman, and child in the US), and the tragic increase in shootings using semi-automatic weapons, gun control has become a contentious issue. In particular, the ownership of so-called "assault weapons," which are slightly adapted military combat rifles, has become a matter of widespread debate.[4]

The response of retail establishments that sell guns and assault weapons has been varied, and largely disappointing. Most retail stores have chosen to keep selling assault weapons and continuing with business as usual, typically arguing that they do not want to risk losing customers, and that owning guns is a legal right and an individual decision.

An exception to this trend has been Dick's Sporting Goods, a large retailer with over 850 stores and over 50,000 employees. Immediately after a mass shooting at a Florida high school, Dick's chairman Ed Stack banned the sale of assault weapons and high-capacity magazines in his stores and refused to sell any guns to anyone under the age of 21 (even those that can legally be purchased at age 18). In addition, he oversaw the destruction of over $5,000,000 worth of assault weapons in inventory, while continuing to call for additional controls on the sale of guns in the US.[5]

We think what Stack did is significant for a variety of reasons, but in the present context it is significant for how it can be applied to the identification of ethical leaders.

While Figure 10.1 shows a simple model, it reflects the point of the gun control story. Ethical leaders and potential ethical leaders have the moral courage to speak up on issues of importance beyond the scope of their specific organization, and you can observe that capacity in the potential leaders around you. Organizations can evaluate their potential ethical leaders using two axes: courage or moral courage, and overall orientation (i.e., metrics vs. the common good). While represented in quadrants, each is more accurately a continuum, where courage is defined by the willingness to speak up on

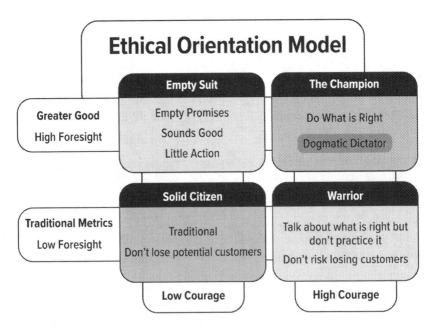

Figure 10.1 Ethical Orientation Model

issues, and overall orientation is defined by what people speak to—the organization's traditional metrics or ethical principles of doing the right thing.

Put another way, do the people you are evaluating for the future:

- speak up in meetings and other settings to share their point of view?
- challenge the decisions of others?
- speak up when they are in the minority?
- raise higher order questions about right and wrong?
- maintain their position when challenged?
- listen to the input of others?

Just as important is what they speak on or speak to. It is probably safe to speak to the traditional metrics—how do we increase profit, how can we better educate our students, or how can I reach more voters. Those who speak to traditional metrics fall in the bottom half of our model, whether they speak with little conviction or a great deal. To be clear, we are not opposed to many traditional metrics. Increasing profits or becoming profitable is crucial to the overall survival of the organization. At the same time, however, you can observe what a person speaks about or to, and how frequently and passionately they speak.

> To be clear: you have to have the moral courage to speak up to matters of right and wrong to be an ethical leader. Silence or second guessing and later criticizing a decision because it did not "feel" right is not moral courage. Moral courage is explicitly speaking out on a topic or demonstrating your position through your actions and behaviors.

Our model allows you to overlay ethical leadership on top of traditional measures of leadership potential which, in turn, raises expectations of enhanced ethical leadership throughout the organization.

Note as well that in addition to our four quadrants, we have added an additional category that we label as the "Dogmatic Dictator." As suggested in our chapter on political leadership, there is a shadow side of some archetypes, and we believe that can be the case in our model. There are individuals who have good or even excellent leadership skills which they combine with rigid, exclusionary ethical systems. These individuals tend to espouse a belief structure that clearly defines right and wrong, is prescriptive about expected behavior, *and* draws clear distinctions between "us" (those who share our beliefs) and "them" (anyone who does not share our beliefs).

Unfortunately, it does not take much effort to find examples of this phenomenon in our world, whether they be politicians, religious leaders, or business leaders. Take a moment to test the concept and see if you or your friends can identify such characters. We suspect that it will not take long for you to do so.

Systematically calling attention to ethical leadership changes the focus of the organization and potentially starts to change the culture. We will return to this concept in Chapter 11 on culture, where we look explicitly at those actions that can reinforce ethical behavior, or conversely those actions that can undermine an emphasis on ethics.

Selection

In the "old days," people were hired or promoted into leadership roles for a variety of reasons. They performed well in their current job (good salespeople would make good sales managers), they seemed to have the "correct" personality, they interviewed well, or perhaps they were a friend of the owner/boss. The list could go on forever, and some of those people were successful while others failed. Following World War II, during which both sides paid more attention to putting the right people in critical roles, the concept of a more systematic and objective approach to hiring began to take hold.

Currently, a good selection process will consist of one or more of the following components:[6]

- A structured interview. Usually consisting of a structured interview guide for the sake of consistency, with questions that elicit critical information. Approaches can include behavioral, situational, hypothetical, or other interview formats.
- Psychometric tests. Valid tests that measure factors such as personality, critical reasoning, and emotional intelligence, to name just a few.
- Simulations. These encompass a broad range of activities that are designed to replicate critical aspects of the target job and to allow the candidate to demonstrate behaviors associated with that job. Case studies, role plays, group discussions, and presentations are typically part of the simulation package.
- Multiple measurement points. Excessive reliance on one interview or one tool is a potential problem. Having multiple interviews and a variety of tools increases the objectivity and the likelihood of minimizing biases.
- Data integration. To mitigate the bias of any one-person, multiple people should be involved in reviewing the data and making a recommendation. While the hiring manager may have the final say, group processing improves the chances of making a good decision.

Given the above and recognizing that no selection system will be 100% accurate or predictive, can you design a system that will help you select ethical leaders? We think the answer is yes, assuming you follow these principles:

- Identify the individual behaviors that are critical to ethical behavior in your organization
- Focus on behavior, not creeds or beliefs
- Use questions or simulations where there is no right or wrong answer
- Use multiple perspectives.

Using the above as guidelines, what might a sample system look like? Below are some possibilities.

In Appendix A we have provided sample ethical leadership competencies and their behavioral components. There are a variety of ways to identify competencies and critical behaviors, ranging from surveys to focus groups and from simple to complex. We offer details in the Appendix as a guide, but it is not the intent of this book to go into the minutiae. For discussion purposes, we will assume the previously identified seven competencies as the basis for discussion.

Based on the above, a relatively simple system might look like the following:

- Two or three behavioral interviews conducted by different interviewers.
- A case study with a presentation to a group of observers. Usually, this is followed by questions by the observers and responses from the participant.
- An interaction simulation. Typically, this would be with the participant acting as the leader interacting with an employee, who would be portrayed by a trained role player.

Given the above, what might each component of the selection system consist of?

1. Behavioral interviews: As noted earlier, the behavioral interview would be a planned interview with specific questions, designed to elicit examples related to specific competencies. While sample interview questions are contained in Appendix A, examples of questions could include:

    1.1   Integrity: Please provide an example of a time when you confronted or disagreed with a decision your supervisor was making.
    1.2   Trust: What do you do to make people trust you? Please provide an example.

    1.3   Empathy: People vary widely. Give an example of someone who is different from you and how you took that into account when you interacted with them.

2. Case studies: In a case study, the individual is typically presented with a business scenario and asked to make a recommendation for a course of action. Most cases are written in such a way that there is no clear-cut right or wrong answer. Cases can be written so that moral dilemmas or ethically ambiguous choices are presented. From a competency perspective, this allows observers to evaluate a moral mindset, fairness, integrity, and courage, among others.
3. Interaction simulations (role plays): Simulations provide the opportunity to see how a candidate handles one-on-one situations. Typically, the participant is given some background information on a peer, boss, customer, or subordinate and given goals to accomplish in the discussion, with no clear definition of right or wrong courses of action. As with case studies, we would add elements of moral ambiguity into those discussions, which would allow observers to see the participant demonstrate empathy, fairness, courage, and moral mindset.

Again, of course, no system of selection is perfect. However, by raising the question of ethical behavior, observing opportunities to demonstrate ethical behavior, and simply paying attention to the issue of ethics, you can increase your chances of identifying ethical leaders and enhancing the ethical culture of your organization.

Developing Ethical Leaders

When we were children, most of us were raised with certain values. While those values may vary by culture, it is safe to assume that most children were raised to value honesty and telling the truth. Often, that value of honesty was also placed in the context of an ethical system such as, "Our family always tells the truth," or, "In our family, a person's word is their bond." Simple, concrete, and understandable—even for a child.

And if this is a common experience for most of us—being raised to value honesty or other similar values—why does our behavior sometimes change in adulthood? In other words, at a very basic level, we know what is right to do and we value that behavior, so why do we ever do otherwise? At the core of a book on ethical leadership lies the implicit assumption that you can develop ethical leaders or develop one's capacity for ethical leadership. But can you? Or better yet, can an organization develop ethical leaders? It is a critical question both for this book and for organizations that purport to be ethical.

This critical question has been debated since at least the time of Socrates, and opinions vary to this day. The nub of the question seems to fall in three areas:

1. **Personal Values.** Part of ethics is personal values. If ethical systems help instill beliefs about right and wrong, to some extent the nature of right and wrong is determined by personal values. Can you identify personal values? The answer seems to be yes. There are various approaches that are helpful for identifying personal values, prioritizing them, and putting them into an informative array. This is not to suggest that you can teach "values"; it is only to suggest that you can foster an awareness of values, which may help guide behavior. Teaching values is more problematic, as noted in the following comments on teaching ethics.[7]

2. **Teaching Ethics.** Can you teach ethics? This is where Socrates weighed in with his "yes," and many others have echoed his position. You can teach codes of conduct, standards of right and wrong, and conflicting systems of ethics, and you can test for comprehension of all of these. There seems to be little doubt that you can teach others a viewpoint of right and wrong (ethics) and test a person's understanding of that system of right and wrong. Indeed, you can go a step further and provide the individual with scenarios or dilemmas that are application based, to provide even greater insight into their understanding of right and wrong. Can an individual take their understanding of an organization's code of conduct and describe how it should be applied in a variety of situations? Again, yes.

   2.1 More and more universities are offering courses in either business ethics or ethical leadership. While the overviews of courses we have seen (admittedly not the entire universe of courses), there is not a lot of data to support those courses carrying over into ethical behavior in the workplace.

3. **Ethics and Behavior.** Here is where the rubber meets the road, and the answer becomes less clear: *Will an individual's understanding of a code of conduct/ethical system, or knowledge of specific values or virtues, result in him or her behaving in a manner that is consistent with that code?* In other words, will my understanding of an ethical system result in me behaving in an ethical manner? Think back to the opening example we used in this chapter on honesty as a refresher.

Let us look at an example for a moment. The Boy Scouts of America ask their scouts to take a simple oath, which states:

On my honor I will do my best to do my duty to God and my country and to obey the Scout Law:

to help other people at all times, to keep myself physically strong, mentally awake, and morally straight.

The Scout Law then goes on to enumerate twelve points or traits of Scouts, including being trustworthy, obedient, kind, and brave.[8]

Mind you, there is absolutely nothing wrong with this oath or the various laws of the Boy Scouts, just as there is nothing wrong with similar organizations that espouse various ideals or values. In fact, most of us would argue just the opposite: that these values are wonderful and should be a model for all. This is true of religious creeds, organization mission statements, or the oath of office for government officials. Their intent is admirable. *But they do not guarantee ethical behavior or action.*

The sad truth is that we can come up with all too many examples of ethical lapses in clergy, business leaders, politicians, and even leaders of the Boy Scouts. All too frequently, people who appear to be ethical make unethical choices. It does not work to simply educate people on ethics and expect that to translate into behavior change.

Why Do Ethical People Make Choices That are Unethical?

That brings us to an underlying question: Why do some otherwise ethical people make unethical choices, while others go through their lives with impeccable reputations and no negative actions? Some of this dichotomy may stem from personality or circumstances. Some people may be hardwired to always make ethical choices, or they may simply have never faced a situation that forced them to make hard choices with significant consequences, although we doubt that. For most people that may be true—they do not face circumstances that challenge their behavior, or they may be dualistic by nature that nothing challenges their absolute, black and white sense of right and wrong.

As a side note, we accept the fact that there are people who do terrible, often criminal, things. There are unethical, amoral individuals whose underlying personality allows them to behave unethically with no remorse or constraints. This book is not intended for them, and any change in their behavior will require a dramatic intervention that is beyond the scope of this book, and perhaps any book.

Still, the harsh reality is that many people—business leaders, clergy, politicians, or employees—who are otherwise ethical make poor choices. Carucci (2016) suggests several reasons why ethical people make unethical choices:[9]

- Organizations create environments where people are forced to make choices they would never have imagined otherwise.
- It is psychologically unsafe to speak up.

- There is excessive pressure to reach unrealistic performance targets.
- Conflicting goals create a sense of unfairness.
- A positive example is not being set.

Looking at it in a slightly simpler manner, Carucci essentially argues that three factors lead to unethical behavior: the culture does not support ethical behavior, performance goals encourage unethical behavior, and leaders do not provide a positive example. In other words, circumstances encourage otherwise ethical people to cut corners, act inappropriately, or make decisions that are unethical by any standard.

We agree.

We think people are fundamentally good, ethical, and honest, although given the circumstances of the day, we sometimes debate that proposition. Given the opportunity, most people will make ethical, honest decisions. But too often, the organizational environment forces them to make decisions that they normally would not have made.

What Can Be Done?

As we have suggested previously in this chapter, we are skeptical about any organization's ability to instill values and ethics through training. While we think traditional training is a building block and a necessary basis for organization ethics, it is not sufficient on its own. And, unfortunately, too many organizations assume that training alone is the answer. Too often, when misbehavior is observed, the organization blames the individual, saying, "We trained them not to do that." In a case like this, the organization has failed to recognize that training alone will not suffice.

Witness the recent #MeToo movement in the US, which saw a number of male sexual predators receive their comeuppance for their atrocious behavior. While we cannot prove it, our guess is that many of these individuals and their organizations went through trainings on sexual harassment, were subject to policies that forbade it, and at some level recognized that what they were doing was wrong, but they did it anyway.

Elsewhere, we have made the argument that hiring ethical leaders and creating an ethical culture is crucial, and we stand by that. However, we also believe there are other ways to encourage ethical behavior and ethical leadership. To put it simply, the problem with traditional training programs is that they are done in a controlled environment, deal with hypothetical situations, and give the participants ample time to process decisions and actions. Because the environment is safe and the scenarios are hypothetical, there are no real repercussions for poor decisions. Additionally (and this may be a good thing), the training is typically done in groups, so there is subtle pressure to conform and act appropriately. Training needs to occur, as everyone needs common information and understanding; however, simply conducting training does not ensure compliance or ethical behavior.[10]

So, what does that mean for developing ethical organizations and ethical leaders. There are several principles that are critical for any development program.

- There needs to be an openness to critical thinking and the freedom to challenge assumptions and decisions. That sounds easy and straightforward, but think about the ethical catastrophes that have been caused or enabled by individuals being unable to speak up and voice their disagreement.
- The program needs to be grounded in actual real-world ethical dilemmas a person or organization may face. Note: We use the term "program" broadly, as we recognize that different organizations will develop different approaches to the ethical process? We believe a suitable program would encompass the following:
  - A clearly articulated mission and values for the organization.
  - The designation of an individual as the Chief Ethics Officer.
  - A written compliance policy that explains the process and procedures for ethical behavior and decision making.
  - Appropriate training on the compliance policy and related topics (i.e., sexual harassment, anti-discrimination policies, etc.) to ensure that employees understand the organization's expectations.
  - Explicit protection for "whistleblowers" who come forward with accusations of inappropriate actions or unethical behavior.
  - Support systems that allow individuals and groups to explore ethical decisions and ethical dilemmas they face in their jobs.
- As much as possible, development needs to take place in real time, either before a decision is made or shortly after the decision as an "ethics review." Just as some organizations conduct loss reviews or similar post-event reviews, so should they conduct ethics reviews to capture learnings, mistakes, and positive experiences.

The program must have the involvement and support of leaders throughout the organization. Leaders must model openness to challenges and be able to both receive feedback and acknowledge mistakes when they occur.

Below are our suggestions:

1. **Traditional Training.** Whether in the classroom or virtually, there is a place for traditional classroom activities. Teaching such topics as compliance, ethical standards, and/or specific topic areas such as sexual

harassment or anti-discrimination is certainly relevant. Individuals in any organization need to be fully informed on expected standards of behavior and organizational norms. Testing to ensure understanding and comprehension of material is certainly meaningful as well.

We consider training to be a necessary precondition for a successful ethical culture, but we consider it insufficient as a stand-alone program. To use a university metaphor, training is an introductory course in ethics that should lead to further courses of study. We believe successful ethical development requires combining traditional training with one or more of the following structured approaches.

2. **Peer Ethics Coaching.** Within a department, peer group, or organization, appoint someone to serve as the ethics coach, perhaps different people on a rotating basis. The role of this individual would not be to pass judgment on decisions, but to challenge the thinking of his or her peers and ask questions. The peer ethics coach would be the designated ethical gadfly. Available for consultation, free to step in and observe or challenge, and given carte blanche to ask, "Is that the right decision?" on a regular basis.

The benefits of this approach can be significant.

- Acting as the ethics coach can be a significant developmental assignment, particularly for leaders who aspire to higher levels.
- The experience is an application of ethics. There is no better ethical development experience than having to challenge others on the ethics of their behavior and actions.
- The approach establishes and supports accountability for behaving ethically and is a visible manifestation of an ethical culture.
- Having more "localized" ethics coaches broadens an organization's approach to and concern with ethical behavior. Rather than relying on a Chief Ethics Officer or Chief Compliance Officer for answers on dilemmas, this approach forces decision making and thinking about ethical issues to lower levels of the organization.

3. **Ethical Study Groups.** University students often create informal study groups to pool their resources, gain additional understanding, and discuss the applications of the material they have been studying. The same approach has merit in the workplace, giving likeminded individuals the opportunity to engage in serious discussion of the ethical and moral issues facing their organization(s).

A program like this could and probably should have at least minimal support from the organization. The benefits to this approach are similar to those of the above options, but here we would also add:

- More time to study ethical issues in depth
- The benefit of having a group of individuals focusing on common ethical issues
- Simple numbers lead to a greater focus on ethics
- Greater ability to request discussions with senior leaders who are making daily ethical decisions.

4. **Ethics Mentors/Counselors.** Many organizations run formal mentoring programs in which high-potential leaders are assigned to an experienced leader who functions as their mentor. Likewise, in many organizations, there are individuals who serve as informal mentors based on their experience or organizational knowledge. We believe such programs should be expanded and formalized to include ethics mentors.
5. **Using Company Intranet or Newsletters to Discuss Ethical Issues.** Writing about an idea in company communications is a powerful means of reinforcing it. Having the CEO or principal leader write about an ethical issue or dilemma he or she faced, or having other senior leaders do the same, is an incredibly potent means of reinforcing an emphasis on moral behavior or doing the right thing.

Developing ethical leaders—or, for that matter, simply encouraging ethical behavior—is a complex task, as evidenced by the failures of some organizations noted previously, stunning ethical lapses in faith-based organizations, or the potential risk that ethical training efforts could turn into indoctrination or brainwashing. It is not an effortless process, even in the best of circumstances. At its core, ethical development requires an openness to critical thinking, diverse ideas, and the willingness to change one's mind. This may be a daunting goal if one considers the general lack of willingness to engage in dialogue and the black-and-white answers so many people rely on in the face of complicated problems.

Developing ethical leaders can be done, but it is a constant process of trial and error. At a minimum, as we have suggested, it requires various approaches and systematic reinforcement and discussion.

We believe that even the best ethical development systems do not exist in an organizational vacuum and will not automatically create or develop ethical behavior and leadership. As we discuss at other points in this book, the talent you select for your organization and the organizational culture you foster have a dramatic impact on ethical behavior at all levels.

Questions for Your Consideration

For aspiring leaders:

1. What does my organization do to encourage ethical leadership and ethical behavior?
2. What can I do to enhance my ethical and moral awareness? Can I put together a personal development plan to do so?
3. Where can I go in my organization or to whom can I go to receive mentoring and coaching on ethical issues I will face as a leader?

For leaders:

1. How can I model ethical leadership and behavior for my group?
2. Where can I get coaching on ethical leadership or developing an ethical culture in my organization?
3. What do I need to do in my department to encourage and develop ethical behavior?
4. What types of feedback do I need to provide to people to reinforce positive ethical behaviors?

For HR personnel:

1. Are we doing the right things to encourage and develop ethical behavior in our organization?
2. Are we doing all we can to develop people as ethical leaders?
3. Are we effectively identifying potential ethical leaders?
4. Are we selecting ethical leaders for future leadership positions?

Notes

1 Alternative Board, "'Culture Eats Strategy For Breakfast'—What Does It Mean?," Alernative Board Blog, April 26, 2021. www.thealternativeboard.com/blog/culture-eats-strategy.
2 Moira Warburton, "Factbox: Jimmy Carter's Biggest Challenges While President," Reuters, February 20, 2023. www.reuters.com/world/us/jimmy-carters-biggest-challenges-while-president-2023-02-20/.
3 "JOSSO 2 by Atricore," n.d. www.shrm.org/resourcesandtools/tools-and-samples/hr-qa/pages/whatsa9boxgridandhowcananhrdepartmentuseit.aspx.
4 Joseph Stepansky, "US Lawmakers Banned Assault Weapons in 1994. Why Can't They Now?" Al Jazeera (Gun Violence News), April 20, 2023. www.aljazeera.com/news/2023/4/20/us-legislators-banned-assault-weapons-in-94-why-cant-they-now.

5 Rachel Siegel, "Dick's Sporting Goods Overhauled Its Gun Policies after Parkland. The CEO Didn't Stop There." *Washington Post*, May 31, 2019. www.washingtonpost.com/business/economy/dicks-sporting-goods-overhauled-its-gun-policies-after-parkland-the-ceo-didnt-stop-there/2019/05/31/9faa6a08-7d8f-11e9-a5b3–34f3edf1351e_story.html.

6 Indeed Editorial Team, "17 Effective Employee Selection Methods To Consider," Indeed.Com, March 11, 2023. www.indeed.com/career-advice/career-development/employee-selection-methods.

7 The Center for Parenting Education, "Using Your Values to Raise Your Children," October 23, 2018. https://centerforparentingeducation.org/library-of-articles/indulgence-values/values-matter-using-your-values-to-raise-caring-responsible-resilient-children-what-are-values/.

8 Boy Scouts of America, "What Are the Scout Oath and Scout Law?" December 16, 2019. www.scouting.org/about/faq/question10/.

9 Ron Carucci, "Why Ethical People Make Unethical Choices," *Harvard Business Review*, September 7, 2017. https://hbr.org/2016/12/why-ethical-people-make-unethical-choices.

10 www.gallup.com/workplace/357113/hard-truths-ethics-compliance-training.aspx.

Chapter 11

Ethical Leadership and Organizational Culture

In a healthy ethical culture, an unethical person is not successful.

(Author unknown)

We hear terms like "company culture" or "organizational culture" frequently these days, particularly as organizations debate whether they will return to the office in the post-pandemic world. Usually, the term culture is brought up in the sense of "We have to maintain our culture, so we are coming back to the office," or some variation on that idea. This implies that culture is a shaping factor, in that it has an influence on the behavior of employees and is crucial for business success. Or, as the unknown author suggests, ethical cultures do not tolerate unethical behavior.

An organization or leader must have the appropriate culture in place if they expect their people to behave ethically. Ethics and culture tend to be addressed tangentially, if at all. For example, Kirk Hanson, the executive director of the Markkula Center for Applied Ethics, says that ethics-based organizations tend to adhere to the following best practices:[1]

1. Strong values statements
2. A well-crafted code of conduct
3. Leading by example (executive modeling)
4. Comprehensive ongoing ethics training
5. Integration of values into work processes
6. Establishment of a confidential reporting mechanism
7. Transparent investigative processes for ethics violations
8. Effective ethics governance
9. Periodic revisions of ethical standards
10. Unwavering focus on constant improvement.

Some of the above—values, leadership, and focus on constant improvement, for instance—may be elements of an organization's culture. Others

DOI: 10.4324/b23260-15

such as ethics training, reporting mechanisms, and a transparent process are more transactional or "check-the-box" statements that, while meaningful from a compliance perspective, may not reflect the organization's culture and its impact on ethical behavior. As we have stated elsewhere, we have no issue with compliance, ethical codes of conduct, or any of the programs that spring from ethics and compliance offices. Quite the opposite. Such programs serve as a necessary foundation for any organization to ensure that employees have the necessary information to behave ethically, and the reporting processes that are usually a part of such programs are crucial. For some employees, these measures alone will be enough to promote ethical behavior. If they understand the rules of the game, they will play by those rules and behave ethically.

However, as we have also noted elsewhere, an organization can have all the best compliance systems in place and check the boxes on all ten items mentioned above, while still having problems with people behaving unethically. It all comes down to culture.

We will talk more about this as we progress in our discussion of culture, but let us summarize several of our key positions relative to culture and ethical behavior:

- Culture is supreme. The culture of an organization will either support ethical behavior or discourage ethical actions, regardless of stated values, beliefs, or data provided by the compliance office or other leaders.
- An organization may have a unified culture that all employees subscribe to, but this overall culture may also consist of smaller subcultures comprised of different departments, office locations, or teams. While they are s subset of a general organizational culture, these subgroups may have radically different cultures than the organization as a whole. Many organizations will describe tension between different functional areas, i.e. differences between the sales group and production, which can be an artifact of different cultures. Likewise, multinational organizations may have subset cultures that reflect the norms and values of the local country.
- There are formal and informal aspects of an organization's culture. The formal aspects tend to be those statements and beliefs that are codified, overt, and public. The informal elements tend to be the stories, heroes, and anti-heroes that are exalted by the employees. While debatable, the informal culture as personified by the comment "that is not how we do things here" is more powerful than the values written on the wall.
- Leaders shape the culture. Leaders can intentionally change a culture by virtue of the visions they share, what they reward, etc. Of course, leaders can also undermine the intended culture through their actions or inactions.
- While leaders have a critical role in shaping the culture, everyone has a responsibility to maintain the culture as well.

Before diving into more detail, let us examine several examples of different cultures and their outcomes:

- In 1986, the USA's Challenger space shuttle blew up 73 seconds after launching, killing all aboard. The subsequent investigation of the accident discovered that several O-rings had malfunctioned and caused the explosion. More notably, it was revealed that the problem with the O-rings was a known issue among NASA engineers, but no one had been able to get the attention of senior leaders about the issue or raise the issue to a level that would lead to the cancellation of the launch. When qualified people do not feel they can bring a serious issue to the foreground, that is organizational culture at work.[2]
- In the time between 2015 and 2018, three US retailers—Nike, Levi Strauss, and Patagonia—each took a public stance on political or social issues that had the potential to alienate a portion of their customer base. Nike used a controversial American football player who had protested police brutality as the face of an advertising campaign; Patagonia took a public stand against President Trump's order to reduce the size of two national parks; and Levi Strauss came out in favor of gun control, making significant charitable donations to support those efforts. These three organizations, among many, have spoken publicly about their values and acted on those values in a way that had the potential to stoke controversy and impact profits. This too is culture at work.[3]
- In 2015, it was discovered that Volkswagen had modified the software in over 11,000,000 cars to falsify carbon-dioxide emission levels—yet the company's stated values included customer focus, respect, responsibility, and sustainability. This contradiction between actions and stated values led to the resignation of the CEO, Ferdinand Piech, and other moves, not to mention the lost confidence of the buying public. This is also culture at work.[4]
- In 1987, Paul O'Neill took over as CEO of the Aluminum Company of America (Alcoa). At the time, he announced (to much criticism) that his and Alcoa's sole focus would be on safety. O'Neill reasoned that if the company was focused on excellence in safety (something every leader and employee could support), then other aspects of Alcoa would become excellent as well. He turned out to be right. After creating a culture focused on safety, when O'Neill retired in 2000, Alcoa was worth five times what it had been when he took over, and its market capitalization had risen to over $27 billion. Meanwhile, Alcoa's plants and people became significantly safer. This is culture and focus.[5]

One of the reasons some people despair over the difficulty of linking the evaluation of an individual's ethics or integrity to actual behavior is that time and time again, the culture one works in either encourages ethical behavior or, through a variety of mechanisms, discourages ethical behavior. Some cultures plainly value ethical behavior and make strong statements to that effect, while others do quite the opposite. This chapter will explore that issue through a discussion of culture, key aspects of an ethical culture, the role of leadership in culture formation, and how one can change or redirect a culture that has gone awry ethically.

Defining Culture

We have all had the experience of walking into a place of business—it could be a restaurant, a dry-cleaning establishment, or a large corporate office—and having an almost immediate reaction to it. You might have a visceral reaction that suggests the place is cold, sterile, or unpleasant. Or, alternatively, you perceive it to be warm, inviting, and friendly. While these perceptions are based on multiple sensory inputs, such a reaction is a quick snapshot of that organization's culture. People who work there may experience it differently, but what you are experiencing is culture, nonetheless.

Likewise, one often hears the term "culture" used to describe different countries and communities. Our focus here is on organizational culture, whether the organization be a faith-based one, a school, or a business. This particular usage of "culture" originated with Deal and Kennedy's 1982 book *Corporate Cultures: The Rites and Rituals of Corporate Life*.[6] In their words, "Organizational culture is the collection of values, expectations, and practices that guide and inform the actions of all team members. Think of it as the collection of traits that make your company what it is." Kennedy and Deal suggest that there are six components of organizational cultures:

- *History.* What are the organizational traditions of the past, and how are those kept alive and honored, or ignored?
- *Values and beliefs.* What are the beliefs and values that are shared by members of the organization?
- *Rituals and ceremonies.* What brings us together, and what do we celebrate? It can be simple as the morning safety meeting or getting together for a beer after work on Fridays.
- *Stories.* What stories do people tell others about employees (good or bad), successes, or failures? Stories are a shared narrative about our values and beliefs.
- *Heroes.* Whose status is elevated or shared as a model for the values of the organization? Who is portrayed as heroic within the organization, and for what reason? Is it the salesperson who made a big sale, or the warehouse person who went the extra mile to get an order from a customer, or the person who consistently greets others with a smile?

- *The cultural network.* Here, Deal and Kennedy delve into the informal network and the roles various people play in how cultural information and norms are shared or subverted.

Johnson and Scholes discuss similar concepts in *The Cultural Web,* proposing six key elements of corporate culture: stories, rituals and routines, symbols, organizational structure, control systems, and power structures.[7] Others have since suggested additional cultural benchmarks such as purpose, values, behaviors, and recognition.

Similarly, according to Albert Pierce, director of the Institute for National Security Ethics and Leadership, the most ethical organizations develop four abilities in their employees: moral awareness, moral courage, moral reasoning, and moral effectiveness.[8]

As we move toward specificity on the variables at play in an ethical culture and how to shape that culture, let us stop for a moment and talk about measurement.

Measuring Culture

In our earlier chapter on selecting ethical leaders, we wrote about the competencies and behavioral anchors one could use to evaluate potential ethical leaders, on the premise that one could interview or observe those competencies. We take the same approach to culture. Culture should be as measurable and objective as possible. Otherwise, how can we determine the state of a given culture, how it varies over time, or where a leader needs to focus his or her energies? Consequently, in the next section, we lay out our approach to the specific variables that make culture measurable.

Any measurement of the ethical status of a culture needs to take several factors into account, assuming that individuals will respond anonymously to a survey:

- Demographic data must be collected so that analysis can be conducted at all leadership levels, employee level, and by location or department.
- Confidentiality needs to be maintained and privacy protected.
- Group and aggregate data need to be analyzed at each level as well as the total organization.

Quantification and actionable results are crucial. It is all too common to hear exaggerated, glowing descriptions of organizational cultures from those organizations' recruiters or senior leaders. To create an ethical culture, a leader needs concrete data to identify gaps and reinforce progress.

While measurement is crucial, we are discussing intangible variables that are dependent on individual perceptions. In this case, the adage that perception is reality serves as our basis for measurement. The gaps that exist between perceptions at various levels of an organization are crucial to both defining ethical culture and developing a plan to improve or sustain it.

Variables of an Ethical Culture

Most, if not all, of the efforts to define the variables of an ethical culture come from a compliance perspective. In other words, they tend to have a law-and-order bias, where the variables you are analyzing relate to upholding the letter of the law and reflect something of a dualistic perspective, where right and wrong are absolutes. As you have no doubt gathered if you have read our book to this point, we take a different approach. Fundamentally, we believe in an approach we shall call "process ethics" where the cultural variables are more about enabling people to discuss right and wrong than they are about defining right and wrong.

What does this mean? At its simplest, it means that two organizations may espouse wildly different beliefs about right and wrong, but if they both go about defining those beliefs through open, transparent discussion, they can both be counted as ethical cultures. Let's look at two examples:

1. Hobby Lobby. Hobby Lobby is a privately owned US-based company that offers a range of supplies for home crafters and hobbyists. The firm is explicitly Christian in orientation and is very transparent about this. They are closed on Sundays; they refuse to carry Halloween supplies, due to the holiday's non-Christian history; and they oppose being forced to provide contraceptive care for employees, as abortion is against the company's principles.[9]
2. Amazon. The American retail giant has long had explicit core values and beliefs which it purports to act on consistently. When the US Supreme Court ruled against abortion, Amazon almost immediately opted to provide funding for its employees who were affected by the ruling by subsidizing travel for abortion and offering contraception access as well.[10]

At face value, the two organizations could not be more diametrically opposed. In the US, one would be considered liberal and the other conservative. One is open all the time and one closes on Sundays and Christian holy days. Furthermore, they are diametrically opposed on social justice issues such as abortion. Still, from an ethical process perspective, one can argue that their approaches are strikingly similar. Both have very clear missions and explicit values that they consistently act on, even when the action risks offending customers. They are willing to demonstrate their respective values in the marketplace, even at the risk of losing revenue, while making no apologies about who they are as an organization and what they believe in. While we may (and do) have strong feelings about which approach is more appropriate, from a strictly process perspective, they are very similar and appear to have clearly defined cultures.

Before delving into the variables of a culture that affect ethical behavior, we must consider the distinction between the formal aspects of a culture and its informal aspects. We define the formal aspects to include those written statements of belief that define the organization, the formalized aspects of reward and recognition, and those rituals that are embedded in the fabric of the organization. These can include mission statements, values, compensation plans, performance management systems, and such events as annual meetings or other regularly scheduled gatherings.

As Deal and Kennedy note, the informal aspect of organizational life has to do with how information about norms, values, and expected actions are transmitted. Much of the "informal network" Deal and Kennedy discuss is built on stories or tribal knowledge. The ethical culture an organization creates in these informal ways can either reinforce or undermine what it formally states about its values. Think of your own experience in your chosen field. Most of us went through some form of training to prepare us for our job where we were exposed to the organization's values, purpose, mission, history, etc., with the best of intentions. The organization wanted us to be good tribal citizens and so did most of us. We want to be valuable contributing members of our organization. And then we went out to our jobs, where all the training we had received and all the expectations we had been provided with were either supported or subverted, or some combination of the two.

That is the informal aspect of culture at work, and, in many ways, it is the more powerful aspect in the shaping of behavior and action. After all, who wants to be an outlier, a naysayer, or the person parroting upper management's perspective? We want to get along with our coworkers, and most of us adapt to that standard. This is certainly true as it relates to ethical behavior and actions. We may believe something our company is doing is unethical, but will we speak up when no one else does? We may engage in unethical behavior because everyone else does or because it is what one needs to do to be successful, but will we stop that behavior or confront others who are engaged in the same behavior? Probably not, although many organizations have created "whistle blower" protection programs to address that specific issue.

An Example

One of us was in sales for a period of time, selling into a very large multinational firm. As part of his work, he read everything he could on the company, pored over its annual reports, subscribed to periodicals that covered the industry, and toured manufacturing plants. As a result, he could quote the organization's values, describe its mission, and outline the company's organization chart. He also understood the company's formally stated needs, decision-making process, and purchasing procedures. He was generally successful with that approach.

However, when he began to seek coaching from some of his contacts on who to talk to, who the decision makers and influencers were, and how the buying process really worked, his sales took off. In other words, gaining insight into the company's *informal* culture and procedures was what led to multi-million-dollar success.

Below, we outline the variables that we think constitute an ethical culture. Each variable contains a definition and two more sample statements (written as if someone was responding to a survey) that illustrate the definition. More sample items on each variable are contained in Appendix B:

Focus. Focus is defined as the organization's orientation to the external world. Some organizations are internally focused on what happens within their facilities or teams. Other organizations may look to doing right by the external world (community, country, climate, etc.), while still others may look inwardly and focus on doing what is right by their stakeholders, customers, and/or employees. Most organizations are probably a blend of these orientations, but they will likely have a dominant focus that drives behavior and action.

- Leadership is primarily concerned with our performance relative to profit and loss.
- The leadership of my organization consciously considers the needs of our local community.

In our chapter on selecting ethical leaders, we drew the distinction between those that focused on traditional metrics (i.e., profit and loss, number of new members, etc.) and those that focused on the "greater good." That becomes an additional aspect of focus. Those organizations that are focused solely on metrics are less likely to be seen by members of the organization as ethical.

Consistency. Does the organization act in a manner that is consistently congruent with its stated values, mission, or objectives? In other words, does the formal stated culture match up with the actual actions that the organization and its leaders take? This can be summed up in the classic admonition, to "walk the talk."

- The leaders in my organization act in a manner that is consistent with the written values of our organization.
- Our compensation system reflects our values and supports making the right decision.

Consistency may be one of the most significant factors in developing or maintaining an ethical culture. A lack of consistency can lead to perceived hypocrisy. If members of an organization perceive its management to be hypocritical, trust and credibility begin to erode.

You can also think of this as a mathematical formula, where ethical culture is the numerator and perceived hypocrisy is the denominator (see Figure 11.1).

The greater the PH, the lower the EC. In other words, let us arbitrarily use a five-point scale where 5 is high and 1 is low, and let us say that the Actual Ethical Culture (AEC) is a 5. How high the AEC is depends on how low the PH value is. If the PH is 1, then the overall ethical culture score is 5. While alternatively, if the PH is 5 then the overall actual ethical culture score is 1. If the ethical culture is 5 and PH is 2, then the overall AEC is 2.5.

Transparency. Often discussed but infrequently practiced, transparency is critical to ethical culture. By transparency, we mean that information, rationale for decisions, and good and bad news are shared openly with all employees and stakeholders. This includes the willingness to admit mistakes and, where necessary, to apologize and make amends. This relates to trust as well, as it is hard to trust leaders who withhold information.

- Management openly shares financial results with all employees and other stakeholders.
- My leader admits when he or she makes mistakes and apologizes for them if appropriate.

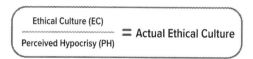

Figure 11.1 Actual Ethical Culture

Certainly, there are limits to transparency, as certain matters need to remain confidential for legal or moral reasons. No one needs to share personal, private information unless they choose to. However, as a rule, we believe an "open book" approach to information works best, and, more importantly, withholding information leads to mistrust, rumors, gossip, and other negative situations that impact the culture.

Openness to disagreement. While openness to disagreement typically gets the most attention in boss/subordinate relationships, it also applies in peer-to-peer discussions. Can I express disagreement with a decision, change, or action without fear of repercussions or recrimination? At the core of this is an atmosphere of mutual respect, where anyone can disagree with another without regard to rank or position when discussing ethical matters. Giving and receiving feedback effectively tends to be a skill associated with this variable.

- I can disagree with a decision my leader has made without fear or concern.
- My peers can tell me that they disagree with an action I am taking.

Too often, organizations or leaders state that they are open to disagreement until someone actually disagrees with them. However, if you are going to have a transparent organization that shares information and reasoning, you must be willing to accept disagreement, particularly if you espouse the notion that multiple inputs are important to a better outcome. This variable implies that whistleblower policies protecting individuals who call attention to ethical issues are probably a good idea.

Orientation to safety. We approach orientation to safety with an eye toward both physical safety and psychological safety. This variable relates to such concerns as sexual harassment, diversity, and inclusion to name just a few. Are my leaders concerned with my overall safety, and do my peers look after one another's safety? While in some ways related to openness to disagreement, orientation to safety focuses on the well-being of everyone in the organization.

- People speak up when they see someone treated in an inappropriate manner.
- My leader demonstrates his or her concern for my safety daily.

Orientation to safety also relates to consistency, as most organizations have printed material in employee handbooks and bulletin boards on the wall stating their views on safety related matters. What the rank-and-file members of the organization typically evaluate in this area, however, is the actual behavior of the leaders of the organization. Does the leader hold true safety briefings at the beginning of each shift? Does the leader confront instances of sexual harassment or bullying? This is a distinct area where actions speak louder than words.

Leader concern. This is a top-down variable perceived most accurately by those lower in the organization. Leader concern addresses two issues: does leadership in my organization care about me as an individual, and are we treated fairly by leadership (this references a concept typically referred to as procedural justice). Wanting to be treated as an individual (i.e., I need time off to take my sick child to the doctor) does not contradict being treated fairly. An individual can believe that exceptions should be made for them and believe that standard should apply to all. It becomes a contradictory concept when different people receive different treatment in similar situations.

- My leader recognizes when I have personal concerns and addresses those concerns.
- Everyone in my group is treated the same way. Leadership does not play favorites.

Leader concern answers the question of whether I am treated as a unique human being. At a basic level, leader concern looks at whether my leader knows me—my needs and wants, my family situation, or what my hopes and aspirations are.

Heroes and villains. This is the storytelling (how people describe the heroes and villains of the organization) variable with a twist. Most organizations tell stories about their heroes and heroines, so to speak, which is a great way to provide information on the culture. In other words, which of its members does the organization exalt? Relative to defining an ethical culture, who one describes as a villain or antagonist is just as important. This does not only apply to competitors but is also applicable if an organization tends to cast external regulators, the government, or some other person or body as the enemy when they narrate the group's story.

- I regularly hear stories about people in our organization who have acted in a way that is consistent with our values.
- We tend to demonize people outside our organization.

This concept is related to two aspects of Deal and Kennedy's work—storytelling and the informal network—with two differences. First, what kind of behavior is made heroic? We often make heroes out of people who go the extra mile, but some organizations may make heroes out of someone who cut corners or lied to beat a competitor to a sale. What you lionize makes a difference. Likewise, who you describe as villains, if anyone, makes a difference. If your compliance group spends a great deal of time and energy making sure the organization is behaving legally and, at the same time, leaders spend a great deal of time complaining about government oversight or taxes, the contradiction is telling.

Rewards and recognition. This variable is closely related to consistency. Much like the storytelling variable, the rewards and recognition variable may contradict the stated values of an organization. While we may state that we value integrity in all we do, the organization may reward results without concern for integrity.

- People in my group are recognized for doing the right thing.
- Financial rewards are tied to living our values on a daily basis.

The most obvious example of this tends to be those behaviors tied to compensation. Does your compensation system reward ethical behavior or encourage cutting corners to meet compensation goals? For a superb and disturbing discussion of this issue, read the book *The Smartest Guys in the Room*.[11] It depicts the rise and fall of Enron, where the system ran amok as people raced to make money with little or no accountability.

Decision making. This factor speaks to how decisions are discussed and what rationale is provided when decisions are announced. The ethical organization discusses whether a decision is right or wrong, beyond whether the decision will be beneficial to the organization. Specifically, it asks, when we are making decisions, do we talk about what is right for our employees, what is right for our community, and what is right morally?

- My leader shares the moral reasoning behind decisions.
- My team discusses whether an action is right or wrong.

Fundamentally, we do not believe an organization can consider itself truly ethical if its decision making never goes beyond the bottom line or compliance. In the narrow sense, it may be ethical, but in the broader sense, it can ignore implications to society, the environment, or the community while considering itself to be ethical.

How Leaders Change Their Culture

Changing an organization's culture is a complex process that does not happen overnight. Change takes concentrated effort over time, and this is particularly true when one is endeavoring to change the culture into something radically new. For our purposes in this section, we have made three critical assumptions:

1. Leaders change the culture. The culture of an organization is the responsibility of its senior leadership. While lower-level leaders and team members have a responsibility to be good citizens of their organization,

senior leaders drive the culture. No culture will change without the commitment and direction of the senior leaders.

   Note: Leaders who oversee small groups or departments within a larger organization can certainly create their own team culture. However, for our purposes, we are focusing on the overall organization, and in that case, senior leaders do drive the culture.

2. While the term toxic culture is not synonymous with an unethical culture, there has been much written on toxic cultures and how to change that is applicable to unethical cultures.[12]

3. As we note elsewhere, transparency is a given in an ethical culture. Therefore, we assume every step of the process should be publicized to the entire organization. For the sake of simplicity, we have eliminated any overt discussion of transparency in each subsequent step, but we assume the actions on each step will be publicized to the entire organization.

The Culture Change Fishbowl

Congratulations—you have decided that you want your organization to be an ethical one. Now think of yourself as fish swimming in a fishbowl, watched by everyone else in your organization. Because that is what it will be like—your every action will be scrutinized, evaluated, and critiqued by those watching you swim in the bowl.

Form a Steering Committee

Ultimately, the leader is responsible for culture change. The leader of any organization is the single most powerful voice providing a direction and vision, along with the will to make the vision a reality. However, success also requires the commitment and input of many others; to that end, we recommend the formation of a steering committee to guide culture change on a day-to-day basis.

   A steering committee should be comprised of a cross-section of employees including leaders, different functions, and all levels of the organization, totaling no more than ten members. The steering committee should be charged with developing plans, monitoring progress, and identifying barriers to success, and it should be in regular communication with the organization's leader.

Measure the Current Culture

It is crucial to identify the status of the current ethical culture, establish a baseline, and identify the gaps in the current ethical culture. Without data, organizations are relying on subjective opinions, which are biased toward expected outcomes. We favor a survey approach to measuring the ethical culture; as quantitative results are provided, you can compare year-over-year data, and shorter "pulse" surveys are possible. But other forms of measurement can be used as well. Among these are:

- Structured interviews conducted by an external third party to provide objectivity.
- Focus groups comprised of randomly selected employees, conducted by trained facilitators.
- Observations by a skilled team of behavior analysts.

Before moving on to action steps, several additional words of potential caution are in order. First the journey toward either creating an ethical culture or sustaining one (i.e., if it is already effective and needs to be maintained as such) means that leaders have to model and practice ethical behavior as part of the process. This means:

- The data must be shared in an open and transparent manner, whether the news is good or bad. It must be shared consistently and transparently in an ongoing process.
- The data must be treated as the "truth" even when it goes against generally held perceptions or is contrary to what senior leadership wants it to be. There may be a million and one reasons why the data shows what it does, but this is not the time for excuses.
- As much as is possible, the results must be shared with all employees, preferably in person. Leaders need to be seen as committed to the change in the culture.
- If there are areas that need improvement, share these specifically, even if they are painful (e.g., if the data suggests that employees think senior management is not open to disagreement).
- There needs to be a commitment to sharing action plans once the data is fully analyzed and digested.

Identify Critical Gaps

There is a tendency in any change effort to try and do too much, too fast. That leads to disconnects, frustration, and resistance. Any effective culture change effort—particularly one centered on ethics—needs to be focused on two or three key gaps that will bring the greatest return on effort and the greatest chance for sustainability over time. Taking the time to identify the crucial gaps revealed by the data and developing a focused plan for those gaps is crucial. While seemingly a simple idea, several thoughts are in order:

- Involve employees at all levels in the process of identifying gaps. This is crucial particularly when there are differences in perceptions of the culture between levels. Remember that leadership may be seen as part of the cultural problem. Involving leaders and others at all levels will build buy-in and commitment in moving forward.
- While it is almost trite to say, focus on those gaps that are the easiest to close first. Build success and sustainability before diving into the more complex gaps that require substantial time and effort.

Change the Focus to Ethics

For any organization to be successful, it needs to meet its core metrics (profits earned, students educated, new members gained, etc.). That is a given. However, with the importance of metrics as a given, changing the ethical culture requires an additional focus. Look again at the story about Alcoa and Paul O'Neill at the beginning of this chapter, as here we are suggesting a focus very similar to O'Neill's. If a leader truly wants to change his or her organizational culture to a more ethical one, it requires the same level of focus that O'Neill placed on safety at Alcoa. Every meeting, every interaction, every decision needs to address the underlying emphasis on "are we doing the right thing?"

You may believe that the above is overly simplistic or even irrational (among the kinder words one could use), so let us spend a few moments reflecting on the possible outcomes associated with a focus on doing the right thing. Here is what happens if you take this approach:

1. You have simplified your message and you have provided something everyone can understand.
2. You have to hold yourself accountable for being ethical. It's hard to tell others to be ethical if you are not modeling that as a leader.
3. Leaders at all levels have to become more transparent, open to disagreement, and caring toward their people in order to model the expected ethical orientation and behavior.
4. Employees are treated as if they matter and become more engaged in the direction of the organization.

On a practical day-to-day basis, there should be an ethics briefing at the start of each day where people are recognized and celebrated for making the right ethical decision, and leaders talk about decisions they have made in terms of right and wrong—not just in terms of profit. If you can include a safety briefing as part of every meeting, you can include an ethics briefing as well.

Commit to Consistency

As noted previously, lack of consistency leads to perceived hypocrisy. It is imperative that the leaders of an organization who are dedicated to changing the ethical culture behave in a way that is consistent with both the organization's values and the objectives of the culture change effort. Leaders need to model the expected behaviors, reinforce adherence to the expectations, and transparently call out lapses in consistency. In short, the leaders of an organization need to "walk the talk" on a daily basis.

> One of the paradoxes of ethical leadership is that some of the great moral leaders of history have not been paragons of moral behavior in their personal lives. Consistent leaders do not have to be saints, but they need to recognize that all aspects of their behavior will be under ethical scrutiny. And they need to be prepared to deal with lapses openly and transparently.

Consistency is driven by leaders at all levels and may be the most critical role they fulfill in a culture change effort. Efforts to change the ethical landscape are doomed if others in the organization do not see commitment and consistency on the part of their leaders.

Align Systems

There are at least two organizational systems that need to be carefully examined to ensure that what they measure and reward is consistent with an ethical culture: the performance management system and the compensation/bonus structure. Without conscious alignment of these systems, culture change can be derailed. Too often, there is a disconnect between the stated values and what is rewarded. The classic example of this is an organization that says it values integrity and treating customers with respect, but rewards its salespeople for the volume of business they bring in, regardless of the methods they use.

At a minimum, the following should occur:

• The performance management system needs to measure individual congruence with ethical behavior. In other words, there needs to be at least one key performance indicator (KPI) that is directly linked to ethical thinking and ethical behavior. Did someone make the right ethical decision? Did they challenge our ethical thinking? Did they engage with others on ethical dilemmas and share their thinking with others?

- Similarly, the compensation system needs to be aligned with ethical expectations, particularly when it comes to bonuses. Individuals should have a portion of their bonus tied to their ability to consistently behave in an ethical manner.

- For organizations that have some formal means of recognition—whether it be a monetary reward or public recognition—what is recognized needs to be carefully examined. Many organizations provide recognition for individuals or teams who have gone above and beyond expectations or who made major contributions to the success of the organization, and we support that concept. Simply put, however, in the context of creating an ethical culture, those individuals or teams who have modeled ethical behavior, made difficult decisions, or acted in other ways the organization was encouraging need to be recognized in the same manner.

Model the Expected Behaviors with Transparency

If leaders are serious about building an ethical culture (and we suspect many are), then they certainly need to model the behaviors they expect from others, as we have noted previously. The difference in building an ethical culture is that they need to be absolutely transparent and open about what they are doing and why. In other words, leaders need to name the behaviors they are modeling overtly and clearly to others.

In effect, leaders need to become both models of expected behaviors and commentators on their own behavior. Think of it as if you are watching a football game on TV. Typically, there is an announcer who describes the action and an analyst who discusses strategy, why plays did or did not work, and what the team was trying to do. Leaders need to become both the announcer, when they share a message, and the analyst, when they describe what they were attempting to do and why.

Think for a moment about how powerful it can be if you, as a leader—after sharing a message, having a coaching session with an employee, or leading a meeting—step back and spend a few minutes doing three things: (1) sharing with others what you were attempting to do and why, (2) asking for their feedback on what you were trying to do, and (3) asking for suggestions about how you could improve.

What is the impact of that action on others and what messages does it communicate?

Align, Coach, or Eliminate Toxic Leaders

Coaching and feedback on supporting an ethical culture will be crucial for leaders at all levels of the organization. We believe that most people and most leaders inherently want to do the right thing. So coaching and giving feedback to those individuals is a simple matter of giving them permission to do that, and most will respond positively.

However, not all leaders can demonstrate the behaviors necessary to lead in an ethical culture, and some leaders—hopefully very few—are amoral, unethical, or uncaring. Employees generally know who these "leaders" are, and how these people are dealt with during a culture change will be watched carefully.

Dealing with potential terminations is an ethical issue, in that most leaders want to be fair, respectful of the individual, and provide opportunities for corrective action. We generally agree with that approach, with the exception of a leader who behaves unethically. That should be a zero-tolerance situation and an unethical leader should be removed from the organization immediately.

Dealing with ethically toxic leaders has a great deal to do with consistency. Others in the organization will watch very carefully how these individuals are handled as a measure of how serious senior leadership really is about culture change.

Track and Report Progress

Progress on establishing an ethical culture should be reported to the organization on a regular basis, including successes and failures. Preferably this should be done via a format that allows for questions and dialogue, although that may not always be possible. In conjunction with these organization-wide communications, we recommend conducting periodic "pulse" surveys of the organization that focus on the specific gaps that are being addressed by the steering committee. While we are sensitive to the dangers of survey fatigue, having concrete data that shows progress or a lack of progress is important.

Celebrate Success

In conjunction with reporting progress, the organization should also periodically stop and celebrate successes. We recommend that this takes the form of celebrating individuals who have made significant ethical decisions or who have acted with integrity against the odds. Being specific about those stories—what the person did, what was different about it, and why it is important—goes a long way toward making change occur.

Plan for Sustainability

Too often, culture change is seen as having an end point; instead, it should be recognized that any change effort is the starting point in a cyclical process. Even if great progress has been made, the critical question becomes, "How are we going to sustain that progress and maintain our new ethical culture?"

Obviously, beginning to work on additional gaps is one way to sustain a change, as it allows for continued focus and attention on the culture. Another way is continuing to recognize and reward ethical behavior, and ongoing leadership attention to the culture is a third.

The steering committee needs to plan for and monitor ethical culture on a continual basis in order to sustain the change.

Summary

If you are successful in changing your organization's focus on ethics, what happens? A lot, not all of which is predictable; however, at a minimum, the following will likely occur:

- Employee satisfaction and engagement will go up. People want to work in an organization that is transparent and does the right thing for the employees, the larger community, and the environment.
- If engagement goes up, so will retention and productivity. There is a lot of research correlating high engagement with improved performance on traditional metrics.
- Focusing on the ethical culture will improve your standing in the local community. People notice when you are contributing to your community and your employees are committed to the direction of your organization.
- You will gain customers or members. While it may be slow, people notice when you practice what you preach.
- At the end of every day you can go home knowing that, while it might not have been perfect, you and your organization did the right thing and made ethical decisions.

Questions to Ponder

1. Do you think your organization's culture is ethical? Why or why not? What needs to be done to sustain the culture or improve it?
2. Are our leaders transparent? Do they model the expected behaviors, etc.?
3. Do we celebrate people behaving ethically? Conversely, are those that behave unethically dealt with?

4. Do we measure or evaluate our culture on a regular basis? Do we track year over year performance?
5. Do our senior leaders hold open discussions about the culture and welcome input and suggestions?

Notes

1 Anne Federwisch, "Toward an Ethical Culture: Characteristics of an Ethical Organization," Markkula Center for Applied Ethics, Santa Clara University, n.d. www.scu.edu/ethics/focus-areas/business-ethics/resources/toward-an-ethical-culture/.
2 The Editors, *Encyclopaedia Britannica*, "Challenger Disaster," *Encyclopedia Britannica*, History & Society, January 14, 2009. www.britannica.com/event/Challenger-disaster.
3 Jim Mintz, "Brand Activism the Breakthrough Concept in Marketing Revisited," Center of Excellence for Public Sector Marketing (CEPSM), October 26, 2018. https://cepsm.ca/brand-activism-the-breakthrough-concept-in-marketing-revisited/.
4 Russell Hotten, "Volkswagen: The Scandal Explained," BBC News, December 10, 2015. www.bbc.com/news/business-34324772.
5 David Burkus, "How Paul O'Neill Fought For Safety At Alcoa," David Burkus (blog), April 28, 2020. https://davidburkus.com/2020/04/how-paul-oneill-fought-for-safety-at-alcoa/.
6 Terry Deal and Allan Kennedy, *Corporate Cultures: The Rites and Rituals of Corporate Life* (New York: Basic Books, 2000).
7 Gerry Johson and Kevan Scholes, "The Cultural Web," 1992. www.mindtools.com/a8im94b/the-cultural-web.
8 Margaret Steen, "Building and Nurturing an Ethical Culture," Markkula Center for Applied Ethics, Santa Clara University, n.d. www.scu.edu/ethics/focus-areas/business-ethics/resources/building-and-nurturing-an-ethical-culture/.
9 Hobby Lobby. "Our Story—Hobby Lobby Newsroom," n.d. https://newsroom.hobbylobby.com/corporate-background#:~:text=Core%20Values&text=Honoring%20the%20Lord%20in%20all,strengthen%20individuals%20and%20nurture%20families.
10 Jeffrey Dastin, "Amazon to Reimburse U.S. Employees Who Travel for Abortions, Other Treatments," Reuters, May 2, 2022. www.reuters.com/business/retail-consumer/amazon-reimburse-us-employees-who-travel-treatments-including-abortions-2022-05-02/.
11 Bethany McLean and Peter Elkind, *The Smartest Guys in the Room: The Amazing Rise and Scandalous Fall of Enron* (New York: Penguin, 2013).
12 Donald Sull, "How to Fix a Toxic Culture," *MIT Sloan Management Review*, September 28, 2022. https://sloanreview.mit.edu/article/how-to-fix-a-toxic-culture/.

Section IV

Thoughts for the Future

Chapter 12

The Future of Ethical Leadership

Sneaking a Peek into the Rabbit Hole

It ain't what you don't know that gets you into trouble. It's what you know for sure that just ain't so.

(Mark Twain—writer, humorist, entrepreneur)

Throughout the process of working on this book, we have been asked why we think the subject of ethics in conjunction with leadership is relevant. This is a somewhat poignant question we have asked ourselves, too. Does ethical leadership matter? If so, on what grounds? What is ethical leadership's merit? Is it a discipline and mindset that can be translated into real behavior, pragmatic decisions, and strategies both personal as well as entrepreneurial? Since it is always individuals who constitute interconnected systems (as in organizational frameworks and networks) that may collide and produce paradoxes, is it a futile endeavor trying to navigate complex organizations with the greater good in mind? Isn't this mission even more futile amidst an ocean of conflicting interests and corporate motives? Numerous times we have asked ourselves whether or not our research originates from our backgrounds in theology, philosophy, politics, and HR management and represents some sort of vain navel gazing.

To cut right to the chase: yes, we do believe this book is a navel-gazing one. We do believe this book naturally has a lot to do with what we believe in and work toward every single day. However, there is a clear transpersonal twist to our take on ethical leadership as well. The fields of ethics and business ethics are concerned with the greater good to be pursued. So, the subject matter is of importance for each and every one of us. The average person will most probably spend 90,000 hours at work over a lifetime as industrial-organizational psychologist and data scientist Andrew Naber found in his research.[1] That is roughly 10.2 years. Against this background, it is the obligation of leaders to make the workplace as ethical, dignified, and purposeful as possible. Organizations, employers, and professional environments ought to grapple with ethical questions, as they do have a

DOI: 10.4324/b23260-17

significant influence on the way people feel, develop, unfold their personalities, and evolve in their perspectives on life and the way they intend to
leave a mark. In our book, we have explored numerous questions such as

- How do I define the common good for my business, and beyond my
  business?
- In what way does it matter for my clients, my employees, peers, the com-
  munity where my business is located, my investors, and my supporters?
- How do I make sound ethical decisions? How do I scrutinize a situation
  and come to a decision that positively contributes to the greater good?
- What incentives can I install and communicate that promote consistent
  ethical behaviors?
- How do we deal with dilemmas? How do we make difficult decisions?
  What happens if identifying ethical issues turns out to be unfavorable
  for your business?
- What kinds of structural conditions or company policies do I need to
  put in place to nurture an ethical culture? How will I track, quantify, and
  monitor the ethical practices of my business?

As Mark Twain conveyed so thought-provokingly in his famous quote on
our certainties, which inadvertently have a dark side as they are biased
by nature, imperfect, and vain: asking questions, challenging yourself and
your organization, practicing some serious ethical navel gazing and implementing corrective action when necessary are key behavioral competencies of ethical leaders and ethical organizations. Such conduct is to the
ethical leader as natural as the duck takes to the water.

Questions and Answers

He who has a why to live for can bear almost any how

(Friedrich Nietzsche)

Let us dwell for a moment on the act of raising questions—questioning
the status quo, welcoming discomfort, and exposing yourself to cognitive dissonance (as the Twain quote above suggests). Asking questions is
representative of a certain mindset. Someone who asks questions to truly
explore, wonder, and delve into matters of interest may also display an
inquisitive mindset—as opposed to a mindset of already having all the answers at hand. Providing answers, of course, is necessary, too. We have
sincerely tried to raise questions and provide some answers to these questions as well in our chapters on ethical culture, maturity levels of cultures,
leadership and love, development of ethical leadership, and pathologies of
leadership. What we deem most important, however, is the entire process

between somebody raising questions and developing answers to those questions. One may label this process as some sort of lucid dialogue, a conscious eliciting of ways to handle ethical dilemmas and how to treat one another. So, dialogue and civil dispute are key—providing answers really comes second in the process.

The Common Good as an Intellectual and Pragmatic Challenge

Regarding the questions posed above, organizations should define their ethical compass as a gauge to commendable as well as questionable conduct of individuals, teams, and leadership. In our view, this is key to uphold rules of compliance, sow the seeds of responsibility, ownership, courage to flag and prevent fraud, and sustain moral integrity. Defining and driving commitment to ethical standards in processes and human interaction plays a relevant role in consolidating the ethical fabric of an entity that exerts influence on society and within the marketplace. We have tried to provide ample evidence of this claim throughout our book. Defining and upholding ethical conduct clearly poses an intellectual as well as pragmatic challenge because ascertaining these standards incurs costs in the time as well as financial departments. In addition, oftentimes ethical leadership is not seen or sufficiently acted upon as part of the real-life tasks to be covered by management. This is what our work as leadership advisors has shown repeatedly. So why is the frequently invoked common good and its definition as well as integration into leadership practice such a massive challenge? In this regard, let us look at one example: it is clear that giga-organizations such as Amazon have radically changed the map of e-commerce. Amazon (which was originally named "Relentless") started as a virtual bookstore, generating profits by gathering data and predicting the consumption behaviors of their customers. Of course, the ambition of such an organization is to offer everything you may desire in one marketplace, and at an affordable price. On the other hand, Amazon has been handling the CIA's cloud computing activities since 2013.[2] The cloud effort, known as the C2E Commercial Cloud Enterprise, builds on an earlier $600 million cloud computing contract that was awarded to Amazon's cloud computing division in 2013.

This, of course, raises massive questions about the concentration of power in one privately run organization, corporatism, freedom, and so forth. Concentration of power is a contentious issue and must be scrutinized. To this end, the common good needs to be defined. It goes beyond mere corporate interest, growth strategies, and efficiency programs. As ethical leaders, we ponder the common good as it impacts our teams, our community, society, future perspectives, culture, and the way we navigate all the systems that comprise the fabric of life. The common good constantly needs to be reflected in business and taken into consideration. Challenges need to be tackled ethically and solved with intelligence, creativity, and sound values-based reasoning that does not solely focus on immediate organizational benefit. Ethical leadership is always more than just that.

Obligation to Render Ethical Decisions

Another question we have frequently raised in our book has been about how to make ethical decisions. This has been discussed in our chapters on the hierarchy of values and the dilemma of authenticity. Ethical leaders must be cognizant of the values they stand for, which, in most cases, can be ranked in a hierarchical order. However, when analyzing decision-making processes and human interaction with an external perspective, quite frequently values are compromised or simply do not lie within the realm of consciousness as biases of different provenience kick in and render objective conduct ineffective. Imagine this situation: one team member has been suffering from a rather intimidating, domineering, seemingly fearless and competitive conduct of another team member. Due to a variety of influencing factors such as interpsychological, team-related (as in systemic), cultural as well as hereditary (implicit rules and conventions usually have come a long way), the team member who feels affected does not voice his or her critique. As we all have probably experienced at some point, there might come a point that such corrective feedback wiggles to the surface and erupts with quite a bit of steam, wreaking havoc. In such a situation, even a long-term relationship may become strained and the person receiving feedback probably will not perceive it as particularly constructive. The person receiving feedback may even *misuse* the concept of appreciation by persisting that the feedback shared hasn't been conveyed professionally—exempting himself or herself of criticism. On the other hand, corrective feedback should be conveyed on a regular basis and must not be subdued. So, when analyzing the instance described above, it would be one-sided to only place the focus on the domineering character. Ethical leaders are not stymied by such scenarios; they take responsibility all along. Clarity and temporary discomfort may have a positive effect and serve the greater good. It may hurt or feel uncomfortable at first but have a cleansing cultural impact in the long run. Reversely, feedback culture (and its corresponding competencies in people) should be promoted and lived up to—across the board and hierarchy. Be that as it may, this example shows that there are hierarchies of values: respect, fairness, appreciation, and relationship-orientation might be values that play a role in the above example. Ethical leaders must see through the fog, take bold action, weigh the consequences, and base their actions on sound values that are organized in a hierarchical order.

The Counterintuitiveness of Ethical Reasoning and Action

Intuition is seeing with the soul

(Dean R. Koontz—author, novelist)

Ethical leaders relentlessly ask themselves what long-term values they aspire to and strive for. This requires intuition, but also the capacity for counterintuitive reasoning and decision making. As Dean R. Koontz expresses with his beautiful quote above: intuitive seeing is done by the soul, and with love. However, many decisions come at a price. When making decisions, values must be scrutinized with respect to levels of selfishness, impact on the immediate community (team, department, and such), impact on the cultural fabric of an organization, impact on individuals, congruency with principles, and possible leeway when it comes to exceptions that may be made as they serve the greater good. Ethical leadership takes time. However, it is a dire necessity to always strive for a better world. Think of the Harvey Weinstein scandal that surfaced after more than thirty years of sexual misconduct, rape, and harassment. Between 2016 and 2017 Weinstein was finally brought to justice.[3] Dozens of terrified women who (most shockingly) were taken aback by the very fact that someone that invincible and untouchable such as Harvey Weinstein was finally brought down and taken on. Many of these women came out and testified that Weinstein had run his companies like a cult or dictatorship. These women had spoken to their agents, other actors, and in some cases even to the press—but they were not given a voice, as it was *just Harvey* and his antics. During the trial, many a director or actor had to admit to having heard of some of the allegations long before Weinstein was taken down by *New York Times* journalists Jodi Kantor and Megan Twohey, and that they had not dared to do anything about it. Some directors—Quentin Tarantino, for instance—admitted to their silence. Many did not.

As discussed in our chapter on hierarchies of values, ethical decision making involves cognizance of values, hierarchies of values, and the courage to act upon these principles, oftentimes not necessarily to your own advantage. That is why ethical decisions might be counterintuitive as well. These aspects must be taken into consideration by any ethical leader. Ethical thinking and acting on your ethical reasoning are not just time-consuming. Ethical leadership is downright risky, unsettling, and counterintuitive as it may jeopardize the status quo of things. In the long run, we believe, ethical consistency is what defines the kind of dignified behavior that drives respect, spiritual richness, longevity of corporations, and the deep-rooted purpose of organizations that embrace their ethical responsibilities.

Incentivizing Ethical Conduct

Write your injuries in dust, your benefits in marble.
(Benjamin Franklin—statesman, diplomat, and polymath)

To continue, let us zoom in on the question what incentives or benefits an organization can install and communicate that promote ethical behaviors? We have discussed how ethical behavior can be described, how it can be considered when developing staff, and in what way it can be utilized to foster a culture that regards ethics as a palpable merit. To call the essentials to mind once more: from our point of view, ethical behavior comes from a place of love. Love engenders compassion, togetherness, acceptance, responsibility, and empathy, as well as the capacity to set boundaries and move on (because it is a wise thing, at times, to let go and depart). Love has a transcendental element to it, as many a religious text has endeavored to capture. The transcendental element is key in the discussion of ethical leadership because we should always bear in mind that immediate personal benefit does not matter—it is the ideals, higher purpose and the greater good we should internalize as our north star when making ethical decisions.

But how to incentivize ethical behavior? To begin with, in critical instances, behavior needs to be read or interpreted from an ethical vantage point. For instance, imagine an employee comes forward after sexual harassment has been experienced, observed, or heard of. Such a choice requires a high level of courage, as sexual harassment and misconduct—or a rather lenient way of dealing with such unacceptable instances—may be the norm within an organization. The whistle blower may be marginalized as he or she counteracts implicitly sanctioned conventions within the system. An ethical leader will not accept such marginalization. The very act of blowing the whistle must be appreciated by the leader—particularly so when such courage kicks off a tiresome process of following things through, eradicating conditions that promote such misconduct, and sowing the seeds of future ethical behavior within the ailing system. Acknowledgment of doing the right thing—especially if it counteracts unhealthy norms within systems—is key.

Now, we all know that there is a plethora of corporate cultures, and that, in all probability, some behaviors at a warehouse will differ from those at a consultancy. The actualization of codes of conduct at a landscaping company will most likely be different from that of a financial institution. There will be parallels, but there will be differences also, which by no means makes one or the other better. The point here is that each organization engenders highly specific conventions. Specific industries have specific styles, modes, rituals, heroes, and ideals. Ethical leaders need to understand this and put behaviors into culturally sensitive perspectives. There is a difference between ethical ideals to be approximated, on the one hand, and the specific actualizations of such codes on the other. It is naïve to assume such actualizations are all the same; this might be explained by affinity biases, social desirability effects or courtesy biases. It is virtually universal, though, to prize dignity, reverence for life, and the creation of conditions where people want to contribute and strive. Furthermore, ethical leaders establish the foundation which promotes peaceful conduct. These ideals must be present and function as determinants of ethical leadership. In other words, ethical leaders navigate the cultural idiosyncrasies and are led by an ethically universal north star at the same time.

Consider the following situation: an inspiring employee works at an international manufacturer of furniture, case goods, and partitioning systems. At a warehouse, a colleague of hers makes explicit, demeaning, and sexualized comments about her. After the incident, she flags this behavior with her superior, who hesitates to take appropriate action and initially states that—although unacceptable—the colleague's conduct basically corresponds with the rough atmosphere generally embraced by staff at the warehouse. So it takes the victim quite some time to convince her superior to address the issue. What would be your take on this critical incident?

Another perspective comes into play when new behaviors are observed and appreciated, based on the sensitization of staff within a particular work environment with all its idiosyncrasies. For instance, if brief discussions or workshops are held as a platform for staff to exchange impressions, perceptions, and ideas with respect to ethical conduct, this might be a viable approach. It is most likely that in the aftermath of such workshops, new behaviors will emerge that serve the organization, make a difference, improve psychological safety, and promote wholesome interactions. In such cases, the new behaviors may be incentivized by positive feedback, recognition, and respect. Such instances may also lend substance to the creation of a commendable workplace culture, which can be further instilled when new employees are taken on board and so forth.

A company from the banking sector decided to set up a training program for leadership development that focuses in part on doing the right thing, acting ethically, flagging misconduct, and dealing with inappropriate behaviors. The program teaches constructive behaviors and strategies for difficult situations. Outside the program, business ethics is discussed on a regular basis, even in meetings and workshops with an entirely different agenda. Employees who have spoken up are given a voice and even the temporary title of ethical ambassador.

Employees who show remarkable ethical conduct and self-regulation when dealing with dilemmas in business may be asked to share their rationale in the context of such workshops. When a challenging negotiation has been resolved, a conflict has been resolved amicably, or ideas have been offered to make the business more sustainable, such instances may be translated into positive cases that exemplify the values of the organization. Such positive cases can possibly be shared by the originators or protagonists who showed exemplary reasoning; consequently, they receive legitimate visibility within the organization, in workshops, or during onboarding trainings.

Moral Dilemmas and Their Ethical Charge

We are between the wild thoat of certainty and the mad zitidar of fact—we can escape neither.

(Edgar Rice Burroughs—writer, author)

Dilemmas are terrible and a blessing at the same time. We believe we shed some light on many such dilemmas in our discussion of ethical leadership. If you observe behavior in a person that is utterly unacceptable and at the same time you know this person is highly influential, what do you do? If you are approached by a client who is strategically relevant but shows behavior and objectives that you deem questionable, what do you do? If you are approached by a client who is strategically relevant but shows behavior and objectives which you deem questionable—what do you do? Say a peer entrusts you with sensitive information, asking you to keep it to yourself, but you know it would be useful to share this information to resolve issues, rectify wrongdoing, or save somebody else, what do you do? Or if a managing director shows consistent selfish behavior but talks frequently about the common good, leadership for a better future, and socially sustainable conduct, what do you do then? All these situations will be trade-offs of some sort. In our view, immediate advantages or disadvantages must be taken into account when taking action. Immediate benefits or lack thereof are one side of the coin. However, dignity and reverence for the right thing play significant roles as well—even if you may take a beating as a consequence. Why else should one intervene when someone else is distraught? Why else would anyone blow the whistle when there is wrongdoing? Why else leave a job over a toxic workplace culture? All these decisions may result in unfavorable consequences for you personally, but they also accrue karma credits, so to speak, making you walk upright and respect yourself when looking in the mirror. The next time you feel uncomfortable or realize your judgment of problematic behavior has been numbed by groupthink, think twice, weigh the options and indeed, consider speaking up. That is ethical leadership of self and others at its very core. Why else did

Gandhi call to peaceful action against tyranny? He was compelled to embrace a most likely personal dilemma: personal safety and integrity versus the peaceful revolution in 1924. Could he have enjoyed a prosperous and somewhat peaceful life as a lawyer? Of course, he could have. But ethical leadership convictions kept him from leaning back. Instead, he leaned in for sure.

Dignity and respect are key in ethical leadership. It involves weighing pros and cons, pondering dilemmas, and trying to resolve these actions that are made from the same fabric historic (and glorified) role-models and their reasoning were. Essentially, there are no differences across history at all but rather the potential to learn from history and become a better person, and eventually an ethical leader.

To conclude, consider this tricky (albeit quite frequent and conventional) situation: an employee decides to leave an organization because he or she got frustrated over certain standards, mindsets, and so forth. Now, the easiest reaction for those left behind will be to externalize and solely seek to pinpoint the (dysfunctional) reasons of the entire situation within the very person who left the pack. This is quite a common response, but it is way off the mark. We are convinced that organizations can learn from such critical incidents, reverse the whole situation, and discuss what might have made the person leave in order to eradicate blind spots and genuinely evolve toward a brighter future. As mentioned above, ethical leadership of self and others may feel counterintuitive at times. It is, however, worthwhile to challenge yourself to become the best version of yourself and develop an ethical culture as an individual influencing the cultural fabric of an organization. Hence it follows, entry interviews are as relevant as exit interviews. Ethical leadership is as key as knowing your craft as a manager. Love and compassion are as relevant as mastering the intricacies of New Work approaches and AI gadgets. Indeed, resolving apparent dilemmas and dichotomies both creatively and with foresight is imperative when you strive to be an ethical leader.

Policies, Structures Encouraging Ethical Behavior, and Our Obsession with Quantifying the Unquantifiable

We should not forget, no matter how we quantify it: "Freedom is not free." It is a painful lesson, but one from which we have learned in the past and one we should never forget.

(Paul Eugene Gillmor—politician)

With regard to freedom, Paul Eugene Gilmor once stated that quantification is not everything. We like to quantify and it is an imperative when steering organizations and our lives. However, our obsession with quantifications (revenue, the steps we walk, health stats, people we have dated and such) comes at a price: it changes our minds and perceptions, may have an impact on mindfulness, and can turn our souls into a bleak wasteland of facts and figures. In the previous chapters on whether or not organizations can develop ethical leadership we have argued that critical incidents displaying the necessity of ethical consciousness are indispensable. Incidents like those given above can be used to discuss such dilemmas, draw lessons learned from them and (re)define ethical criteria. We have also made the case that different levels of foresight and courage foster ethical behavior on varying levels of personal maturity. We raised questions such as: Does somebody speak up in meetings and other settings to share their point of view? Will somebody challenge the decisions of others? Will somebody speak up when they are in the minority? Does somebody truly listen to the input of others? Such questions and the corresponding behaviors must be taken into consideration when leaders are developed or given feedback from an ethical standpoint. Codes of conduct and compliance rules are practical tools put in place to reward or rectify unethical behavior (or compliant versus uncompliant to use more common business vocabulary). From our point of view, ethics and ethical behaviors must be an integral part of personnel reviews, possibly promotions and/or vertical developments, competency models (focusing on courage, fostering culture, driving meaningful change, and so forth), workshops, and townhalls.

As our culture's obsession with facts and figures leads to the (mostly unconscious) assumption that things which cannot be measured do not really exist or bear significance, let's take a look at some quantifiable data. Last year, a survey conducted by the Association of Certified Fraud Examiners found that US organizations lose an estimated 7% of their annual revenues to fraud.[4] That is equivalent to more than $1 trillion of the 2008 gross domestic product. There are real, recurring and significant returns, however, for organizations that base their actions on a strong sense of ethics. Ethisphere has been publishing its list about the world's most ethical companies for decades now. Those companies' stock grew at a rate more than double that of the Standard & Poor's 500 over the past five years.[5] That makes sense when you consider that organizations with superior ethical track records can attract the talent and customers they need to sustain their growth far more easily and with less expense than those burdened by questionable reputations.

A study done jointly by Stanford University and the University of California at Santa Barbara recently found that 97% of recent MBA grads polled said they would be willing to make a financial sacrifice of nearly $15,000 a year off their starting salaries to work for a company that practices good corporate social responsibility and ethical business conduct.[6] Ethisphere conducted research which suggests that if staff trust their leaders, over 90%

of employees will perform as whistle blowers. If people do not trust their leaders, that percentage falls to 60%.[7] Key performance indicators—such as *return on ethics* (ROE)—and their integration into the mindset of controllers, steering committees, or HR as well as structures that promote ethical conduct will incur considerable cost, to be sure. However, you may radically reverse the way you look at things and consider this idea instead: ethics, or the price of right, are essentially priceless. Once a reputation is lost or severely damaged, no amount of money can buy it back. We believe that what is most important about an ethics program is not what it costs but what it is worth in terms of the reputation, financial resources, and human capital it protects. Ethical leaders understand this paradigm and act upon it.

The Future of Ethical Leadership: Relevant Trends to Be Considered When Leading Ethically

Consistency requires you to be as ignorant today as you were a year ago.
(Bernard Berenson—art historian)

Bernard Berenson may be an advocate for change and transformation when thinking about the above observation. From our vantage point, ethical leadership takes extra time and is strenuous. So why bother? First off, we would like to share some basic considerations. In both our work and our research, we found that many organizations do want to contribute to the greater good, and that they place this intention alongside other ambitions such as driving growth, expanding, being innovative, promoting diversity, and serving the client. In our own experience, the discussion of ethical matters must be intensified, as oftentimes these conversations are merely lip service with no or too little action behind it. It is an interesting fact, for instance, that companies have been scaling back diversity, equity, and inclusion (DE&I) roles since 2022.[8] Isn't this interesting? Tens of thousands of companies putting an extra focus on DE&I-promoting roles, using rainbow colors for their corporate logos (think Starbucks, Deutsche Telekom, Apple, IBM, Visa Inc. or BlackRock). We have stumbled across organizations that borrow people with a diverse ethnic background for glamorous corporate photo session. At the same time, DE&I roles are being decreased after? According to Revelio Labs, a New York City-based company gathering and evaluating data to assess workforce developments, "DE&I roles began diminishing at a faster rate than non-DE&I positions in 2021 and this trend continued to accelerate during layoffs in 2022."[9] This is madness.

So, the pressing question can be asked whether organizations simply revved things up DE&I-wise in the wake of the BLM movement, and now that the matter does not seem to be as present anymore, those newly established roles are already being reduced.[10] Strategies that involve ethics are complex, as they cannot and must not exclude questions about the impact a certain product or service may have on society. Such strategies and discussions thereof may involve politics—and many an organization has banned political discussions amongst employees based on sound reasoning (peaceful work environments, productivity, organizational swiftness, and such).[11]

Another issue, of course, is the question about whether or not—or to what extent—decisions in this context can be democratic. If they can, this will impact organizational efficacy, as discussions on relevant issues will require time. If they cannot, this means that a few people's decisions will be imposed on others, which may compromise motivation and retention. In a nutshell: such questions take time. And leadership takes time. Anyone who has transitioned into a leadership role will most likely confirm this. Alas, though, ethical leadership takes even more time.

So, the all-important question still keeps on vexing the self-reflected leader: why bother? Why is ethical leadership something you should strive toward and integrate into your business to safeguard its future? Why does ethical leadership make sense, and why is it one of the future trends of the twenty-first century?[12] We tried to shed some light on these questions and provide answers as well as some food for thought. What we have not embarked on so far is to sneak a peek at the future and give some perspective. The above questions are particularly poignant, as they concern the future. There is ample evidence in society, generations, and external circumstances that necessitate change. It is our conviction the corporate and social spheres are in dire need of ethical leadership. So, it is time to take a closer look at future trends and developments.

Research on Future Developments and Trends: The Most Pressing Trends and Developments

We have no right to assume that any physical laws exist, or if they have existed up until now, that they will continue to exist in a similar manner in the future.
(Max Planck—theoretical physicist)

As we have postulated on many an occasion throughout our book, ethical leadership is key now and will become even more important in the future. To understand this assertion, let us zoom in on the most significant and meaningful trends humankind will face in the decades to come. Trends are characterized by their duration for several decades, their ubiquitous character (as they affect economics, coexistence, consumption, values, politics, etc.), globality (as truly significant trends will emerge worldwide at some point), and finally complexity (as trends gain evolutionary traction owing to their highly dynamic interdependencies).[13]

In most cases it is hard to give a clear answer as to where exactly trends originate from. In many cases, however, they are formed from several similar and simultaneous phenomena that reinforce each other. As an example, look at the seemingly simultaneous rise of conservative populism around the world (a trend which we will discuss further down). Furthermore, megatrends appear all over the world, with different characteristics. Austrian Zukunftsinstitut Consulting created a wonderful overview, wrapping up the most relevant megatrends of the future.[14]

Furthermore, one needs to be aware of certain biases when studying trends. From our point of view, it is grossly inaccurate to believe that progress mostly originates in the so-called Western world and that economic change is generally initiated in the industrialized countries. This is Western hubris stemming from the tendency to put oneself in the center of the universe. For instance, when it comes to innovations in the area of non-cash payments, it is worth looking at African countries such as Kenya that play a pioneering role in this regard. If you want to know which trends are taking place in the area of urbanization, you are well advised to look at developments in Asian megacities such as Guangzhou, Shanghai, Chongqing, or Seoul. And regarding electric vehicles, Tesla may be the company with the greatest pioneering spirit and the greatest impact, but the actual breakthrough of e-mobility has long since taken place in China.

So, what are megatrends of the future? We believe that—among others—the gender shift, health, glocalization, connectivity, New Work, mobility, neo-ecology, individualization, sustainable energy generation, multipolarity (in geopolitical terms), the challenges of political division, silver societies and/or aging, global warming, wealth disparity, urbanization, and knowledge management are some of the trends that will shape the future. Clearly, this is not a comprehensive or all-encompassing list, and it is not meant to be. Let us zoom in on some of these megatrends and ask ourselves the question, in what way and to what extent is this trend relevant to ethical leadership?

Silver Societies, Health, and Aging: Seniority Trumps!

For instance, silver societies will play a more and more relevant role in the future. People around the world are getting older and staying fit longer. Medicine is progressing at a dizzying pace, and people's access to it is increasing, too. If you work out at the gym you will most probably be surrounded by health-enthusiasts of all ages. Pictures of Jean-Claude van Damme, Arnold Schwarzenegger, Winona Ryder, or Heidi Klum staying in shape are all over the place— and leave their mark when it comes to our idea of maturity, potential, and beauty. Consider the fact that it used to take decades for new vaccines to be created. Developing the COVID-19 vaccines was achieved within a year. This is mindboggling and raises a multitude of questions. In stark contrast, it took two decades to develop the chickenpox vaccine.[15] Furthermore, innovative technologies play an ever-increasing role: biotechnology, 3D printing, AI, nanotechnology, the use of big data and combinations of the above are all emerging approaches to further stir up, revolutionize, and improve the healthcare system. These advances further propel demographic change. This presents societies with considerable challenges indeed. On the other hand, it also creates great opportunities for a new sociocultural vitality.[16] In order to successfully master this demographic transformation, new social and economic framework conditions are needed as well as a new approach and position toward aging. Ethical leaders are cognizant of the challenges and opportunities to be considered when dealing with the silver society, their needs, and the value they bring to the table. Their toolset encompasses inclusive approaches, smart ways to sensitively manage knowledge, as well as approaches to leverage and make the most of diversity.

Individualization: Me, Myself, and I

Another central cultural principle of our time is reflected in the megatrend of individualization: self-actualization (think Maslow) within a uniquely designed individuality. Individualization is propelled by the increase in personal freedom of choice and individual self-determination. The relationship between *I* and *we* is being renegotiated. In addition, the importance of new communities is growing, which will give individualization a new face in the future. Clearly, there has never been a more extreme time than ours in the twenty-first century, where the use of platforms—accessible by virtually everyone—suggests and promotes individuality, uniqueness, and boundless self-fulfillment. The only thing you need to do is open LinkedIn, Instagram, Twitter, TikTok, Reddit, or whichever platform is to your liking, start browsing, and present yourself in the most charming light possible (taking pictures of yourself helping others, working out, donating money to charity, getting vaccinated, or checking out the latest sustainable fashion). With the help of social media, people have started revolts and grassroot social movements (think of BLM, the Arab Spring, Die Letzte Generation, MeToo, or the New Hope Movement in Malaysia). Such tendencies play a role in the workplace as well—and not just because of their potential to cause distraction. People seek individual purpose and do not necessarily value money over everything else.[17] Sustainability, our social footprint, political awareness, ethical culture, future forms of coexistence, high levels of soft (or real) skills in leaders, and the need for psychological safety are on the rise—and ethical leaders will play an increasingly important role when it comes to such individual needs.

Climate change and Sustainability: Time Is Ticking

Have you ever heard of the Doomsday Clock? The Doomsday Clock has been maintained since 1947 by the Bulletin of the Atomic Scientists. It serves as a symbol that epitomizes the probability of human-made global catastrophe, taking into account geopolitical conflicts, pollution, nuclear risk, and so forth. Whether we like it or not, emerging scientific data supported by the majority of international researchers is relentlessly pointing toward a very real and urgent peril: human-caused climate change. The effects are unsettling: increases in average temperature, significant rise of sea levels, mass extinction (the sixth one is well underway—and clearly human-made), reduction of the snow and ice cover, plastic pollution of the oceans (think of the Great Pacific Garbage Patch), heightening of the acidity of the oceans, all of which only further increase the rate, intensity, and duration of extreme events all over the world. Hence follows, climate change is impending and certainly no conspiracy to further subjugate the masses as control necessitates anxieties. Climate change is a real threat to life on earth and action must be taken. Ethical leaders must be role models in this regard. All too often, trendy neo-ecology promotes sustainability (jobs, products, food, clothes, and such), ecological consciousness, and all the politically correct behaviors that follow. Frequently, this seems to be more of a shiny surface than a real and radical conviction. Trends such as so-called *workations*—where employees travel to distant locations to enjoy the summer breeze by the ocean whilst working from their hip, remote workstations—are anything but sustainable. Separately packaged power-foods presented in show-offy cardboard boxes at the office are pseudo-sustainable. Venerating the Enlightenment as the historic period that effectively removed the shackles from humankind and paved the way for delightful progress and infinite joy is plain ignorance, considering rampant mass extinction and record levels of plastic pollution that have held sway over the environment for the past decades.[18] Praising e-mobility as the holy grail without taking into consideration its ecological and social impacts (on rare earths and metals, for instance) must be considered one-sided. Hence follows, it is imperative that ethical leaders sneak a peek into the proverbial rabbit hole every once in a while, which basically means to be critical thinkers who do not take things for granted or at face value only.

Political Division and Divisiveness: Potential Repercussions in the Workplace

To seek simple answers is an understandable human desire. However, this holds true for level-minded consideration and broad analyses. Famous pre-Socratic Greek philosopher Thales (623 BC–c.548 BC) coined the phrase "nothing is more active than thought, for it travels over the universe."[19] Even though it is true that hardly a lifeform is as aggressive as humans are, it is also true that one beautiful characteristic of humans is the act of thinking. If one observes the political discourse and how it has developed over the past decade or so, one can observe that extreme takes on the world we live in are ever-present. This, of course, has always been the case to some degree. However, when taking a closer look at the political debates of recent years, the tone and actions have become harsher and are anything but the result of cool reasoning: more and more right-leaning, reactionary political developments are surfacing, and oftentimes the strategy is more to vilify and damage the other camp than to engage in levelled political discourse. This phenomenon could be perfectly observed during the discussion of COVID measures between 2019 and 2022/2023—and this does not only hold true for the so-called alternative media but applies to the established media in equal measure. In the US, the utter culmination of these extreme developments could be observed in the attack on the Capitol on January 6, 2021, in which at least seven people lost their lives. In Europe, such developments can be observed in France, the Netherlands, Germany, Poland, or Hungary, where far-right voters have surged in numbers this decade, which clearly affects political discourse.[20] Figures such as Marine Le Pen, Björn Höcke, Oleh Tyahnybok, and Geert Wilders come to mind. Ethical leaders ought to be aware of this development. Indeed, there are companies that have successfully banned political discourse from the workplace. We are uncertain whether this is the right measure to be taken. Our point is not so much about managing potential political discourse in the workplace. On the contrary, our main contention is that positions can be spread more broadly on the standpoint spectrum. This may result in a generally heated atmosphere that may find its way into (professional) domains formerly perfectly disconnected from such heat. The challenge here is that ethical leaders are advocates of level-headed reasoning who can navigate the perilous shoals of these rough seas. Fostering a space where solution-oriented discourse is possible and psychological safety is given is a key competency of ethical leaders.

Ubiquitous Connectivity and the Way We Work

The connectivity megatrend describes the dominant basic pattern of social change in the twenty-first century: the principle of networking based on digital networks and infrastructures. Network-based communication technologies are fundamentally changing the way we live, interact, work, and do business. They reprogram sociocultural codes and create new lifestyles, behavioral patterns, and business models. Thinking back to the COVID pandemic between 2019 and 2023, connectivity helped many organizations to survive. However, the sole focus on virtualized communication also illustrated the meaning of *social animal*. Virtual connectivity cannot replace real interaction—or can it? In our consulting work, many leaders have shared their concerns with us about the use of social media during working hours and the distractive effect it can have on employees' single-mindedness and focus. Is it fair to regulate this, or will employees perceive this to be an affront and ample proof that an employer does not keep up with the times? Such questions must be explored and managed by ethical leaders.

Gender Shift, Evolution of Values, and the Need to Find Passage Through Shallow Waters

The gender shift must be concerned as a significant and almost omniscient development, and it will most likely not wane in the near future. Traditionalists and progressives discuss it alike (think of Ben Shapiro, Matt Walsh, Aisling Swaine, Jacinda Ardern, or Michael Kimmel). Gender does not necessarily predetermine a person's biography and identity anymore. In addition to this, from our vantage point, acceptable behaviors in society and certainly in the workplace have changed drastically over the past decades. Furthermore, the traditional social roles ascribed to men and women in society are becoming less socially binding. Gender loses its fateful meaning and is no longer the sole relevant determinant regarding individual biographies. Changing role models and emerging gender stereotypes are causing a radical change in business and society toward a new culture of pluralism. Daniel Coyle's *The Culture Code* strictly focuses on the significance of vulnerability that expresses itself in humbleness, the ability to apologize, and concepts such as servant leadership.[21] This would have been unthinkable in the 1980s. What the discussion around the gender shift also causes at a more conceptual and perceptual level is a kind of abolition of binary boundaries (think of terms such as non-binary, fluid, and so forth). One might say that new conventions are created that redefine what is acceptable and what is not. Think of behaviors that are clearly indicative of pathology (see our chapter on the pathology of leadership) such as neuroticism, lack of self-consciousness, sense of entitlement, utter lack of fear, overconfidence, lack of empathy, overly intense experience of emotions, excitement-seeking tendencies, or lack of agreeableness—these behaviors will keep on existing. However, the mindset, conventions, and ideals that are evolving nowadays will become more and more unforgiving of such deviations. We believe that ethical leaders who thrive on the management of dilemmas—and dilemmas do have to be managed, considering the rapidness with which values are evolving at present—will play an imperative role when weighing the pros and cons in this regard.

The World Obsessing About Vr And Ai: Who Draws the Short Straw?

Taking the above dynamic mélange of trends that affect us all into account, it becomes abundantly clear that ethical leaders are and will increasingly become a valuable commodity—especially when AI is further being injected into society. The notions of justice, accountability, and guilt will have to be discussed when cars, lorries, airplanes, and so forth are being operated by AI entirely. When AI causes casualties in a car accident, monitoring programs fail to prevent hydrogen tanks in airplanes from exploding, or a drone distracts a pedestrian who gets injured as a consequence, who is to blame? Such instances must be anticipated a priori—and this can be done by leaders equipped with a lucid ethical mindset. If you visit Harvard lectures on justice, you will be bound to deal with the question of guilt at some point. When AI is involved, the matter changes dramatically. Think of Elon Musk who has been obsessing about the neural link for years now (in fact, one of his many companies is actually called Neuralink). The definitive objective: connecting the human brain to computer systems. Probably most of us have watched one of the many SciFi movies where the protagonist sees through barriers, scans the rugged terrain, or swiftly learns how to fly a helicopter (think *The Matrix*, for instance). This can, of course, be a reality, and partly already is, considering night vision, VR hardware, holograms and such. All of this can be used for good (surgery, simulated interrogations, architecture, interior design, tourism and so forth). However, it is an obsession to attain utter control, safety, and predictability as well, and cannot and should not remedy all the deeper ailments of humankind. There are realities such as social credit systems or the omnipresence of surveillance cameras as well—conditions that must be questioned and discussed. So, when it comes to the promises of salvation ascribed to AI and VR, it is all too likely that such an excessive supply of data and analysis of input will impact human behavior. It will be up to us alongside ethically sensitive leaders to navigate the ensuing consequences. From our point of view, ethical leaders should be able to resort to ethical reasoning and well-balanced weighing of different scenarios: on the one hand, no blind veneration, and on the other, no utter rejection.

Cooking Up Ethical Leadership: A Recipe for the Greater Good

> *You know, I have seven children, so I guess I know some things about life.*
> (Stevie Wonder—singer-songwriter)

In the present book we have tried to approach what we think are necessary conditions and competencies to be developed, reflected, and trained in order to lead ethically. Giving guidance to others is a creative and profound

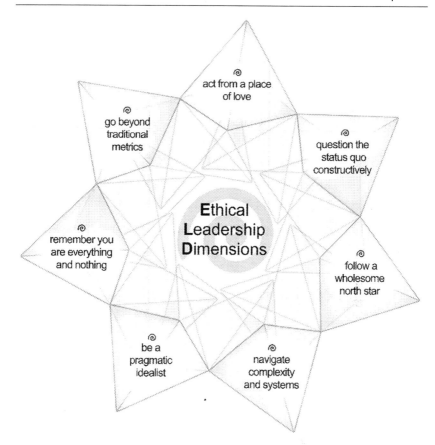

Figure 12.1 Ethical Leadership Dimensions

act—just like Stevie Wonder indicated when reminding us that raising children is educational and an incredible experience. Raising children is an ethical act as well—and it requires (in an ideal world) personal maturity. In simplistic terms, maturity is the level each one of us must attain that can be characterized as the best version of ourselves. For the sake of clarity, we would like to suggest the following steps to be taken into account when aspiring to become the best version of yourself in ethical terms. This model is by no means exhaustive; it is simply some inspiration for you, to be adjusted to suit your personal needs.

We believe that the findings, insights, and ideas we scrutinized in working on this book can be cast into a model consisting of *seven elements* in order to attain the highest level of ethical leadership (see Figure 12.1). The respective dimensions are interdependent and interconnected. No hierarchy is given, but rather a fully integrated network of dimensions influencing each other.

1. It is key to act from a place of love when it comes to making ethically sound decisions. Placing human life above everything else (as many a religious text does) is an outdated position. Acting from a place of love most probably engenders eye-level, psychological safety, natural belonging, and truthfulness, and it will foster a sense of cohesion. Love opens your heart, clears the mind, reduces anxieties, and possesses the power to heal you and those you encounter in life. It helps you let go, forgive, move on, and admit you were wrong. *Love is everything.*

2. Ethical leaders ask questions and do not propagate their viewpoints non-stop. This does not mean you mustn't position yourself clearly and unequivocally. However, there is also a mindset of listening which radically reduces ego and opens yourself up for the other side. Furthermore, ethical leaders *question the status quo* in order to strive for a better world within and without their own organization.

3. Ethical leadership needs a *wholesome north star*. Praising the beauty of homo sapiens' tools and toys incessantly is a perversion and certainly no wholesome prospect. Life is more than tools. Ethical leaders create a sound and non-aggressive coordinate system that generates peace, coexistence, and sustainability, and certainly takes soft factors such as dignity as well as reasonable progression into account.

4. No matter how much some people crave simplicity in architecture, furniture, literary style (think Hemingway), and strategy, simplicity is usually the result of complexity reduction. Now, the ideal here could be that the development is always from complexity to simplicity. However, evolutionists such as Richard Dawkins maintain it ought to be the other way around: start with simplicity and then move to *complexity*. Be this as it may, life is complex and there usually are no simple answers. The development may go both ways—from simple to complex or from complex to simple. As the butterfly effect has proven so elegantly, there is no action without an effect. Your actions have consequences in the systems surrounding you. Ethical leaders bear this in mind before going forward, they share ethical insights as Zen Masters, and they focus on what they can possibly influence.

5. *Pragmatic idealism* is a poignant oxymoron. On the one hand, it is imperative to strive for a wholesome ideal, a better future, equal pay, better corporate cultures, an innovative edge, and so forth. On the other hand, ethical leaders are pragmatic in the purest sense of the word. They do not complicate things but make decisions. They weigh the options, the pros and cons, the risks and contingencies—then they make a plan and, most importantly, they execute it. Our cultures overestimate

pragmatism and we dare to disagree (also bearing in mind the above acknowledgment of complexities). Life is both striving for higher ideals, on the one hand, and putting things into action on the other, both pragmatically and efficiently. Focusing too much on either extreme is a distortion of reality.

6. *Memento mori* is an artistic and symbolic trope, reminding us of the fact that we will cease to exist one day. Vanity is futile. The Grand Leveller will take it all. Being too self-centered can be considered the shadow side of every warrior, leader, or innovator. The concept has its roots in the philosophies of classical antiquity and Christianity, in which it functioned as an antidote to hubris and arrogance. In a way you are *everything* (because you are entrapped within yourself) and you are *nothing* (you move into a different state one day). Ethical leaders put things into perspective: driving the business, fostering culture, and offering great solutions to clients are relevant tasks, but these things need to be contextualized without the usual business pathos. There are more important things than today's meeting, a stakeholder conference, or solving a technical problem. Think about it.

7. Ethical leaders must go *beyond traditional metrics* and take all the above points into consideration and act upon them. Being a great leader who inspires others, embraces life (and not just human life), drives the business in a wholesome way, considers how others feel around himself or herself, and makes others thrive goes beyond KPIs, objectives and key results (OKRs), and strategy implementation. Leadership is an interpersonal phenomenon—and ethical leaders take responsibility for their environments to prosper ecologically, economically, socially, and spiritually.

Clearly, the headline to this section is a bit over the top, and intentionally so. As stated above, life is complex and cannot be captured by a model provided in some book on ethical leadership. However, we strongly believe (and would like to encourage you accordingly) that integrating the above dimensions wholeheartedly will help you develop into an ethically more mature person or leader. This requires contemplation, working on yourself, discipline, asking for advice, and being humble. The merits, however, are priceless.

Advocates of Becoming: Learning from the Past and Extrapolating Essentials into the Future

I am no bird and no net ensnares me: I am a free human being with an independent will.

(Charlotte Brontë—novelist, poet)

In her groundbreaking book *The Greats on Leadership: Classic Wisdom for Modern Managers*,[22] internationally acclaimed author Jocelyn Davis directed readers' attention to more than twenty-five centuries of practical leadership wisdom. From Shakespeare she derived the capacity for dealing with dilemmas, from Machiavelli she took the competency of initiating and driving disruptive change, from ancient philosopher Sophocles she took the meaning of true power, and from Pericles and Lincoln she extrapolated the gift of skillful communication. We can relate to Jocelyn's approach completely. As Goethe wisely noted, "he who is not able to account for 3,000 years, will dwell in darkness eternally and live from day to day only."[23] We do not intend to venerate or glorify particular historic personalities to make our point. If anything, the lives of Mahatma Gandhi, Frederick Douglass, Harriet Tubman, or Mother Teresa have been tainted as well, if you dare to look closely and move away from our institution's glorifications. However, it is key to understand that—to a certain extent—all of us bear the wisdom, trauma, and experiences from our forebears within ourselves. Epigenetics, for instance, is a discipline researching this very phenomenon. Jung called this the collective unconscious, and linguists like Chomsky explored and developed Indo-Germanic theories that unveil parallels between languages originating in the eastern limits of Bengal and those originating on the western shores of Europe. We are interconnected regarding consciousness, language, intellect, and our shared past.

Ethical leaders can be connoisseurs of the past, they may handle the intricacies of future possibilities, they ground their decisions on sound ethical foundations, they nurture the courage to speak up, and they foster a culture where others feel safe to do the same. The Earth Overshoot Day marks the date when humanity's demand for ecological resources and services in a given year exceeds what Mother Earth can regenerate in that year. In 2022, it fell on July 28.[24] This is dire news and marks one of the reasons why we believe the world is in need of mature, loving, self-critical, and visionary ethical leaders. Aside from this unsettling news, doing the right thing and encouraging others to become the best version of themselves is a profoundly ethical act. This is not for the sake of self-actualization only—it is about striving in a dignified and wholesome way. Ethical leaders are *advocates of becoming* and lovers of (all) life—and we hope to have contributed a pragmatic as well as thoughtful impetus to the field of ethical leadership, as well as the equally perilous and joyful journey of self-discovery, personal development, self-challenging, and change that ethical leadership must be.

Notes

1 "One Third of Your Life Is Spent at Work," n.d. Gettysburg College. www.gettysburg.edu/news/stories?id=79db7b34–630c-4f49-ad32–4ab9ea48e72b.

2 Frank Konkel, 2014, "The Details About the CIA's Deal With Amazon," *The Atlantic*, July 17, 2014. www.theatlantic.com/technology/archive/2014/07/the-details-about-the-cias-deal-with-amazon/374632/.

3 Jodi Kantor and Megan Twohey, "Harvey Weinstein Paid Off Sexual Harassment Accusers for Decades," *The New York Times*, April 30, 2021. www.nytimes.com/2017/10/05/us/harvey-weinstein-harassment-allegations.html.

4 *Report to the Nation on Occupational Fraud & Abuse* (Association of Certified Fraud Examiners, 2008).

5 Carlos Baez, "Ethisphere: Data and Community for Leading Integrity Programs," Ethisphere: Good. Smart. Business. Profit.®. March 13, 2023. www.ethisphere.com/.

6 Darreonna Davis, "How To Change An Email Signature In Outlook," Forbes, July 15, 2023. www.forbes.com/sites/darreonnadavis/2023/07/15/how-to-change-an-email-signature-in-outlook/?sh=54e2cb043f74.

7 Aarti Maharaj, "New Data from Ethisphere Says Employee Perceptions of Senior Leadership's Behavior Has Dramatic Impact on Employee Reporting of Observed Misconduct," Ethisphere: Good. Smart. Business. Profit.®. November 20, 2019. https://ethisphere.com/culture-report-press-release/.

8 Diversity Officers Hired in 2020 Are Losing Their Jobs, and the Ones Who Remain Are Mostly White," NBC News. February 27, 2023. www.nbcnews.com/news/nbcblk/diversity-roles-disappear-three-years-george-floyd-protests-inspired-rcna72026.

9 Matt Gonzalez, "Why Are DEI Roles Disappearing?" *SHRM*, March 17, 2023. www.shrm.org/resourcesandtools/hr-topics/behavioral-competencies/global-and-cultural-effectiveness/pages/why-are-dei-roles-disappearing-.aspx.

10 Gonzales, "Why Are DEI Roles Disappearing?"

11 Kritti Bhalla, "Google Bans Political Debate To Tackle Work Culture Issues," *Inc42 Media*, August 25, 2019. https://inc42.com/buzz/google-updates-guidelines-bans-political-debate-to-tackle-work-culture-issues/.

12 Jacob Morgan, "Leadership Trends You Must Know: Morality, Ethics, and Transparency," Jacob Morgan, December 25, 2021. https://thefutureorganization.com/leadership-trends-you-must-know-morality-ethics-and-transparency/.

13 Christian Nordqvist, "What Is a Trend? Definition and Example," *Market Business News*, April. https://marketbusinessnews.com/financial-glossary/trend/.

14 "Megatrend-Map," Zukunftsinstitut, June 1, 2023. www.zukunftsinstitut.de/artikel/die-megatrend-map/.

15 Natalie Colarossi and Taylor Ardrey, "How Long It Took to Develop 13 Vaccines in History," *Business Insider*, May 8, 2023. www.businessinsider.com/how-long-it-took-to-develop-other-vaccines-in-history-2020-7#measles-mumps-and-rubella-mmr-8.

16 "Demografischer Wandel und der Megatrend Silver Society," OVB Holding AG, December 5, 2022. www.ovb.eu/blog/artikel/megatrend-silver-society-der-demografische-wandel-in-europa.html.

17 Samuel A. Chambers, *Money Has No Value* (Berlin: De Gruyter, 2023), 45.

18 Alistair Walsh, "What to Expect from the World's Sixth Mass Extinction," *Dw.Com*, January 12, 2022. www.dw.com/en/what-to-expect-from-the-worlds-sixth-mass-extinction/a-60360245.

19 Patricia F. O'Grady, *Thales of Miletus* (New York: Routledge, 2022), 101.

20 "Europe's Shift Right," Reuters, n.d. http://fingfx.thomsonreuters.com/gfx/rngs/FRANCE-ELECTION-FARRIGHT/010040TK1SP/index.html.

21 Daniel Coyle, *The Culture Code: The Secrets of Highly Successful Groups* (New York: Random House Business Books, 2018).

22 Jocelyn R. Davis, *The Greats on Leadership: Classic Wisdom for Modern Managers* (Boston, MA: Nicholas Brealey; Reprint Edition, 2018).
23 Johann Wolfgang von Goethe, *Gesammelte Werke* (Cologne: Anakonda Verlag, 2015).
24 "Earth Overshoot Day," n.d. www.genevaenvironmentnetwork.org/resources/updates/earth-overshoot-day/.

Appendix A

Sample Competencies and Interview Questions

(Possible questions are in italics under each competency)

Integrity. Integrity means that an individual must not only be able to speak the truth, but is willing to do so in situations where he or she may be challenged. Integrity is speaking the truth without regard for consequences.

Behaviors:

- Speaks up when others remain silent.
- Holds to his or her position in the face of opposition.
- Speaks even when he or she knows there will be opposition or knows his or her position will be unpopular.

1. *Please provide an example of a time when you disagreed with a decision that leaders above you had made. What did you do? What was the result?*
2. *We all make mistakes at various points and often times we learn from mistakes. Talk about a mistake you made, what action you took on that mistake and how you learned from it?*
3. *At various points we may see people do things that we think are unethical. If you have had that experience, what did you do about it? How did that work out?*

Moral Courage/Willpower. Courage is a willingness to act on beliefs and values, to stand up to authority or others when he or she believes the decision or action is unethical or morally wrong. Courage is the strength of conviction to act regardless of the potential outcome or consequences. Moral courage may also be seen in its absence, as in "he failed to stand up for what was right and allowed the group to rule unchecked."

Behaviors:

- Makes his or her beliefs public and transparent.
- Supports others who speak up or share thoughts that oppose the views of others.

- Willing to challenge the moral or ethical aspects of proposed decisions.

1. *Tell me about the hardest decision you have had to make in the last twelve months. What made it hard? How did you gather information? What process did you use to make the decision?*
2. *Have you ever seen something at work that violated the company values or ethics? What did you do about it if anything? What made you choose that course of action?*
3. *Tell me about a time when you saw a co-worker doing something wrong. What did you do about it?*

Trust. Trust speaks to the ability to act in a consistent, predictable manner. Others can rely on your consistency of action and thought. Others can rely on you to honor commitments and promises. It also means taking personal accountability for mistakes and errors without blaming others.
   Behaviors:

- Builds positive relationships with individuals and groups.
- Acts in a consistent, predictable manner.
- Walks the talk. Lives up to commitments and takes accountability for his/her actions.

1. *Tell me about a time when you went into a new situation and had to build trust. How did you proceed? What were the results?*
2. *Tell me about a time where you had to build credibility with peers or upper management. Tell me about the situation, what action you took and the results you obtained. How did you know you had gained credibility with the group?*

Treats Others with Concern and Fairness. Fairness focuses your decisions by strongly considering the impact of decisions on others to include all stakeholders. It treats others with fairness and balance, and does not play favorites but applies a consistent, caring manner to all. Fairness places people above profits. In the literature this concept is often referenced as procedural justice.
   Behaviors:

- Applies organizational standards of fairness and justice to members of the organization equally.
- Does not "play favorites" in making decisions.
- Within the limits of confidentiality, explains the rationale for decisions that are made about individuals or groups.

1. *Tell me about a time when you had to mediate a conflict between two others people. What did you do? How did you resolve the conflict?*

2. *People can be annoying. Tell me about a time when someone annoyed you. What did they do to annoy you and how did you deal with the person?*

Empathy. Demonstrating empathy shows that an individual understands the concerns and feelings of others and anticipates how they will respond to your actions and decisions. It takes that into account and prepares for it. This shows up frequently in models of emotional intelligence.

Behaviors:

- Adapts his/her messages to the needs and concerns of others.
- Actively anticipates how others will respond to issues and acknowledges their concerns.
- Actively listens to others and reflects back both the content and feelings behind the statements of others; often summarizes his/her understanding to check for understanding.

1. *Tell me about the most difficult co-worker you have had to work with. How did you handle this person? If you were successful in resolving your differences, what did you do?*
2. *Tell me about a time where you felt someone had not listened to you. How did you respond to that? What did you say to the person who was not listening?*

Moral Mindset/Moral Competence. Moral mindset demonstrates curiosity about the nature of right, wrong, and fairness. It goes beyond rules and procedures to ask, "What is right?" and acts on that view. It is aware of how others may perceive and judge the nature of right and wrong, and is not limited to organizational norms, going beyond those norms to ask, "What is just?"

Behaviors:

- Engages others in discussions of right and wrong.
- Constantly curious about ethical issues when making decisions.
- Acts on his or her values and applies those values to decision making.
- Refuses to act on decisions he or she believes are unethical, immoral, or illegal.

1. *Tell me about a time you asked a leader why and how they made a particular decision. Why did you ask them about it? How did they react?*
2. *We all debate right and wrong with our friends and colleagues. Tell me about the last time you did that at work. What was the situation? What did you say? Did the group reach agreement?*
3. *Tell me about a time where you felt strongly that someone was being treated unfairly or inappropriately. Did you take action on that? Why or why not? What action did you take? What was the result?*

Acts with Transparency. Transparency shares what you're thinking, reasoning, and your rationale for decisions openly with others. It shares factual data and information that does not violate any personnel privacy issues or concerns. Transparency builds trust and reliability in the eyes of others. It's a willingness to share personal feelings and reactions as well.

Behaviors:

- Shares his or her thinking and rationale behind decisions.
- Provides data that supports the decision-making process.
- Share personal feeling about the decision being made including doubts and fears.
- Willing to listen to and hear contrary opinions.

1. *Tell me about a situation where you had doubts about a decision made by upper management. Did you share your concerns? With whom and how?*
2. *Tell me about a time when you were leading a team and candidly expressed your thoughts about the project you were working on (whether those thoughts were positive or negative). How did you express your thoughts? What were the reactions?*

Critical Reasoning. Critical reasoning can be defined as the logical and intuitive processes one uses to sort through data and arrive at the final decision. In the context of ethical leadership, critical reasoning also applies to the analysis of right and wrong relative to the decision being made and incorporating ethical considerations in the final decision.

Behaviors:

- Can sort through the assumptions that others are using relative to decision making.
- Will evaluate various options by considering both traditional and ethical factors.
- Makes decisions that are ethical, moral, and legal.

1. *Tell me about a moral dilemma or a situation where right and wrong were not clear, that you faced at work recently and what you did about it. How did you resolve the situation?*
2. *Not all situations have clear cut answers. Tell me about a time where you had to choose among a variety of possible solutions to a problem. What steps did you take to analyze the situation? Did you involve others? What factors drove you to the final solution to the problem?*

Appendix B

Measuring the Ethical Culture

(Ethical Culture Assessment)

Note: Below are key ethical culture factors and sample statements which are part of the Ethical Culture Assessment (ECA). The ECA provides a measurement of an organization's ethical culture by soliciting feedback from employees, leaders, and senior leaders. More information on the ECA may be obtained by contacting the authors. Bulleted items represent sample statements from the ECA

Focus. Focus is defined as the organization's orientation to the external world. Some organizations are internally focused on what happens within their facilities or teams. Other organizations may look to doing right by the external world (community, country, climate, etc.), while still others may look inwardly and focus on doing what is right by their stakeholders, customers, and/or employees.

- My leader admits when he or she makes mistakes and apologizes for that if appropriate.
- Leadership shares the reasons behind decisions openly and honestly.
- My team provides constructive feedback to one another.

Consistency. Does the organization act in a manner that is consistently congruent with its stated values, mission, or objectives? In other words, does the formal stated culture match up with the actual actions that the organization and its leaders take? This can be summed up in the classic admonition to "walk the talk."

- My leader acts in a manner that is consistent with the written values of our organization.
- Senior leadership walks the talk on values and ethics.
- Senior leadership stresses ethical behavior at all levels

Transparency. Often discussed but infrequently practiced, transparency is critical to ethical culture. By transparency, we mean that information, rationale for decisions, and good and bad news are shared openly with all employees and stakeholders. This includes the willingness to admit mistakes and, where necessary, to apologize and make amends.

- My leader admits when he or she makes mistakes and apologizes for that if appropriate.
- Leadership shares the reasons behind decisions openly and honestly.
- My team provides constructive feedback to one another.

Openness to Disagreement. While openness to disagreement typically gets the most attention in boss/subordinate relationships, it also applies in peer-to-peer discussions. Can I express disagreement with a decision, change, or action without fear of repercussions or recrimination? At the core of this is an atmosphere of mutual respect, where anyone can disagree with another without regard to rank or position when discussing ethical matters.

- My leader encourages me to speak up when I disagree with a decision or action.
- My leader listens to me when I disagree and lets me know his or her reaction.
- Leadership openly encourages disagreement.

Orientation to Safety. We approach orientation to safety with an eye toward both physical safety and psychological safety. This variable relates to such concerns as sexual harassment, diversity, and inclusion to name just a few. Are my leaders concerned with my overall safety, and do my peers look after one another's safety?

- My leader demonstrates his or her concern for my safety daily.
- My team treats one another with respect.
- Senior management is concerned about my physical safety on the job.

Leader Concern. This is a top-down variable perceived most accurately by those lower in the organization. Leader concern addresses two issues: does leadership in my organization care about me as an individual, and are we treated fairly by leadership (this references a concept typically referred to as procedural justice)?

- My leader shows interest in who I am as a person.
- Everyone in my group is treated the same way. Leadership does not play favorites.
- Senior leader is concerned about my well-being.

Heroes and Villains. This is the storytelling (how people describe the heroes and villains of the organization) variable with a twist. Most organizations tell stories about their heroes and heroines, so to speak, which is a great way to provide information on the culture. In other words, which of its members does the organization exalt?

- My leader speaks negatively about others.
- My team talks about others they do not respect.
- Leadership tells stories about people who have been successful.

Rewards and Recognition. This variable is closely related to consistency. Much like the storytelling variable, the rewards and recognition variable may contradict the stated values of an organization.

- Financial rewards are tied to living our values on a daily basis.
- My leader provides consistent feedback and reinforcement.
- My compensation is based on my doing the right thing.

Decision Making. This factor speaks to how decisions are discussed and what rationale is provided when decisions are announced. The ethical organization discusses whether a decision is right or wrong, beyond whether the decision will be beneficial to the organization. Specifically, it asks, when we are making decisions, do we talk about what is right for our employees, what is right for our community, and what is right morally?

- My leader shares the reasoning behind decisions.
- My team discusses if an action is right or wrong.
- Leadership talks about what is morally right and wrong.

Index